"The *Resilience* book is an extraordinary manual that combines theory and practice, biology, psychology, spirituality, and social sciences to offer the complete science and knowledge of not just survival in times of suffering and tragedy but learning to thrive and find higher purpose. Our brains are created by genes but sculpted by experiences. This book covers both the science of epigenetics and neuroplasticity, and shows that our biological organism can be redesigned for joy and optimal integration of body, mind, and spirit."

Deepak Chopra, MD, FACP, FRCP, *New York Times* bestselling author

"To paraphrase the bumper sticker, 'stuff happens,' and it is how we respond to adversity that matters. Steven Southwick, Dennis Charney, and Jonathan DePierro show us how, provide an expert's guide to the science, and offer practical advice for navigating life's challenges. In this deeply personal book, replete with juicy and often harrowing details of extraordinary hardships faced by both themselves and others they know, they provide living examples that will inspire. *Resilience* is a beautiful book that will benefit everyone."

Richard J. Davidson, PhD, author of the *New York Times* bestseller *The Emotional Life of Your Brain*

"This superb third edition has everything. It is chock full of graphic anecdotes about people who successfully overcame overwhelming challenges. It provides a comprehensive explication of the ten key elements of resilience. It describes the latest behavioral and neuroscientific research underlying each of these elements. And it provides very practical and doable tips that should enable each reader to practice resilience and thereby enrich their own life. What makes this book so special is that it succeeds at presenting a huge amount of information in an engrossing conversational style accessible to all readers. The authors even share some very personal experiences to illustrate important points. This extraordinary volume ends with a moving tribute to the late Steve Southwick, for whom the book is the capstone to a remarkable career."

Matthew J. Friedman, MD, PhD, Emeritus Professor of Psychiatry, Geisel School of Medicine at Dartmouth; Emeritus Executive Director, National Center for PTSD; Emeritus Director, National PTSD Brain Bank, US Department of Veterans Affairs

T0061878

"Sometimes it seems like trauma defines our age. This book reminds us that resilience is an equal and opposite force. Blending personal stories, cutting-edge science, and clinical insights, *Resilience* provides a comprehensive and rigorous tour of how we recover from trauma, whether that trauma is from a pandemic, a terrorist attack, or a personal tragedy. For anyone interested in a deep understanding of how humans can triumph over profound adversity, *Resilience* is an essential text."

Thomas Insel, MD, Cofounder and Executive Chair, Vanna Health; former Director of US National Institute of Mental Health; author of *Healing: Our Path from Mental Illness to Mental Health*

"*Resilience: The Science of Mastering Life's Greatest Challenges* encapsulates beautifully the literature on the psychological, biological, and neuroscientific perspectives on stress and the individual's response to it. Written by accomplished clinical investigators, this edition highlights and integrates what we know about resilience, and what we still need to know in order to enhance what we clinicians offer those exposed to unimaginable adversity. This book belongs in the library of every clinician, investigator, and teacher committed to understanding what paths one might take when traumatic events occur."

Terence M. Keane, PhD, National Center for Posttraumatic Stress Disorder, Behavioral Science Division, and Boston University Chobanian & Avedisian School of Medicine

"*Resilience: The Science of Mastering Life's Greatest Challenges* presents distilled lessons from three pioneers of the study of human resilience and psychological traumatization. Its messages are simple, profound, and easy to integrate into one's personal coping style. The third edition of this outstanding book is expanded and updated. It is also a wonderful memorial to one of its authors, Steven Southwick, MD. He was a beloved and respected figure in the world of stress research."

John Krystal, MD, Chair of Psychiatry at Yale School of Medicine

"There is no resilience without adversity. Unfortunately, we live in a dangerous world. This book, written by world leaders on the science of resilience, is a must-read for everyone. Certainly, professionals who help others through stressful or traumatic experiences would profit from the knowledge shared, but every single person will learn how to manage challenges better. The authors include very easy-to-read, clear suggestions backed by decades of neuroscience research and from the stories of multitudes of resilient survivors. Every clinician from novices to experienced clinicians has something to learn from this gem. The lessons in this book are what we should teach our children."

Barbara Olasov Rothbaum, PhD, ABPP, Director of the Emory Healthcare Veterans Program and the Trauma and Anxiety Recovery Program; Paul A. Janssen Chair in Neuropsychopharmacology; Department of Psychiatry, Emory University School of Medicine

"Southwick, Charney and DePierro have written a moving and inspiring book with practical suggestions for achieving resilience that are supported by the latest research. The book is dedicated to one of the authors, Dr. Steve Southwick, who dealt so heroically with an aggressive cancer that took his life before this book could be published. The last chapter provides a beautiful tribute to Steve's scholarship and humanity. But Dr. Charney, as well, speaks of his own journey to resilience after being shot by a former faculty member who had been terminated for academic misconduct. The book reminds us that we all have to reckon with challenge at some time, and that such reckoning is facilitated by attitudes and skills that we can develop. It is a book that teaches stories and science. Given the challenges of the last few years, including a global pandemic that resulted in a massive sea change, it is a welcome salve."

Rachel Yehuda, PhD, Mount Sinai Professor in Psychiatry and Neuroscience of Trauma

Resilience

Life presents us all with challenges. Most of us at some point will be struck by major traumas such as the sudden death of a loved one, a debilitating disease, or a natural disaster. What differentiates us is how we respond. In this important book, three experts in trauma and resilience answer key questions such as: What helps people adapt to life's most challenging situations?, How can you build up your own resilience?, and What do we know about the science of resilience?

Combining cutting-edge scientific research with the personal experiences of individuals who have survived some of the most traumatic events imaginable, including the COVID-19 pandemic, this book provides a practical resource that can be used time and time again. The experts describe ten key resilience factors, including facing fear, optimism, and relying on role models, through the experiences and personal reflections of highly resilient survivors. Each resilience factor will help you to adapt and grow from stressful life events and will bring hope and inspiration for overcoming adversity.

Steven M. Southwick, MD, was Glenn H. Greenberg Professor Emeritus of Psychiatry, PTSD, and Resilience at Yale University Medical School and Medical Director Emeritus of the Clinical Neuroscience Division of the National Center for PTSD of the US Department of Veterans Affairs. Dr. Southwick was one of the world's leading experts in psychological trauma and human resilience. His collaborations with Dr. Dennis Charney led to foundational discoveries about the biology and treatment of post-traumatic stress disorder, and factors that support resilience. His own resilience while fighting advanced prostate cancer for five years was an inspiration to his friends, colleagues, and family. He passed away on April 20, 2022, and this book, which he worked on through his final weeks, is dedicated to his life and legacy.

Dennis S. Charney, MD, is Anne and Joel Ehrenkranz Dean of the Icahn School of Medicine at Mount Sinai and President for Academic Affairs for the Mount Sinai Health System. Dr. Charney is a world expert in the neurobiology of mood and anxiety disorders. He has made fundamental contributions to our understanding of the causes of anxiety, fear, and depression, and among his discoveries is use of ketamine for the treatment of depression – a major advance in the past fifty years of clinical care. He also focuses on understanding the psychology and biology of human resilience, which has included work with natural disaster survivors, combat veterans, and COVID-19 frontline healthcare workers. He has over 600 publications to his name, including books, chapters, and academic articles. In 2016 he was the victim of a violent crime that tested his personal resilience.

Jonathan M. DePierro, PhD, is Associate Professor of Psychiatry at the Icahn School of Medicine at Mount Sinai and Associate Director of Mount Sinai's Center for Stress, Resilience, and Personal Growth. Dr. DePierro, a clinical psychologist, is an expert in psychological resilience and the treatment of trauma-related mental health conditions. After many years working with individuals impacted by the 9/11 terrorist attacks, he now focuses on supporting the mental health needs of healthcare workers. Having experienced extensive bullying throughout his childhood, he learned important lessons about resilience that continue to inform his clinical and research work.

Steven M. Southwick, MD
Dennis S. Charney, MD and
Jonathan M. DePierro, PhD

Resilience

The Science of Mastering Life's Greatest Challenges

Third Edition

CAMBRIDGE
UNIVERSITY PRESS

CAMBRIDGE
UNIVERSITY PRESS

Shaftesbury Road, Cambridge CB2 8EA, United Kingdom

One Liberty Plaza, 20th Floor, New York, NY 10006, USA

477 Williamstown Road, Port Melbourne, VIC 3207, Australia

314–321, 3rd Floor, Plot 3, Splendor Forum, Jasola District Centre, New Delhi – 110025, India

103 Penang Road, #05–06/07, Visioncrest Commercial, Singapore 238467

Cambridge University Press is part of Cambridge University Press & Assessment, a department of the University of Cambridge.

We share the University's mission to contribute to society through the pursuit of education, learning and research at the highest international levels of excellence.

www.cambridge.org
Information on this title: www.cambridge.org/9781009299749
DOI: 10.1017/9781009299725

© Steven M. Southwick, Dennis S. Charney, and Jonathan M. DePierro 2023

This publication is in copyright. Subject to statutory exception
and to the provisions of relevant collective licensing agreements,
no reproduction of any part may take place without the written
permission of Cambridge University Press & Assessment.

First published 2023

Printed in the United Kingdom by TJ Books Limited, Padstow Cornwall

A catalogue record for this publication is available from the British Library.

A Cataloging-in-Publication data record for this book is available from the Library of Congress.

ISBN 978-1-009-29974-9 Paperback

Cambridge University Press & Assessment has no responsibility for the persistence or
accuracy of URLs for external or third-party internet websites referred to in this publication
and does not guarantee that any content on such websites is, or will remain,
accurate or appropriate.

Contents

Acknowledgments

This book would not have been possible without generous contributions from the many inspiring individuals who granted us permission to interview them and share their stories with our readers. Their stories make up the heart and soul of this book, and it was our privilege as authors to learn from them. They have become our role models. We are particularly appreciative to the faculty and staff of the Mount Sinai Health System, who responded with creativity, strength, and courage beyond words to the COVID-19 pandemic. Mount Sinai was the epicenter of the epicenter. In this book, some of these remarkable individuals share their stories.

Many friends and colleagues helped us as we formulated ideas about resilience for this new edition. We wish to thank Deb Marin, Vansh Sharma, Craig Katz, Adriana Feder, Eric Nestler, and Robb Pietrzak, all of whom provided guidance on specific chapters. Sydney Starkweather provided invaluable editorial assistance.

Our families have been a tremendous support. Jonathan would like to thank his wife, Vivian Khedari-DePierro, for providing vital comments on the text.

We wish to thank the many professionals at Cambridge University Press who edited and published the book, including Catherine Barnes and Lori Handelman. Jessica Johnson provided all the original artwork new to this third edition.

Finally, this book is dedicated to the memory of Steven Southwick, MD. We thank Bernadette Southwick for inspiring us to write the best book possible and enabling us to keep Steven in our hearts and minds. Bernadette provided important background information, particularly for the epilogue. Dr. Steven Southwick was a role model to so many, a towering figure in the field of resilience research, and will never be forgotten for his kindness and caring for all who came to him in time of need. Gone too soon.

DSC and JMD

1

. . . . .

What Is Resilience?

Even before the COVID-19 pandemic, serious traumas were remarkably common. Studies estimated that 69–90 percent of people would experience at least one serious traumatic event during their lives (Goldstein *et al.* 2016; Kilpatrick *et al.* 2013). Examples of these events include violent crime, domestic violence, sexual assault, child abuse, a serious car accident, the sudden death of a loved one, a debilitating disease, a natural disaster or war, or military combat. Though they are not often "counted" in these epidemiological studies, other stressors can have a devastating impact on well-being, including racial discrimination, emotional abuse (e.g., bullying or chronic insults or invalidation by caretakers or romantic partners), and homelessness.

We know that any one of these events can throw our lives into turmoil. For some, the stress of the event will become chronic, lasting for years. They may undergo a dramatic and lasting change in outlook, becoming withdrawn and angry. Some people will become depressed or develop post-traumatic stress disorder (PTSD). But what we also know is that this is far from the full story. Over our careers, the three of us have devoted much of our research and clinical work to defining, measuring, and fostering the missing piece – the human capacity for resilience.

What is *resilience*? While it has been defined in many ways by experts (Southwick *et al.* 2014), we see it as *the ability to weather and recover from adversity*. Here are a few important points about resilience to keep in mind while you are reading this book:

1. *Resilient people have faced challenges.* You cannot say a person is resilient unless they have had challenges thrown their way – they must be resilient *to, from, or following* some stressful or traumatic event.

2. *Resilience unfolds over time.* How someone is coping immediately after a traumatic or stressful event may not tell you very much at all about their resilience – because it is a process that unfolds over days, weeks, months, and years.

3. *Feeling distress does not mean someone is not resilient.* Resilient people may experience psychological symptoms such as depression, recurring upsetting memories, or intense self-blame following traumatic events – while still carrying on with important facets of their lives. Resilience can also be seen in the process of recovery from medical or mental health conditions.

4. *Resilience often involves growth.* Often people who go through challenging life events say they have grown in some way as a person and have a greater sense of personal meaning in life. This change, like many in life, can come after or during significant emotional pain.

5. *Resilience can differ across the life span.* One way of thinking or acting might be more helpful at one point in someone's life, but not at another. Think about a child who has no one to turn to in their life – they need to be self-sufficient and scrappy to survive and thrive. But when they get older and have more people around them who care for them, reaching out and asking for help in tough times would be a marker of personal resilience (Bhatnagar 2021).

6. *Resilience occurs in context.* Adaptation to stress depends not only on the individual but also on available resources: family, friends, specific cultures and religions, communities, societies, and governments. Many of these resources are outside a person's immediate control. We will return to this point at the end of this chapter.

Throughout the book we also draw upon events in our own lives that have informed how we think about resilience. Dennis Charney, dean of the Icahn School of Medicine, played a key role in directing Mount Sinai Health System's response to the COVID-19 pandemic. In 2016, well before the pandemic, he was shot by a former employee and had to undergo intensive rehabilitation. Steven Southwick battled advanced cancer for five years and helped family members through their own medical challenges. Jonathan DePierro, the third author for this new edition, experienced extensive bullying in childhood that led to periods of depression. He was the first person in his immediate family to finish college and ultimately earned his PhD in clinical psychology. While this book mostly focuses on the many resilient people we have interviewed, you will hear a bit more about our life experiences in later chapters.

How We Became Interested in Resilience

Over the years, all three of us have examined the negative impact of having lived through overwhelming traumas. We started from the perspective of studying a psychiatric diagnosis – post-traumatic stress disorder. In our research, we learned a lot about how the body's stress response is overactive in individuals with PTSD, and how this contributes to a range of potentially disabling symptoms. We treated Vietnam veterans who endured decades of emotional pain from their combat experiences.

But we often wondered too about survivors who seemed to somehow cope effectively with the negative effects of stress. These people either did not develop stress-related symptoms or if they did then they carried on and harnessed resources to support their recovery. The term "resilient" described these people well.

When we got started focusing on resilience, little was known about it. We had many questions and set about trying to answer them. Here are some of the things we wondered: What factors can help protect individuals from developing persistent symptoms following traumatic events? Is there something unique about their nervous system or genes? Have they been raised in a special manner? What about their personalities? Do they use specific coping mechanisms to deal with stress? If we learn more about how they dealt with stress and trauma then will these lessons be helpful to others? Can someone learn to become more resilient?

Alongside many carefully designed research studies, some of which involved thousands of people, we were also interested in hearing individual stories of resilience. We decided to interview people who stood out to us as tremendously resilient. In the previous two editions, we shared stories from Vietnam prisoners of war (POWs) and United States Special Operations Forces instructors, 9/11 survivors, and other individuals who had not only survived enormous stress and trauma but had somehow endured or even thrived. Then, the COVID-19 pandemic, coming two years after our second edition of this book was released, provided an undeniable example of human resilience. Growing attention to racial injustice in the United States and geopolitical unrest added layers uncertainty, stress, and trauma. These more recent world events raised more questions: Did what we had learned about resilience "hold up"? How could we as authors, clinicians, and human beings learn from these jarring experiences?

You may have picked up this book because you have your own questions about resilience, or because you are struggling through a challenging event in your life. We hope that you find it helpful for the challenges you face now, and those you will no doubt encounter in the future. In the next sections, we will give you a preview of what is to come.

Ten Resilience Factors

Most of us will never become a prisoner of war, need a heart transplant, or step on a landmine, but we will inevitably face our own personal tragedies. Fortunately, to withstand, overcome, and grow from these experiences, we do not need to have superior genes, nor do we need to take a "tough as nails" approach to life or have trained with elite military units. But we do need to prepare ourselves, for life has a way of surprising us with adversity when we least expect it.

We know of no better way to learn about tried-and-true methods for becoming more resilient than listening to and following the advice of people who have already "been there." In our interviews with resilient people, we heard recurrent themes. The people we met

1. Confronted their fears
2. Maintained an optimistic but realistic outlook
3. Sought, accepted, and provided social support
4. Imitated sturdy role models.
5. Relied on an inner moral compass
6. Turned to religious or spiritual practices
7. Attended to their health and well-being
8. Remained curious, pushing themselves to learn new things
9. Approached problems with flexibility and, at times, acceptance
10. Found meaning and growth during and after their traumatic experiences

The next ten chapters focus on each one of these factors in more detail. In each chapter, we share personal stories, the latest scientific research, and practical suggestions for building resilience in your own life. We also recognize that our list is by no means definitive or complete and that other factors certainly contribute to resilience. Here are a few stories that have inspired us and informed our thinking about the ten factors.

Resilience Following 9/11

The terrorist attacks of September 11, 2001 were horrifying and disorienting events for hundreds of millions of people. While most everyone who was alive then can remember when they heard the news of the attacks, there were also those who witnessed it up close, lost someone close to them, or directly responded to help in affected areas such as Ground Zero in lower Manhattan. Jimmy Dunne's compelling story provides just one example of individual resilience after 9/11.

On the clear, balmy morning of September 11th, Jimmy was enjoying a much needed day off work. But quickly his relaxation gave way to fear. He was stunned to learn that planes had crashed into the World Trade Center. His thoughts immediately turned to his work colleagues and dear friends who he knew were there. United Airlines Flight 175, a Boeing 767, struck the South Tower between the 78th and 84th floors, trapping hundreds on the floors above (Dwyer *et al.* 2002). His company, the financial services firm Sandler O'Neill, was located on the 104th floor.

Jimmy's worst fears were confirmed. Nearly one-third of Sandler's employees died that day. Among them were Jimmy's close friends and fellow managing partners, Chris Quackenbush and Herman Sandler. There were forty-six widows and widowers, and seventy-one children who lost a parent. The firm's operations systems were also crushed: all the company's paperwork and computer systems were destroyed. Through his grief, Jimmy decided to be a role model for his remaining staff: "The moment I heard what the terrorists wanted, I decided to do exactly the opposite. Osama Bin Laden wanted us to be afraid. I would show no fear. He wanted us to be pessimistic. I would be incredibly optimistic. He wanted anguish. I would have none of it."

Dunne made a series of momentous decisions. He and his staff would "do right by the families" by paying the salaries of the deceased employees through December 31, 2001; extending bonuses and healthcare benefits; setting up an education fund; and providing mental health counseling. They also decided to find a way to carry on with business, despite the long odds. By September 17, the day the New York Stock Exchange reopened, the firm was already set up in a temporary office. Dunne and his team saw rebuilding the firm as a moral imperative – a way of honoring their lost colleagues. Dunne's heartfelt emotion was the driving force in his rescue of the firm. From the day of 9/11 onward, he and his team had a clear sense of purpose that guided every decision.

Throughout the book, we will share more about the two decades of research on the resilience of individuals affected by 9/11, including those living and working in lower Manhattan and those who responded or volunteered on the rescue and recovery efforts.

Resilience during COVID-19: Firsthand Accounts from Mount Sinai

As of early August 2022, when this chapter was written, approximately 6.4 million people worldwide had died from COVID-19. In March and April 2020, New York City became one of the global epicenters of the pandemic. You can probably remember being worried about your health or that of your loved ones in these early days, as the pandemic swept the globe. During this time, healthcare workers across the city helped to care for extremely ill patients, fearing that they would get infected and pass the virus on to their own families while doing their vitally important jobs. We lost colleagues, including from among our staff at the Mount Sinai Health System.

The pandemic was exhausting, terrifying, and traumatizing. Studies have shown increases in depression, anxiety, and loneliness, particularly during the early waves, which will need to be addressed for many years to come. Healthcare workers on the front lines of the pandemic, like their counterparts responding to 9/11 twenty years earlier, shouldered a heavy emotional burden. Our team began to survey healthcare workers early on. From that work, we know that 39 percent of frontline healthcare workers taking care of patients with COVID-19 at Mount Sinai Hospital reported significant symptoms of anxiety, depression, or PTSD (Feingold *et al.* 2021). It is a stark reminder that these individuals are humans first and providers second; and they were at the epicenter of the epicenter, making tough decisions and witnessing so much suffering and death.

Firsthand Accounts from Mount Sinai

Throughout the pandemic's many waves, there have been many examples of creativity, community support and collective strength, and determination. The human need for comfort and connection shone through the catastrophe. For example, amid clear risk to their own lives, healthcare workers across the country held up phones so that patients' families could say their goodbyes. Shauna Linn, a physician assistant at Mount Sinai during the first wave of the pandemic, shared this with us:

> It was very terrifying emotionally, but also extremely meaningful and powerful because you felt like you were the only connection this person has to their loved one. I wasn't really mediating it per se. I just felt like I was kind of a vehicle through which she could see her mom, and I tried not to editorialize it or intervene too much, but I just tried to give her mom some, you know, hold her mom's hand, give her mom some tactile connection that she wasn't able to do. (Earle 2020b)

From our surveys of frontline healthcare workers, we learned about many factors that helped people cope, including social support from family, friends, and leaders; finding small positives amid the suffering; and having a sense of purpose (Feingold *et al.* 2021; Pietrzak *et al.* 2020). We will refer to this growing body of research many times in later chapters of the book.

In April 2020, one of us (Dennis) summarized the resilience factors he observed within the Mount Sinai community:

> One is a positive sense of optimism, which is not easy in these times, but our doctors and our nurses … have a sense of optimism that they're up to the task and that ultimately, we will prevail. That this will end at some point, and we will get back to normal activities. And I think they will look back upon this time and place as being, as Winston Churchill said, their Finest Hour. That when they were challenged, they were up to the challenge, did spectacular work … I would [also] say support is very important. You have to function as a team now. You've got to be able to rely on each other 100 percent to take care of the patients that we're responsible for … And I've heard this a lot from our staff and that is – this is what they are trained to do … And a lot of them have the attitude: "If not us, who? Who's going to do it?" (Earle 2020a)

The experiences of our healthcare workers called us to action – we knew we had to use what we had learned about resilience to be of immediate help. In April 2020, we opened the Mount Sinai Center for Stress, Resilience, and Personal Growth (CSRPG). The primary mission of this unique center is to support the resilience of all Mount Sinai Health System employees, students, and trainees. Based on the same ten factors described in this book, CSRPG's staff have used resilience training to support both healthcare workers and the community at large in New York City (DePierro *et al.* 2020, 2021). We partnered with many pastors in New York City in creating a resilience-building program for their congregants. Later on in the book, we will share the experiences of one of these pastors, Reverend Dr. Thomas Johnson, who helped lead Canaan Baptist Church in New York City through the worst parts of the pandemic.

A Nation Shows Resilience: The 2022 Invasion of Ukraine

In the years since the second edition of this book was published, there has been rising global uncertainty. War and persecution in multiple countries, including Venezuela and Syria, have fueled a refugee crisis. We saw one stunning example of a conflict with global implications when, in February 2022, Russian forces invaded Ukraine without provocation. A major global superpower bore down on a country whose military was comparably smaller. Over 20,000 Russian troops poured into the country, along with thousands of tanks, missile platforms, and armored personnel carriers. Ukraine did not back down – it faced its fears, with the clear mission of protecting its citizens and its land. Those who could stay took up arms to defend cities block by block, allowing over a million people to flee.

As the world looked on, and no other country directly intervened, Putin's anticipated early victory was upended by the bravery of the Ukrainian people. As of the fall of 2022, they are still fighting. This spirit has been best exemplified in part by the words and actions of their president, Volodymyr Zelenskyy. Declining an offer to evacuate the country for safety early in the invasion, he stated, "I need ammunition, not a ride." On March 8, 2022, in a virtual speech to the UK Parliament, he echoed British Prime Minister Winston Churchill's inspirational words, saying: "We will fight till the end, at sea, in the air. We will continue fighting for our land, whatever the cost."

Later in the book, we will hear from Dr. Preethi Pirlamarla, a Mount Sinai cardiologist, who provided medical aid as part of a relief effort in Poland, near the Ukrainian border.

Extraordinary Experiences of Military Service Members

Many years ago, we sat down for in-depth interviews with former US prisoners of war. Most of those we spoke with were pilots who had been captured when their planes were shot down over North Vietnam. After ejecting from disabled burning fighter jets flying at speeds of greater than 400 miles per hour, they parachuted into the jungle. After being captured, they were often paraded through crowds of hostile villagers before being interrogated, beaten, and tortured. They were given meager portions of barely edible food: a chicken head in grease, a piece of bread covered with mold, the hoof of a cow, an occasional tiny piece of pig fat, or a handful of rice that might be full of rat feces, weevils, or small stones.

All the POWs we interviewed were deeply affected emotionally by their imprisonment, isolation, and torture. Many developed trauma-related mental health conditions and had trouble adjusting to civilian life when they got back home. However, they also discussed how they gained a greater appreciation of life, closer connections with family, and a newfound sense of meaning and purpose because of their prison experience. From their stories of survival, we learned that social support, having a moral compass, and physical fitness were important, as were other strategies.

In addition to POWs, we spoke to members of the United States Special Operations Forces, including retired Rear Admiral Scott P. Moore. From him, we learned that failure is not something to fear because it can make us stronger.

Examples from Other Individuals Facing Life's Challenges

In addition, we interviewed people from all walks of life who faced or continue to face a range of difficulties. Here are a few examples.

Congenital medical issues:

- Deborah Gruen, born with spina bifida, won bronze medals in swimming in the 2004 and 2008 Paralympics. She competed as a member of Yale University's women's varsity swim team and graduated from the university *summa cum laude*, attended Georgetown University Law School, and went on to a career with a prestigious law firm.

Life-altering injuries:

- Dr. Jake Levine, an athlete since early childhood, sustained ten sports-related concussions that developed debilitating aftereffects; after daily grueling rehabilitation, he contracted a near fatal heart infection while researching PTSD and resilience in Japan. He

13

completed medical school and is now starting a residency at Mount Sinai to become a physician specializing in physical rehabilitation.

Global conflict:

- Dennis Chung and his family fled persecution in Vietnam, crammed on a boat with hundreds of others. He started with nothing in the United States, and ultimately saved and borrowed enough to start his own restaurant in lower Manhattan. Dennis put his two children through college and graduate school. His son, Tony, is a biomedical sciences graduate student at the Icahn School of Medicine.

The Science of Resilience

Now that we have defined resilience, we want to say a little bit about what we have learned about the biology behind it. Our research has shown us that physiological responses before, during, and after traumatic events all play a role in resilience. We will focus on three different components: (1) the brain, (2) the autonomic nervous system, and (3) hormones.

Let's start with the brain. Many brain regions have been associated with resilience (see Figure 1). It is important to say here that, as with most human experiences, we have a limited understanding of the true complexity of what is happening in the brain – often, we have a snapshot of the brain at one point in time, during lab experiments that might not match someone's real life experiences very well. Here are a few key brain regions you should know about:

- The *amygdala* is involved in our fear responses and learning which situations are safe and which are dangerous. We will say more about learning (and unlearning) fear responses and the role of the amygdala in Chapter 3. People with PTSD and a range of anxiety disorders have overactivity in the amygdala – their alarm bells are going off constantly even when there is no threatening situation in front of them.

- The *prefrontal cortex* (PFC), which is often referred to as the brain's "executive center," facilitates planning and rational decision-making. It helps to regulate emotions and acts to keep the amygdala in check. When you are feeling very anxious and decide to text a friend or go for a run, that is your PFC helping you carry out a plan to feel better. In conditions like PTSD, the prefrontal cortex is thought to be underactive, leaving the individual with raw, unchecked experiences of fear, sadness, anger, and guilt.

- The *hippocampus* plays a critical role in learning, forming new memories, and regulating the stress response. Learning from experience and recalling helpful memories of past success play an undeniable role in resilience as we understand it. We also know from laboratory studies that chronic uncontrolled stress may lead to damage to the hippocampus, complicating recovery.

- The *nucleus accumbens*, sometimes referred to as the "pleasure center"; in association with another part of the brain called the ventral tegmental area, it mediates the experience of reward and the avoidance of punishment. It is associated with the pleasurable effects of food, sex, and drug abuse.

These brain regions and a few others will be mentioned in due course. As you read, you can come back to Figure 1 to remind yourself of where in the brain these regions are located and what functions they serve.

Next on our list is the autonomic nervous system or ANS. It is, simply put, a set of nerves throughout our body that send signals to our organs and muscles. The ANS has two branches that work together: the sympathetic (SNS) and the parasympathetic (PNS) nervous systems. Whether we are running from a bear in the woods or doing laps around a track, the SNS sends out signals to use up energy and get us moving quickly. When the SNS is doing its job, your blood pressure

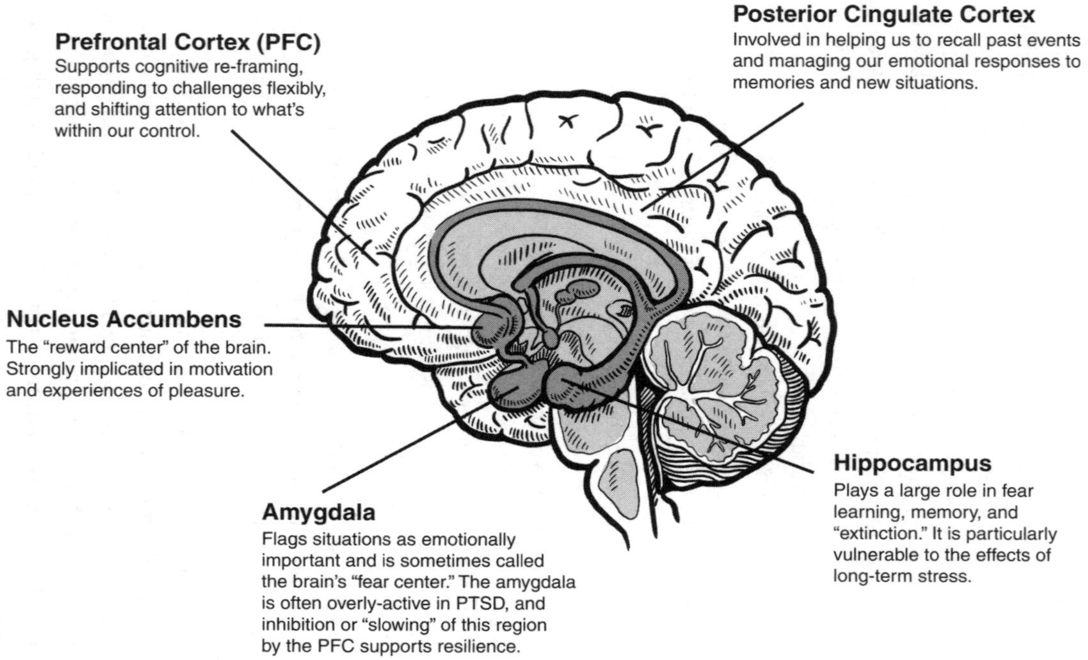

Prefrontal Cortex (PFC)
Supports cognitive re-framing, responding to challenges flexibly, and shifting attention to what's within our control.

Nucleus Accumbens
The "reward center" of the brain. Strongly implicated in motivation and experiences of pleasure.

Amygdala
Flags situations as emotionally important and is sometimes called the brain's "fear center." The amygdala is often overly-active in PTSD, and inhibition or "slowing" of this region by the PFC supports resilience.

Posterior Cingulate Cortex
Involved in helping us to recall past events and managing our emotional responses to memories and new situations.

Hippocampus
Plays a large role in fear learning, memory, and "extinction." It is particularly vulnerable to the effects of long-term stress.

Figure 1 Regions of the human brain

and heart rate go up, digestion stops, and you sweat. But you cannot stay like that forever. The PNS is involved in recovering from stress, and in making and storing energy for the next time a response is needed. For healthy functioning, it is beneficial for the SNS to have a robust temporary response to stress but for you to recover quickly.

Throughout the book we will also refer to various hormones and neurotransmitters that are involved in our stress response and resilience.

- *Cortisol* is a stress hormone that helps the body produce the energy it needs by facilitating the creation and release of glucose (a form of sugar)
- *Epinephrine*, also known as adrenaline, is released by the adrenal glands under conditions of stress. It accelerates heart rate and widens airways as part of the fight-or-flight response to make more oxygen available.
- *Norepinephrine*, also known as noradrenaline, is also part of the SNS. It facilitates alerting and alarm reactions in the brain, and is critical for responding to danger and for remembering emotional events.

Cortisol in particular plays a big role in the hypothalamic–pituitary–adrenal (HPA) axis, which responds to stress with a complex set of reactions. This cycle involves the hypothalamus and pituitary gland, both buried deep in the middle of the brain – and the adrenal glands – which sit atop the kidneys. Cortisol is known as the "stress hormone" because it is released for a short time during stressful situations, and it helps the body to gather the energy it needs to respond. Later in the book, we will also talk about oxytocin, which is a hormone associated with maternal behaviors, social communication, trust, social support, and anxiety reduction.

Our understanding of how these systems support resilience can be likened to shifting gears in a car. You know that when you come up to a steep hill, you must push hard on the accelerator pedal to get up and over it. But once you're over the hill, you must let go of that pedal and work the brakes, or risk losing control of the car. People who are resilient can pump the gas when they need to – by having a clear biological response to the challenging situation – and can slow down and recover when the situation is over. Individuals with PTSD may have problems with some of this biological flexibility; to keep the comparison going, they may be still pumping the accelerator pedal many miles past the hill.

Genetics and Epigenetics

Are we biologically "stuck" with what happened to our parents, grandparents, or far distant relatives? Articles, books, and TV shows mentioning *intergenerational transmission of trauma* have become increasingly common. Luckily our colleagues, including Dr. Rachel Yehuda and Dr. Eric Nestler, are closely involved in careful scientific work in this area. To help you understand what we do and don't yet know about the intergenerational transmission of trauma (and resilience), we should first say a bit about genetics.

The genes we share – that make us all human beings and that make each of us slightly different – are inherited from our parents. But, in the womb, and certainly after we are born, we begin to have experiences that also shape us. We call this the "environment." We are raised by parents or other caregivers. We experience successes, hardships, and life-threatening events – some completely on our own and some with our family.

Scientists have asked the obvious question: Do our genes drive our emotional well-being when we encounter life's challenges or is it our environment? The answer turns out to be that both are important. In a longitudinal study involving over 3,000 adult twins – both identical (monozygotic) and fraternal (dizygotic) – researchers found that genetic and environmental factors had roughly equal contributions to the development of PTSD. But for resilience, environmental factors (such as positive or negative life events) had a slightly bigger impact than genetics (Wolf *et al.* 2018). From this we learn that resilience is not just the opposite of PTSD. It also reminds us that it is not only what happens to us in our lives (including some things that are completely outside our control) but also the things we choose to do that contribute to our resilience.

There's one more term you need to know – *epigenetics*. This is the study of how the environment impacts the functioning of genes. Imagine a string of lights hanging from your ceiling – those are your genes. Simply put, epigenetic changes would be equivalent to flicking a switch to turn any one light off or on. It does not change the string of lights itself – just how parts of it operate for a time. Many things (traumatic life events, diet, exercise, even meditation) can trigger relatively small epigenetic changes that turn some genes on and others off within specific brain regions. These changes could change how someone acts or feels.

We learned about epigenetics in part from research with rat mothers and their babies ("pups"). Just as for humans, there's variability in how these mothers raise their young – in particular, some rat mothers lick and groom their pups more than other mothers do. This turns out to be quite helpful later – pups who got more licking and grooming tended to be less fearful and calm down faster in lab experiments. In other words, they were more resilient. When scientists tried to understand how parenting influenced pup behaviors, they discovered that the highly groomed pups had helpful changes in the *activity* of genes related to the HPA axis (which we talked about in the last section) in their brains – mediated by epigenetic mechanisms. A mother's behavior did not change the gene itself, but what the pup did (O'Donnell & Meaney 2020). You might have caught that these changes occurred after the pups were born.

If life experiences can impact how genes function, can we also pass along certain biological protections or risk factors to our children before they are even born? In other words, is there scientific evidence for the intergenerational transmission of trauma? Our colleague Dr. Yehuda has done foundational work studying epigenetic changes in the children of Holocaust survivors and individuals impacted by the 9/11 terrorist attacks (Yehuda 2022). This "transmission" is extremely challenging to study; it often involves looking at stress-induced epigenetic changes within sperm or eggs prior to conception to make inferences about even just one generation. Dr. Nestler's work with mice has shown a *very small* impact of a father's life adversity on their pups' stress resilience, transmitted through changes in the father's sperm (Cunningham *et al.* 2021).

A few words of caution. The scientific evidence we have around intergenerational transmission in no way matches up with the intense excitement (or dismay) that has erupted over the past few years. We know that it is the physical genes (our DNA sequence) and our own life experiences that are likely to have the largest impact on our physical and emotional well-being, *not* stress-induced epigenetic changes passed from parents to children.

You should also know that the research we mentioned focuses on the activity of genes that *may* influence how you respond to stress; it does not show that PTSD as a diagnosis is "transmitted" genetically or through epigenetic mechanisms. Finally, because any stress-induced epigenetic changes do not change the structure of our genes, we have every reason to believe that positive life events and behaviors within our control, including those mentioned later in this book, could reverse them. Biology is not destiny.

Neuroplasticity

In several chapters, we mention neuroplasticity. Neuroplasticity refers to the ability of the brain and the rest of the nervous system to reorganize its structure, function, and connections in response to new experiences. While many of us think of the brain as an organ that remains unchanged during adulthood, neuroscientists have found that brain structure changes from moment to moment, hour to hour, day to day. When cells in the brain are actively used, they transmit their messages more efficiently and form more connections with other cells. On the other hand, when brain cells are not stimulated, they die and are "pruned" away.

In research dating back to the mid-1990s, neuroscientists found compelling evidence of changes in the brain among professionals as they honed their craft. For example, researchers studied wind instrument players and found enlargement in areas of the brain responsible for lip movement. Further, the greater the number of years of musical training, the more pronounced the brain changes (Choi *et al.* 2015).

Another line of research focuses on the impact of mindfulness meditation, which is thought to build awareness and acceptance of the present moment, including bodily sensations, and may improve the ability to cope with stress. A recent study of brain changes following mindfulness practices (Pernet *et al.* 2021) found that there is a reliable increase in the volume of the right insula – a part of the brain thought to be involved in body awareness – after meditation practice. We see, then, a match between what people practice and the brain area that increases in size as it is called upon more.

In some way, each of us has the power to change the structure and function of our brains. The key is activity. By repeatedly activating specific areas of the brain, we can strengthen those areas. In other words, by systematically following the advice of the individuals in this book, virtually anyone can become more stress-resilient – even in small ways.

Everyone Has Strengths – Some People Have More Resources Available to Them

When we began to study resilience thirty years ago, we assumed that highly resilient people were somehow special, even genetically gifted. We assumed that resilience was rare, reserved for a select group of unique individuals. We were wrong. Resilience is common. It can be witnessed all around us, and for most people it can be enhanced through learning and training. Millions of people all over the world exhibit resilience in their responses to challenging events and circumstances of all kinds. Most of us have been taught to believe that stress is bad. We have learned to see stress as our enemy, something that we must avoid or reduce. But the truth is, when stress can be managed, it can be motivating, and even necessary for personal growth.

And yet we need to acknowledge that building resilience and bouncing back is easier for some than it is for others. Some severe medical and mental health challenges people face may make it hard to put into practice the advice we offer in this book. For example, someone who is experiencing an episode of major depression may be weighed down by the profound sadness and sense of hopelessness, lack of energy, and loss of interest in life. Someone who has suffered a traumatic brain injury may have difficulties implementing plans on their own and may struggle with extreme mood swings. People with these conditions who want to practice the skills associated with resilience would certainly be advised to work with a trained professional.

At the same time, we should also acknowledge the reality of privileges that may be conferred by race and certain other identities in our society. Further, those of us with resources such as financial security, a stable career with good health and leave benefits, and a rich social support network can leverage these resources when the unexpected happens. People who lack these resources may fall into what psychologist Stevan Hobfoll (2001) has called a "loss spiral." One problem can compound another. For example, if a family already under financial strain loses a parent who is the primary earner, the surviving family members may be forced to scramble for ways to pay for food and housing. A financially secure family may have the resources to address their grief and loss in many ways (such as by paying for counseling, hosting a funeral to honor their loved one, and taking time off from work or school to reevaluate their life priorities).

This does not mean that those with fewer resources should give up, but it must be recognized that they will have a more difficult road to travel. Understanding these limitations may allow us to be more patient and understanding with ourselves or with others who are striving to recover from trauma.

We hope that the words and deeds of the generous individuals in this book will be as inspirational to you as they have been to us, and that these individuals will serve as role models for you as you face the upcoming challenges of your life. When we have encountered challenges in our lives, each of us has turned to conversations we had with those individuals. As clinicians treating patients with post-traumatic symptoms, we have also been privileged to witness how they connected to personal strengths amid intense suffering. We try to follow their advice by learning from a specific attitude, style of thinking, emotion, or behavior that helped them.

2
· · · · ·

Optimism
Belief in a Brighter Future

2

Optimism
Believing a Brighter Future

Optimism ignites resilience, often providing the energy that drives us to face our challenges head-on. It facilitates an active and creative approach to coping with challenging situations. How do we define optimism? Optimism is a future-oriented attitude that includes confidence that things will turn out well. Optimists also believe that they can have a positive impact on their own lives, and what they do each day matters. Pessimists, instead, see the future as dim. They believe that terrible things will happen to them and doubt that they can achieve their goals. They tend to be bogged down by negative thoughts – which is, of course, exhausting. In other words, optimists and pessimists have vastly different expectations. Because they see the world differently, they also act very differently.

Scientists have developed ways to measure optimism. One commonly used optimism questionnaire is the Life Orientation Test Revised (the LOT-R), which includes statements such as "In uncertain times, I usually expect the best," and "I hardly ever expect things to go my way" (Scheier *et al.* 1994). The LOT-R measures what scientists have called dispositional optimism (also called trait optimism). Akin to a core part of someone's personality, this tends to be stable from one situation to another. While some of the highly resilient people we interviewed for this book displayed trait optimism, for others optimism depended on the situation. Still, they managed to build on whatever small glimmers of optimistic thinking they could find.

Of the many people we interviewed, Deborah Gruen is perhaps the one who best exemplifies the spirit and power of dispositional optimism.

Deborah Gruen's Story

Deborah's challenges, including a condition known as spina bifida, became evident at birth. Her father Jeff told us: "She had a large tumor at the base of her spine, about the size of a half grapefruit … There was some movement of her legs – but not a lot. She moved her hips and toes and feet, but it wasn't normal movement … I couldn't believe it."

A few hours later they learned that Deborah's vertebrae were malformed and pressing on her spinal cord. She was immediately taken to surgery. Once the spinal canal was widened by removing the impinging vertebrae, Deborah's condition improved rapidly. Still, there was no assurance that she would ever walk. There was also a real possibility that her condition would worsen year by year and put her at risk for chronic problems such as impaired bladder and bowel functions.

After two weeks in neonatal intensive care, Deborah came home. Because her spine was so unstable, she was fitted for a "clam shell." This was a cast made of molded plastic with Velcro hinges that extended from her neck to the top of her thighs. When Deborah was formally named and blessed at the synagogue as an infant, the rabbi ended his prayer with the words, "And may we all dance at her wedding." Susan, her mother, whispered to Jeff, "I hope so."

To her parents' relief, Deborah began to develop normally in many ways: feeding, swallowing, smiling, and occasionally moving her legs. Months later, she had another long but successful surgery to untether her spinal cord. Three weeks after this surgery, Deborah was rushed to the emergency room and admitted for yet another surgery. She ultimately had five operations within her first few years of life.

With time, Deborah's condition stabilized. However, her physical growth and motor development were compromised. Even though – or perhaps because – there were countless distressing and heartbreaking potential scenarios, the Gruens eventually learned not to fret about the future, but instead to help Deborah negotiate the present. They did their best to treat Deborah as they would any other child. But they also knew that Deborah was not like other children.

When Deborah was a preschooler, a family friend invited her to a swimming pool. Susan reluctantly agreed. Would the other kids welcome Deborah? Could she keep up with them? Susan recalls:

> *So she got into the pool and as her mother, I'm dying, because, oh my God, everyone is looking at her. What's going to happen? Well, nothing happened. She swam, she did great, she gets out of the pool just like everybody else. Probably one of the kids picked her up, hugged her and then it was on to the next little game.*

Despite predictions that Deborah would never walk, she gradually learned to do so with canes. Deborah continued to swim, first for fun and then competitively. In 2004, at age 16, she competed in the Summer Paralympic Games in Athens, where she won the bronze medal in the 100-meter breaststroke. Valedictorian of her high school graduating class, Deborah went on to attend Yale University, where she competed on the varsity Women's Swimming and Diving Team. By 2010, she had won medals in nearly a dozen international swimming competitions, breaking records along the way.

Emerging from such a rough beginning and living with a lifelong challenge, how has Deborah Gruen succeeded in so many areas of her life? In part, she has optimistic parents. They never gave up hope, provided unconditional love and support, treated Deborah like any able-bodied child, and expected others to do the same. Her sister Michelle served as a role model who protected Deborah when necessary while also pushing her to face her fears and achieve her goals. Friends never excluded Deborah from their activities, even if it meant waiting for her. Most important of all, Deborah was and remains an optimist herself.

Blind Optimism Doesn't Work

Contrary to popular belief, optimism does not mean blindly ignoring life's problems or viewing the world through "rose-colored glasses." Instead, what we are talking about in this chapter is what Karen Reivich and Andrew Shatté (2003) refer to as "realistic optimism."

Like pessimists, realistic optimists pay close attention to negative information relevant to any problem they face. Unlike pessimists, they do not remain focused on the negative. They don't get bogged down in things they cannot change.

Many other researchers have documented examples of unrealistic optimism. Tali Sharot and colleagues (2007) described the "optimism bias," where people often say that their personal risk of negative life events (such as getting into a car accident or coming down with a serious illness) is lower than that of their peers and that their chance of good things happening is higher. In short, there is a natural urge to feel special, which can bring temporary comfort but is a risky thought to hold unchecked.

Blind Optimism: Some Words of Caution

Former POW Admiral James Stockdale clearly recognized the dangers of blind or "rosy" optimism. He shared his misgivings in a speech to the class of 1983 at the United States Military Academy at West Point:

We pretty much knew each other's outlook and most guys thought it was really better for everybody to be an optimist. I wasn't naturally that way; I knew too much about the politics of Asia when I got shot down. I think there was a lot of damage done by optimists; other writers from other wars share that opinion. The problem is some people believe what professional optimists are passing out and come unglued when their predictions don't work out … babbling optimists are the bane of existence to one under stress. (Stockdale 1979)

During an interview with a special forces instructor, we asked about optimism among their teams of elite "operators." The instructor replied:

We can't afford to have a really negative pessimist on one of our teams because pessimism is infectious and brings everybody down … All it takes is one guy getting excited and negative about something we can handle that causes other people to doubt the situation or the leadership … If one of our guys is too pessimistic, we try our best to work with him, but if he can't get it right, then we remove him from the team … If you want to be on one of our teams and you don't have optimism, then you better figure out how to get it.

Members of the special forces are problem solvers. They know that with the right tools and training, much can be accomplished. But they are not *blind optimists* or in Stockdale's words, *babbling optimists*; instead, they take calculated risks and have a clear sense of the obstacles to their goals.

Humanitarian Hellen Keller likely would have similarly cautioned against blind optimism. She believed that her own brand of optimism was the product of years of deprivation and hardship. Born in 1880 in a small town in Alabama, she contracted a life-threatening infection when she was nineteen months old and nearly died. When Helen began to recover, her family rejoiced, not yet knowing that the illness had left her permanently unable to hear or see.

The next five years were marked by temper tantrums, with fits of violent and uncontrollable behavior. In 1887, when Helen's parents had reached their limit and seriously considered institutionalizing their daughter, Anne Sullivan came into Keller's life. Sullivan persisted in the daunting task of teaching Helen to communicate so that "the barren places between my mind and the minds of others blossomed like the rose" (Keller *et al.* 2003, p. 43).

If not for Anne Sullivan's optimism, Keller might have lived her entire life in severe isolation. Eventually, Helen learned to associate words with objects, feelings, and concepts. With Sullivan's creativity, Helen learned to understand letters and words traced on her hand and then to read Braille. Her progress was so rapid that within a few years she became a "phenomenon," receiving widespread publicity.

After four years of study at the Cambridge School for Young Ladies, Keller applied to Radcliffe College. Doing so unexpectedly tested her resilience: Keller was informed only a day or two before the entrance exam that the math portion would be given in a style of Braille unfamiliar to her, so that she had to learn an entirely new set of symbols overnight.

Radcliffe admitted her. There, Keller began to write about her life and her philosophy. In her essay "Optimism," she described a type of happiness that people ordinarily seek, what she called "false optimism":

> Most people measure happiness in terms of physical pleasure and material possession. Could they win some visible goal which they have set on the horizon, how happy they would be! Lacking this gift or that circumstance, they would be miserable. If happiness is to be so measured, I who cannot hear or see have every reason to sit in a corner with folded hands and weep. (Keller 1903, pp. 12–13)

Keller saw herself as happy and optimistic, continuing: "If I am happy in spite of my deprivations, if my happiness is so deep that it is a faith, so thoughtful that it becomes a philosophy of life, if, in short, I am an optimist, my testimony to the creed of optimism is worth hearing." Keller saw adversity as a prerequisite for real optimism.

How Does Optimism Increase Resilience?

Barbara Fredrickson, a psychologist from the University of North Carolina at Chapel Hill, has developed what she calls the broaden-and-build model of positive emotions (Fredrickson 2013). Fredrickson sees that our emotions, both positive and negative, are closely tied to our focus of attention and behavior. Emotions such as anger, fear, and disgust help us to survive by preparing us for danger. They do this by activating the sympathetic nervous system, which increases physiological arousal. This "fight–flight" reaction narrows our visual focus and tends to restrict our behaviors to those that are essential for attacking or fleeing.

Positive emotions, in contrast, have been shown to broaden our visual focus, our thoughts, and our behavior. When people experience positive emotions, their thinking tends to become more creative and flexible. By broadening attention and action, positive emotions can contribute to our creativity, physical health, relationships with family and friends, our ability to learn new things, and our psychological resilience (Alexander *et al.* 2021).

This capacity to "broaden and build" can help people cope with stress. Those who frequently experience positive emotions can step back from a messy situation and see it from multiple perspectives. They use three coping mechanisms: positive reappraisal; goal-directed, problem-focused coping; and finding personal meaning in ordinary events. We will briefly discuss these coping mechanisms now and elaborate on them later in the book.

First, when optimists broaden their attention, they increase their capacity to positively *reappraise* situations that initially seem negative. The process of reframing allows them to approach hardship as a challenge and to find opportunity embedded in adversity. Realistic optimists do not deny the difficulties they face, but they do tend to look for a "silver lining." This point is exemplified in the infamous words of Littlefinger on *Game of Thrones*, who stated, "Chaos isn't a pit. Chaos is a ladder." As any fan of the show can attest, this royal advisor was an expert at seeing opportunity in the stickiest of situations.

Deborah Gruen is a master at reappraisal. When she received her early acceptance letter from Yale, she was ecstatic. Her long hours of studying and grueling workouts in the pool had paid off. Gaining acceptance to a college like Yale is no small feat. Amid her excitement, as she read and reread the admissions letter, Deborah noticed a website with profiles of the applicants who had accepted early admission. She felt intimidated by their level of accomplishment and worried that she would not be able to measure up. But soon she reappraised the situation by thinking about how interesting her new classmates were and how much fun it would be to get to know them.

A second characteristic of optimists is that they tend to cope with stress by actively trying to solve problems where they can. Research has shown that optimism and positive expectations tend to promote striving toward a goal; pessimism and negative expectations are associated with feelings of helplessness that may lead to avoidance and procrastination. When we talk in the next section about optimism and health, you will see that the action-oriented nature of optimists leads to them having better outcomes.

A third characteristic of optimists is that they are more likely than pessimists to feel happy with their life and see it as meaningful. In a recent study, adults who were optimistic and had more positive feelings had greater life satisfaction. This study also showed that other factors related to optimism, including having gratitude and a sense of meaning in life, were also important contributors to life satisfaction (Oriol *et al.* 2020).

To sum this all up, optimism orients people to the positive aspects of life, helps them focus on sources of meaning and purpose, and fuels active problem solving. Working on your optimism in even a small way can have a significant impact on your daily life – how you see the world and how you face challenges that come up.

Optimism is Good for Your Physical and Mental Health

Optimism has widespread implications for physical and mental health. It may be one component of having longer, happier lives. A recent meta-analysis found that optimism was related to lower risk of "all-cause" mortality, the risk of dying for any reason. It also showed that optimistic adults also had a lower risk of having a stroke or developing heart disease over time (Krittanawong *et al.* 2022). The benefits of meta-analysis like this one, which included over 200,000 participants, is that it combines data from many studies to see if an effect is reliable and strong. It is fair to say, based on their results, that optimism's impact on health outcomes is robust.

Although researchers do not fully understand the mechanisms by which positive emotions benefit physical health, it is likely that the immune system and hormones such as cortisol and growth hormone are involved. It is also likely that optimists in general choose healthier lifestyles than pessimists do; they may adopt healthier eating patterns, exercise more, drink less alcohol, enjoy a more supportive social network and be less likely to misuse substances.

Optimism also protects against some of the negative effects of stress. A landmark study of former Vietnam prisoners of war found that optimism soon after coming home was the strongest predictor of well-being, contributing to a lower risk of having PTSD when they were reassessed nearly twenty-five years after their release (Segovia *et al.* 2015). In our work at Mount Sinai, we saw that health-care workers with lower dispositional optimism were more likely to have persistent distress over the first nine months of the COVID-19 pandemic (Peccoralo *et al.* 2022).

How Optimists and Pessimists See the World

Each day, we are exposed to lots of information – what we think, hear, talk about, and see. So that we are not immediately over-whelmed, we must selectively focus on what is most important to us. The brain does this by drawing our attention to situations that are negative or dangerous, and to situations that are positive and can bring pleasure. That which brings pleasure, such as food and sex, keeps us alive, while what is dangerous, such as a snake or a stranger, may threaten our survival. Our attention to the negative is typically stronger than attention to the positive. We see this in the practice of medicine, where there has been a long focus on group discussions of mistakes or near misses (e.g., "morbidity and mortality conferences"), but not successes.

Our natural attentiveness to danger protects us, but also makes it more difficult for us to be optimistic. It's so much harder to see the joy in a world where the media intentionally focus on stories about war, global warming, crime, epidemics, terrorism, and other frightening events. Media executives know their neuroscience: Bad news grasps attention.

But people vary on just how much they focus on negative situations and ignore positive ones, and this has been called "attention bias." For example, compared to optimists, people who are chronically anxious or pessimistic tend to focus even more on potentially negative or threatening information and avoid focusing on potentially positive information. Their brains are overtrained to see threats and sometimes even turn positive information on its head and make it negative. For example, a person with depression who gets a promotion at work may focus on the weight of increased responsibilities and all that can go wrong, rather than the opportunities and increased salary. On the other hand, while non-anxious or optimistic people notice and pay attention to relevant negative information, they are drawn toward pleasant or positive stimuli, and easily imagine what can go right. People with depression or anxiety often struggle to remember good things, because when they happen, they do not focus on them long enough to make a strong and lasting memory.

How Optimists and Pessimists Interpret Positive Events

Researchers, including Martin Seligman (2006), have found that pessimists and optimists employ quite different *explanatory styles*. When difficult things happen to pessimists, they tend to believe that the negative consequences will last forever and will impact many areas of their lives. They commonly describe the event using words such as "always" or "never," making broad negative generalizations.

Optimists, on the other hand, tend to respond to adverse events by viewing the consequences as temporary and limited in scope. They are more likely to use words such as "sometimes" or "lately" when talking about their situations. Optimistic people tend to have an internal locus of control, believing that they can influence events in their lives; pessimists, by contrast, may have an external locus of control, believing that what happens to them is dictated by luck, fate, or other forces outside their control.

Let's start with some everyday examples. A pessimist whose romantic relationship falls apart might conclude that he will fail in all future romances, that his non-romantic relationships are also doomed, and that there is nothing he can do to change things. One of us (Jon) had a similar reaction taking college-level calculus. One failed first test triggered thoughts of "never being able to do this" and "not being smart enough," and led to discouragement and avoidance of further studying. He considered changing his major. This is a common pattern. When pessimists face a stressful situation, they tend to blame or criticize themselves, underestimate their abilities, and overgeneralize the nature and extent of the problem.

What about optimists? An optimist whose romance fizzles may conclude that he and his partner were not well suited for each other, that he has learned from the experience – making it more likely that his next romantic relationship will work out – and that he possesses the necessary qualities and skills to succeed in future relationships. Had Jon been more optimistic when faced with that first bad grade, he would have seen it as *only one* setback that did not predict many to come and sought additional support. Perhaps he would have tried to challenge the thought that he was an outright failure with many examples of classes where he excelled straightaway. When challenged by life, optimists tend to do a better job of seeing problems as solvable, create positive appraisals about themselves, and focus on their strengths.

Pessimists and optimists tend to employ opposite explanatory styles in good times, too. In response to positive events, pessimists often view their gains as temporary and specific to the event. They might see a personal accomplishment, like an award or promotion, as sheer luck – having nothing to do with their abilities. Optimists, on the other hand, take pride in their accomplishments, and see their personal abilities as stepping stones to future success.

Four Ways to Become More Optimistic

What about those of us who are not born optimists? If we did not inherit "optimism genes," is it still possible to become more optimistic? Fortunately, for most of us the answer is yes. Based on a large body of scientific evidence together with many interviews we conducted over the years, we suggest four ways to increase optimism:

1. Focus attention on the positive things around us.
2. Intentionally focus on more positive or helpful thoughts, and do not dwell too long on negative ones.
3. Reframe the negative and interpret events in a more positive light.
4. Behave and act in ways that build positive feelings.

If we repeatedly focus our attention on the negative, think negative thoughts, interpret events negatively, constantly complain, worry, and act as if we are miserable, we will tend to see the world as a dark and threatening place. But if we pay attention to both the positive and the negative, ignore irrelevant negative information, let go of the negative that we cannot change, interpret information in a more positive light, and take action to solve problems that are solvable, then we will tend to see the world as exciting, challenging, and hopeful.

Focus on the Positive

Researchers have developed ways to train people, particularly those who struggle with psychiatric symptoms, to change their attention biases. Often, the purpose of this training is to build a habit of noticing the positive more. One technique for doing this is called cognitive bias modification (CBM), which uses computer or smartphone games to change the biases in attention that occur without our conscious awareness. One version of CBM involves training participants to respond quickly to a symbol that comes up on the screen in the same place that a picture of something positive (such as a puppy) or neutral (such as a coffee mug) had just appeared. Participants learn to attend more to the parts of the screen where the positive or neutral pictures are shown: If their attention is already there when the symbol comes up on that part of the screen then they win in the game. A recent review shows that CBM is associated with small improvements in symptoms for individuals with anxiety disorders, though its potential for treating depression is less clear (Fodor *et al.* 2020).

But we don't need a computerized game to refocus our attention. We can do it by talking about positive things with others, focusing on what is going well – including the small moments of beauty in our lives that are easily missed.

Shifting Your Focus: Lessons from Dr. Lala

In a June 2021 podcast interview, Dr. Anu Lala, a Mount Sinai cardiologist, talked about how she focuses on the positive with a patient in her care who is experiencing heart failure and needs a transplant.

So with this particular patient who I became very close with, we would start the day off with, let's talk about all the things that are working. So your brain is working. We're having this conversation right now … Your lungs are working, you're not on oxygen. Your kidneys are working … You're able to write and communicate with your family. You're able to walk, your bowels are moving. Your liver is working. And then, yeah, your heart is not functioning well, and that's why we need to replace it. But when you contextualize it like that, I'm not sugar-coating anything by any means, but I am hopefully allowing for recognition of all the things that are working. And I think that's true of life. When you only focus on what's not working out in your life, then you feel like, oh, woe is me. Why me? Pity party sort of situation. But when you try and shift your attention to what is working and have gratitude for what is working, I think it allows for more acceptance for the challenge that you're faced with. (Earle 2021)

Margaret Pastuszko, president of the Mount Sinai Health System, learned to focus on the positive – the beauty of the "here and now" – from her daughter, who has many medical challenges, including limited eyesight.

Her losing her eyesight makes me look at things differently. I look at the trees that are flowering and I think, She can't see them. And a sunrise or sunset. And you think back before you realized that somebody you love can't see them and can't appreciate them. How many flowering trees do you remember? How many sunsets do you remember? Well, believe me, right now, I remember every single sunset and every single flowering tree because you pay attention. You just pay attention [to] experiencing what's in front of you as opposed to always thinking, Oh, I'll do it tomorrow.

Part of focusing on beauty, joy, and success is mentally making space for them. You can do this by seeing challenges you face with perspective, which dials down the negative emotions that come with them. Again, Margaret shared the positive influence her daughter has had:

If you have so many challenges, you would look from the outside and say, Why? Why get up? Why do this? Why do that? This is too hard. I can't do this. And if she doesn't complain, how dare I, right? I don't have any of the challenges she does. She's just been a shining example of what it is to have a spirit that looks at everything with positivity.

And because of that, she changes people's lives and I find that just so fascinating. Somebody who doesn't need to publish a book. You don't need to be a Nobel Prize winner and yet you manage to change people's lives. And you do it with just engagement, compassion, and love. And I've seen her do it over and over again and she's really changed me. I would be a very different person now, I'm sure if it wasn't for her. I'm grateful.

Cultivate Positive or More Helpful Thoughts

A second technique for increasing optimism is to train ourselves to focus on positive or more helpful thoughts in the moment and to avoid dwelling on negative ones. Each time we recall a positive memory and stay with the emotions that come up in us, we make a new memory trace in our brain and build a mental habit of positive thinking. Intentionally increasing your positive emotions activates parts of the brain associated with pleasure (Grosse Rueschkamp *et al.* 2019).

Lew Meyer used positive thinking during his four and a half years as a Vietnam War POW. Optimism did not come naturally for Meyer, but by accessing memories of his life at home with his wife, he trained himself. "We had this book in our house," he says. "My wife Gail read it and reread it and quoted things and pushed me and pushed me. I started reading it. Then I ended up occasionally skimming through it and looking for a certain chapter ... I started rereading it [in my memory] in solitary."

There are many ways to "stick with" positive emotions (Heiy & Cheavens 2014). Here are a few:

1. *Expression* Show your positive feelings more, through smiling or laughing, or saying out loud what is making you happy.
2. *Attention* Fully immerse yourself in the present moment using all five senses, taking it all in. Play upbeat music to stay with the positive feelings and even make them stronger.

3. *Future focus and reminiscing* Remind yourself of a time you felt joy in the past or thinking about future situations where you can anticipate feeling great.
4. *Replaying* Go through all the details of the positive event over again in your mind.
5. *Reward* Celebrate accomplishments with something special to mark the occasion, including having a favorite meal or making a social media post.

You can also hold positive memories in mind by writing them down in a journal or on a sticky note. Having these to refer to in tough times can remind us that negative emotions come and go. One of us (Jon) often tells his staff to save positive emails they have received (e.g., including praise for a job well done) in a special folder and to read them on a bad day. If they do this then they can remind themselves that challenges are temporary and that positive moments can outweigh tough ones.

Interpret Events Positively or More Realistically

A third technique to enhance positive emotions and optimism focuses on changing our explanatory style, the way in which we interpret experiences in our life. We can learn to confront and challenge negative thoughts that are unrealistic or exaggerated.

Many people make destructive statements about themselves (e.g., "How stupid can I be!" or "I blew it again!") during trying times and setbacks, but psychologists have observed that optimists are highly skilled at refuting or in some cases ignoring these negative statements. Optimists often employ strategies that are used in cognitive behavioral therapy (CBT) – the "gold-standard" psychotherapy for many kinds of mood and anxiety disorder. In CBT, therapists teach that negative interpretations of situations fuel feelings of depression and fear. We will go into more detail about lessons from CBT in Chapter 10.

An optimistic coping style can involve not only increasing positive thoughts and refuting negative ones but also affirming the coexistence of both. This work supports the views of James Stockdale and Helen Keller, who both describe the power of realistic optimism that focuses on the positive without denying the negative.

In practical terms, here are some self-help tips for building a more positive explanatory style.

When Something Bad Happens

- Remember that these difficulties won't last forever. Take one day at a time. Where now there may only be pain, over time good things will return.
- Think about the parts of your life that are stable and about things that are going well. The situation may be impacting only one area of your life, and it's important to see it in that perspective.
- Think of strengths and resources you can use to help deal with the problem.
- Notice what is good, for example, acts of kindness by those who recognize your struggle.

And When Something Good Happens

- Give yourself credit for whatever part you played in making it happen.
- Allow yourself to feel grateful for whatever part you didn't play in it – the efforts or generosity of others, or just simple good luck.

- Get the most out of it by "savoring" the moment. Think of ways of holding on to the positive emotions, by taking pictures, sharing the joy with others, or reflecting on the "win" in your mind.

As we will discuss more fully in Chapter 10, on cognitive and emotional flexibility, sometimes it is helpful to ask yourself specific questions to challenge negative beliefs. These questions include:

- What is the evidence for this negative belief?
- Is there a less destructive way to look at this belief?
- What are the implications of this belief?
- Am I catastrophizing or exaggerating the potential negative impact of the situation?
- Am I overgeneralizing, by assuming that this situation has broad implications for my future when it does not?
- How useful is my pessimistic approach to the problem?

Behave in Positive Ways

Finally, a fourth way to enhance positive emotions and to decrease negative ones relies on changing behavior rather than attention or thoughts. Even sticking to small daily routines can build self-confidence and lead to bigger successes.

Put Simply: Make Your Bed

In a wildly popular commencement speech (tens of millions of views on YouTube as of mid-2022), Retired Admiral William H. McRaven, who was formerly in command of all United States Special Operations Forces, states:

If you make your bed every morning you will have accomplished the first task of the day. It will give you a small sense of pride and it will encourage you to do another task and another and another ... And, if by chance you have a miserable day, you will come home to a bed that is made – that you made – and a made bed gives you encouragement that tomorrow will be better (University of Texas at Austin, 2014)

44

Behavioral activation is a therapeutic intervention that has been used to successfully treat depression (Forbes 2020). It is based on the idea that behaviors affect mood, and that depression is often fueled by too much reinforcement for depressive behaviors (e.g., avoidance and withdrawal, crying, repetitively talking about sadness, staying in bed) and not enough reinforcement for non-depressed behaviors (e.g., exercise and social connection). The therapy typically involves increasing positive behaviors and reducing negative behaviors. Psychologists often refer to these, respectively, as activation behaviors – those that accomplish goals and increase a sense of mastery – and avoidance behaviors – those that keep the person "stuck" in a negative place.

This intervention works from the outside in: Act first, then changes in your feelings come later. It might remind the reader of the old adage, Fake it till you make it. Behavioral activation seeks to reduce negative emotions and increase positive emotions by creating opportunities for people to feel better. For some people, this means getting back into exercise; for others, it means showing up at parties even though they don't "feel like it" and are concerned they will be judged. Based on behavioral activation research, we can recommend the following, either on one's own or in conjunction with a therapist.

- *Activity monitoring* Keep a written record of your daily activities. Over time, this record will likely show an association between activation behaviors (doing things that could bring you joy) and increased positive feelings. It might also show stretches of inactivity (e.g., days at a time "binge-watching shows" and ignoring invitations to go out from friends) that are likely to make you feel more unhappy.
- *Assess goals and values* Say or write down your values and goals, which may then serve as motivators that help you to sustain activation behaviors. Where do you want to be, emotionally, in a month or a year? What is most important to you in your life?
- *Activity scheduling* Use a daily planner to set aside time for activities that are consistent with your values and goals, and that you find

increase your positive mood. You don't need to block off hours at a time – even a few minutes reading a long-neglected book or the easiest setting on your exercise bike or treadmill counts.

Not all the above techniques will be effective for everyone, but we hope readers will find at least some of them to be helpful.

The Neuroscience of Optimism

Overall, we also know that engaging with positive emotions like optimism, humor, and joy activate the brain's "reward network," including the nucleus accumbens. The boost of the neurotransmitter dopamine before, during, and after these activities marks a pleasurable experience, helps lay down positive memories, and motivates us to do more (Tabibnia 2020). Research shows that remembering positive events that happened to you, thinking about good things that can happen in the future, and enjoying activities in the moment (e.g., winning money) all reliably activate the reward network in non-depressed individuals. In depressed individuals, this circuit does not "come online" as much in any of those situations – the "spark" isn't there. Jump-starting this circuit, first with little activities, is the key to the broaden and build model and behavioral activation-based treatments.

BUILDING CONFIDENCE

As we mentioned earlier in this chapter, there are many potential ways to enhance realistic optimism and positive emotions. Here is a quick summary of what we have covered so far:

- Focus attention on the positive things around us.
- Cultivate positive thoughts and refuting negative thoughts that are unrealistic or exaggerated.

- Increase positive and reduce negative (avoidance) behaviors.
- Spend time with optimistic and supportive people.
- Engage in meaningful and altruistic pursuits.

A note of caution is in order. Individuals who suffer pronounced alterations in mood, such as those with major depression, should seek help from a qualified professional, who can assess and treat the mood disorder. Therapy for actual mood disorders like depression can often include combinations of counseling and medication, such as antidepressants. Specific recommendations for diagnosis and treatment of depression are beyond the scope of this book.

Conclusion

From this chapter, we hope you have learned that realistic optimism fuels action. Optimists balance acknowledging challenges and avoiding unnecessary risks with pushing themselves to grow. Realistic optimism is the middle ground; on either side of it are potential pitfalls. For example, we know that being overly optimistic can sometimes lead to crushing disappointment when things don't work out as you expect; similarly, only focusing on the negatives, such as things that are not working out, can contribute to paralyzing worry and depression. As Winston Churchill once said, "The optimist sees the opportunity in every difficulty. The pessimist sees the difficulty in every opportunity."

3

• • • • •

Face Your Fears

3

F ear is a basic human emotion – meaning that it is a core part of who we are as human beings. Fear even strikes individuals who are widely admired for their courage. South African dissident Nelson Mandela reported that during his years of imprisonment and struggle against oppression, "I learned that courage was not the absence of fear, but the triumph over it. I felt fear myself more times than I can remember, but I hid it behind a mask of boldness. The brave man is not he who does not feel afraid, but he who conquers that fear" (Mandela 2012).

Facing the Unknowns of the Pandemic

The COVID-19 pandemic brought fear to the forefront for many people around the world. Healthcare workers, especially those caring for patients in the first wave in early 2020, faced uncertainty and the fear of becoming sick and infecting their families, and saw extremely sick patients for whom there was no viable treatment. Several Mount Sinai nurses described their experiences in a May 2020 episode of the Road to Resilience podcast:

> *March 17th [2020] we really saw COVID-19 for the monster that it was. I remember a point that day that we had five resuscitations at the same time. And I was the resus nurse that day and I was running from room to room to room and I realized that it was almost already seven o'clock and the next shift came in. We didn't eat, we didn't drink, we didn't go to the bathroom. It was just nonstop. And I worked at Ground Zero, was deployed to Puerto Rico and worked at a FEMA hospital, worked fourteen-hour days for fourteen days, and it was like the first time that I really felt like this was a disaster, like a real disaster. – Madeline Hernandez, RN*

> *[A]fter the first day, I cried. I was shaking. I didn't know whether I was going to be able to pull through. I felt like, I don't know if what I was doing was right or proper. And it made me anxious as to whether I could easily get this and bring it home to my family. – Manuel Corpus, RN (Earle 2020)*

We hope that the stories we profile in this chapter will help normalize experiences of fear, build an awareness of mental health conditions where fear can take the driver's seat, and empower you with some resources to face fear and uncertainty in your own life. The core message is that to become more resilient, *eventually we will need to face our fears.*

The Science of Fear

We begin this chapter with science, because we believe that knowing a little bit about the biology of fear will deepen your understanding of the survivor stories that follow. You probably already know that when we encounter something that frightens us, we react with the urge either to defend ourselves or to run away. This response happens well before we consciously notice it. Fear does us a great favor: it prepares us to react to danger.

Our fight–flight response is mediated, in part, by a group of chemicals called catecholamines (which include epinephrine, norepinephrine, and dopamine). The nervous system releases these chemicals in response to perceived danger. Catecholamines shut down blood flow to the digestive system, which slows during dangerous situations, and instead diverts blood to the heart and muscles, which are needed for fighting or fleeing. Our reflexes sharpen and blood flow to capillaries decreases, to reduce bleeding if we are wounded.

In the brain, norepinephrine (a catecholamine) stimulates multiple brain regions, including the amygdala. It helps us to orient toward potentially dangerous information, and then zero in on the most threatening things in our immediate environment, such as a weapon or an attacker's fist. Increased levels of norepinephrine in the amygdala also makes memories formed during dangerous situations especially strong and sometimes unforgettable.

Thinking back on your own life, out of the countless experiences that you have had, which ones do you remember the best? You remember experiences that were emotionally charged and elevated your norepinephrine was elevated; that is, when you were happy, sad, angry, and especially – afraid.

Fear Conditioning

Not only do people tend to remember emotionally arousing and traumatic events better than emotionally neutral events; they also tend to remember the context in which the events occurred. The brain's limbic system links the fear that accompanies a traumatic event to sights, sounds, odors, time of day, weather conditions, and other ordinarily neutral things that are present during the frightening event. We may not be consciously aware that all these things can trigger a fear response just on their own.

This process, known as classical conditioning, is familiar to those who know the story of Russian physiologist Ivan Pavlov. Seeking to study digestion in dogs, Pavlov measured their saliva flow when they were fed meat powder. He noticed that the dogs salivated even before being fed, as soon as they heard the researcher's footsteps. The dogs had associated the footsteps with getting meat powder, so that the footsteps alone caused the dogs to salivate. This process works similarly in humans exposed to stressful situations: We can have a conditioned fear response to things that should be harmless (such as the sights, smells, and sounds of a park) if they were part of a traumatic event (being attacked). Even things not so clearly related to the trauma can become fear-inducing: Police officers who responded to Lower Manhattan on September 11, 2001 have told us that they avoid bridges, tunnels, and even the entire borough of Manhattan over twenty years later. Life can become limited while trying to avoid being triggered.

Why does the brain have a mechanism to strengthen memory for dangers and the conditions under which the dangers occur? The answer is survival. Your brain is built to predict danger – to quickly learn what is threatening and what is safe. In fact, these memories may last a lifetime. Simply put, in PTSD, this system is too good at its job; it sends signals that potential threats are everywhere, and the person may never feel truly safe.

Can We Prevent or Undo Fear Conditioning?

Once we live through a terrifying experience, does that mean that we will be haunted by fear-conditioned memories of the experience for the rest of our lives? Fortunately, no. The story of Al DeAngelis' skydiving trip provides one example.

On Memorial Day in May 1989, 26-year-old Al DeAngelis and several friends drove to a small New Jersey airport to skydive. None of them had ever been skydiving before, so to prepare for static-line jumping (parachuting without a partner), they had each trained for four to six hours to learn how to leap out of a plane, deploy a parachute, and land.

When they arrived at the airport, they were surprised at the condition of their plane. The exterior was patched together and there were no seats. Despite numerous attempts, the engine failed to turn over. The pilot had to call for a jump-start out on the runway. Eventually, the engine started, and the plane took off, but before it reached a cruising altitude, it was shaken by an enormous explosion. Al and his friends were immediately covered with oil, and the cabin filled with smoke. He shared:

I couldn't even see the guy next to me or in front of me. As soon as this happened, the pilot screamed "Mayday!" He was trying to get control of the plane … The jump master was totally panicked, screaming and running back and forth – that's why I remember it so vividly, because I thought, of all the people in the plane, he is the one who is supposed to be the calmest.

When the smoke inside the cabin briefly cleared, Al could see the jump master opening the side door. Al remembers thinking, I'm either going to burn to death or get thrown out of the plane. Somehow, despite the chaos and blinding smoke, the pilot, who had spent years flying large jets for a major airline, successfully landed the burning plane in a rural field. Everyone jumped out and raced away from the wreckage.

After Al and his co-workers were medically evaluated by emergency medical technicians, they were offered an ambulance ride to the nearest hospital. But each refused; all they wanted to do was go home.

> *As we were driving back to the airport, I started getting really nervous, and I got nervous to the point where I started to shake a little bit. So, we got to the airport, and I told my friends, "I am going up on the next flight." I said, "If I don't go up on this next plane, I am never going to get in an airplane again, let alone skydive again." They thought I was crazy.*

When Al told the skydiving company that he wanted to go up again in the next available plane, they were amazed but they agreed.

> *When they began to put the parachute on me, I started to shake so much that my knees – like in a cartoon or in a movie – were quivering to the point where I couldn't stand. So, I sat down on a table and they strapped the chute on me while my knees were shaking. I was trying not to. I did not want them to see it; I was wearing a jumpsuit but I was shaking … Then they gave us a few minutes, and I kind of got myself together so that I could stand up.*

> *As I was walking towards this airplane, which, again, looked a little shady, the new pilot jokingly said, "I heard you guys were in a crash. I don't think we'll get in another one." So, I got on the plane, and as we started to taxi and take off, I am telling you … I never felt so motivated in my life. I just wanted to get to the door and jump out … when I landed, it was probably the greatest feeling that I have had in my entire life.*

Al learned one of the most important lessons in facing fear: get back at it as soon as possible. Why was Al able to return from his terrifying outing feeling good? Research shows that new memories remain malleable for a brief time after an event. If we intervene during this window of time, when the new memory is "unstable," it may be possible to alter consolidation of the memory.

But what happens if you don't get back on the plane right away? Is it too late months or even years later? The answer appears to be no. Research suggests that every time a memory is retrieved, it becomes amenable to change for a brief period. The process is called reconsolidation. As we have seen, this process plays a key role in psychotherapy (Lane *et al.* 2015). When a patient recalls and reevaluates the past with the guidance of a psychotherapist, the new memory is different and – one hopes – more realistic and less upsetting.

Recently, Megan Speer and her colleagues demonstrated this concept in an elegant series of experiments (Speer *et al.* 2021). They had participants recall negative events from their lives (e.g., a car accident). Participants were split among four groups, who either (1) described one positive thing that happened due to the event, (2) focused on the negative impact of the event, (3) discussed the date and location of the event only (the basic facts), or (4) played a game that had nothing to do with the memory. Those in the "positive" condition felt more upbeat emotionally when recalling the event one week later. The researchers also found, in more experiments, that these effects may last up to two months, and that the new "reframed" memories for those in the "positive" condition activated different parts of the brain than the original ones. Memories and the emotions that go with them are not, as you might think, set in stone. We can use that knowledge to help manage our fears.

Extinguishing Unhelpful Fear Responses

The process of overcoming a learned fear is called extinction. It involves the brain structures that we discussed earlier (the amygdala, prefrontal cortex, and hippocampus). To extinguish a fear-conditioned memory, a person must be exposed to the fear-inducing situation in a safe environment, lasting long enough for the brain to form a new memory. Tolerating the situation with the support of a therapist conveys that the fear-conditioned situation is no longer dangerous.

Several treatments for anxiety and trauma-related disorders work – at least in part – by promoting extinction. These therapies encourage the patient to confront fear and anxiety head-on. To understand why such treatments are effective for disorders such as PTSD and phobias, it is important to note that avoidance is a hallmark of anxiety disorders. Although it is natural for trauma survivors to avoid situations that remind them of the original trauma and therefore make them anxious, avoiding such situations prevents them from recovering and learning that the past (threat) and present (safety) are different.

One of these therapies involves careful exposure to reminders of the trauma – both reviewing the memories and confronting situations in one's life that are feared (and avoided) because of the trauma (Foa 2011). For this reason, this therapy is called prolonged exposure, or PE. In the imagination component of PE, patients are asked to recount the traumatic experience with eyes closed and in as much detail as possible, describing sights, sounds, smells, and sensations, as well as what they were thinking and feeling. These sessions are recorded, and the client then listens to the recording repeatedly. Clients face reminders of the trauma in their life by making a "hierarchy" of situations that make them afraid and pushing themselves to face one situation at a time. This action helps remind them that they are safe now, and no longer need to avoid. The fear that comes along with the trauma memories gradually settles down; further, PTSD symptoms tend to improve a great deal in this treatment. Understandably, for some people with PTSD who start PE, the fear becomes too overwhelming, and they do not complete the course of treatment.

Cognitive processing therapy (CPT), a highly effective treatment for PTSD (Resick *et al.* 2016), also involves confronting fear. It uses the Socratic method of teaching, in which the teacher poses questions and the student, by answering them, learns new ways of understanding. CPT focuses on emotions such as anger, humiliation, shame, guilt, and sadness, which can fuel anxiety and fear. It is common for individuals who have survived traumas to believe, for example, that they could have done something to prevent the traumatic event or parts of it, even if such actions would have been impossible. They tend to blame themselves and to imagine that others blame them as well. For example, a person who was mugged may have unrealistic beliefs, such as: I shouldn't have gone to the ATM that night. A therapist using CPT asks questions aimed at helping the patient to arrive at the more realistic conclusion that they could not have predicted that a robber would choose that ATM on that evening, and that the blame lies with the robber and not with the patient.

Janine Solejar's Story

You do not necessarily have to undergo therapy to transform or extinguish a fearful memory. Our friend Janine Solejar shared:

I was fourteen and we had just gotten a horse for Christmas named Macy. One Sunday my sister brought Macy out in our driveway so the whole family could take turns riding. I felt very confident as the older sister, so I decided to ride down the street instead of just staying in the yard.

Apparently, Macy saw this as a chance to escape – or maybe she was having a fear response of her own? Anyway, she took off at a trot, then a canter, and then a full-out gallop. I tried to pull the reins and yell Whoa! as I'd been taught, but it didn't work. She just kept running faster and faster. A car went by and spooked her even more. At that point I was totally panicked ... Finally, after what seemed like forever, Macy lunged in a mud puddle and I fell off. Landing on the pavement felt like a great relief to me. A man who had been working in his yard ran over and asked if I was all right. I started reciting my name and address, like an automated recording.

That night we were watching TV and Bonanza came on. Someone jumped on a horse and started galloping away, and I started shrieking and put my hands over my eyes and had to get up and run out of the room, I had such an overwhelming feeling of panic seeing that man on the galloping horse ... I knew in my head that he was an actor and it was all just staged for TV, but at the gut level that didn't matter. I was sure he was going to fall off, and I didn't want to have to watch. I was afraid of all horses after that.

Although Janine's traumatic experience lasted only a few minutes and did not result in any permanent injury, she continued to fear horses and reminders of horses. However, like Al DeAngelis, Janine found a way to confront her fear several years after the mishap.

When I was seventeen, I was visiting some friends, Ruth and Barbara, who had a horse named Danny that they assured me had always been very gentle and was now quite old and didn't even have any teeth anymore. They encouraged me to try riding again ... I was shaking so badly I had trouble mounting, and then I think I just sat there kind of frozen while Ruth and Barbara walked Danny around their garden for about ten minutes. I was still pretty shaky when I got off, but after that I was OK around horses. I was even able to enjoy riding again. To this day, more than forty years later, I still feel fear when I relive the memory of the runaway, but it doesn't paralyze me.

Janine faced her fears until the intense fear subsided – the intense negative emotions associated with riding horses *extinguished*. In fact, decades later, Janine rode a horse again and the horse bucked. However, "My training kicked in ... I automatically kept my weight on the stirrups and held my seat. When the horse stopped bucking, I was shaken but not too scared to continue the ride."

A Special Kind of Fear: Fear of Failure

One of the most common fears we hear about and have experienced ourselves, at one time or another, is the fear of failure. This fear is so great that you might not even take measured risks, because you do not want to be embarrassed by the outcome or you do not think you stand a chance of getting what you want. You might be afraid of making even a minor mistake, out of fear that you will be "found out" or "exposed" as not expert enough – this is what is known as impostor syndrome.

Retired Rear Admiral Scott P. Moore is pretty experienced in high-pressure situations. A US Navy SEAL and expert climber, he served as commander of the Naval Special Warfare Development Group, one of the top commando units in the world. Even in retirement, he continues his pursuit of high-altitude climbing.

At the time of our interview, he was just getting into the planning of a complex goal of "attempting a series of peaks with increasing summit altitudes, and culminating with a climb in Pakistan over 8,000 meters." He attempted Everest in 1989. His team succeeded after Ricardo Torres made it, the first Mexican citizen to summit. They also suffered a climbing death when Torres' partner, Phu Dorje Scherpa, disappeared from the summit ridge.

In June 2021, Scott, his 23-year-old daughter, several former teammates including an Army Ranger, and friends set out to climb Denali, North America's highest peak. He documented the climb in a series of blog posts on the website for SEALKids, a non-profit that helps Navy SEAL children overcome academic struggles. What he shares below is an adapted version of his final post:

> We had a spectacular failure ... At 19,500 ft, 800 ft from the summit ... we decided to turn back. Going any further could have been even more dangerous for us, causing us frostbite or worse. The good side is we were close to the top of North America, the views were absolutely amazing, it was a gift that we were even standing there, and I knew it. We were living the best we could live, even if we came up short.

> Mountain climbing is possibly the most direct example of having a goal, and then attempting to achieve that goal. Most serious climbers succeed on about half of their attempts. There are many reasons why they fail ... But they always come back and try again.

It's the same thing with life. We often don't achieve the goal we have on the first attempt, or early in our efforts. We can get cut from a sports team, fail a class, not get selected for a group, or a number of other examples. As someone who has experienced all of those examples, and even failed to summit Mt. Everest decades ago when I had the summit in my sights, here's what I have learned. Each time we set a goal, and set out to achieve that goal, we improve as a person. We learn the most when we fail. Failing is part of life, and if you really want to grow as a person and become someone you aspire to be, you better get used to failing ...

As Richard Branson has said, "Challenge is the core and mainspring for all human activity." Anything that's ever been invented, or achieved, was failed at many times before it was achieved. It's the way anyone achieves anything, by trying, and failing, until you finally succeed. You learn from your failures, most importantly, about yourself (Moore 2021).

Practical Applications: Learning to Face Fear

Learning to face fear is essential for resilience. We challenge ourselves to live for a while outside our "comfort zone" and learn that we can accomplish amazing things. Some of these techniques focus on thinking while others focus on behaviors.

FACING FEARS

Here are the strategies we will focus on in the rest of this chapter:

- Change the way you think about what you fear: View fear as a learning opportunity, a chance for personal growth.
- Learn more about what you fear.
- Learn skills to help you manage fear, like deep breathing techniques.
- Face fear with support from friends, colleagues, leaders, and/or spiritual guides. They can metaphorically (or literally) provide the nudge you need to get going.

View Fear as an Opportunity and Guide

Medic and special forces instructor Mark Hickey believes that fear is good because it keeps him on his toes and serves as a platform for developing courage, self-esteem, and a sense of mastery. When Hickey experiences fear, he often thinks, "I'm scared, but I can learn from this," or "This is a test that's going to make me stronger." During dangerous missions or training exercises, he feels "apprehension and excitement mixed with fear," and as he puts it: "I think that fear is good because it keeps you sharp. They say when you don't become afraid at all, that's when mistakes start happening, when you take things for granted. When you still have that little bit of fear, you recheck your equipment. You make sure things are as they should be."

Indeed, a certain amount of fear is adaptive. There is a well-established relationship between stress and performance. Think about a test you've taken in school. If you have low levels of stress, you may not do as well, perhaps because you don't feel the drive to prepare or have at least some mild worry thoughts in your head about failing. But, if instead you are overwhelmed by stress, you might procrastinate studying or frantically cram, freezing and forgetting everything when you sit down to take the text. The middle ground, having moderate and manageable stress, may fuel peak motivation and sustained attention.

From a neuroscience perspective, under normal non-stressful conditions, moderate levels of catecholamines, such as norepinephrine, enhance functioning of the prefrontal cortex. However, when brain catecholamine levels rise too high, they tend to take the PFC "off-line," meaning that it no longer adequately inhibits the amygdala. At that point, the fight–flight response prevails, and the individual may panic and become impulsive.

Focus on the Goal or Mission

Many of us who are facing fear waste precious time and resources by focusing too much on potential negative and catastrophic scenarios and by fretting about the unknown. Instead, special forces instructors teach soldiers to concentrate on goals and on the mission of the group, even when they are grappling with fear. Former special forces instructor Tim Cooper recommends that soldiers ask themselves these questions: What are my goals? What is my mission? What is the mission of my group? He goes on: "In order to meet my goals and accomplish my mission, I know that I must make a choice: either back down and fail or face this fear and forge ahead. It's that simple." When Tim advises a frightened trainee who is about to make his first night parachute jump from 20,000 feet, he tells them to concentrate on their personal goals and remember that they are part of a team with a shared mission:

> Look, I need you out there right now. You need to be helping me, I need you involved in this. Don't worry about it, dude, I'm afraid too. This is an unnatural act for humans; otherwise, we'd all be flying to work, we'd all be flying home. Bottom line is: I understand your nervousness … But you have to think, there's a bigger task, there's a bigger goal and it's bigger than you and it's bigger than me. We have to go out and get a job done. And I need you as a part of this, so, come on – let's you and I go ahead and knock this out.

The special forces instructors we interviewed also recommend several behaviors that they have found helpful in dealing with fear. These include acquiring as much information as possible about what is feared, learning, and practicing the skills necessary to face the fear, developing a plan and a back-up plan, confronting fear in the company of a friend or colleague or spiritual presence whenever possible, and taking a calculated leap of faith.

Many healthcare workers responding to the early waves of the pandemic told us that while they were afraid, this situation is exactly why they entered the profession – and were prepared to take on the challenge and try to save as many patients as they could. They had a mission and relied on one another to complete it.

Learn More About What You Fear

Information has been described as the antidote to anxiety (Everly *et al.* 2022). Former Navy pilot and Vietnam POW Al Carpenter knows the importance of recognizing and learning about what is feared. He says:

> A big part of true fear is the fear of the unknown, when you don't know what's gonna happen to you. You can't anticipate, but you think it's gonna be horrible. But most of the scenarios that we, as combat pilots, might face, we have already learned about from other people [instructors and colleagues], from our own experiences, or whatever. So we were prepared.

In the military, fighter pilots or special forces team members are required to complete many hours of classroom-based study focused on emergency procedures and problem solving. The goal is to expose soldiers to as many potential mission scenarios as possible so that they will not be surprised by the unknown. The military believes that knowledge is power. To master fear successfully, first learn as much as possible about what is feared.

Healthcare providers also know the importance of training. They run through high-stakes situations over and over, with mental and physical checklists, simulations, and close observation – well before skills are tested on critically ill patients. When the crucial moment comes, fear is still there, but they can lean on their established procedures to know how to handle (most) every possibility. They also know that their senior mentors have "seen it all" and that they can lean on their wisdom.

Leadership Training Pays Off

We saw the importance of training when the Mount Sinai Health System faced the COVID-19 pandemic. Though, of course, nothing could completely prepare us. Dr. Mirna Mohanraj, a critical care physician, shared how an intensive leadership training course she had done in 2019 helped her when her unshakable ICU director Dr. Janet Shapiro got sick, and she had to assume "command" of the unit.

> I'd done [the leadership course] over 2019 basically … As you go through [the training], you can see how you might apply it and you want to think about ways to put it into action and make it part of your daily practice. But I'll be the first to admit it's not like I got through that course and suddenly was a phenomenal leader now.
>
> But I used it all. I used it all and some of it was instinctual because I had experience and learned about it. Some of it I had to look up. But it was everything from learning how or practicing how to influence, practicing how to build rapid trust, practicing how to strategize change management. I mean you name it. I literally could flip through the pages of the course and be like, "Okay, I have literally practiced every single skill that we have learned in this course" … I was just kind of stuck in this crazy situation and just trying to rely on what experts have demonstrated in the past to work.
>
> When all else failed and when I was really feeling insecure and challenged and unknowledgeable, I know this sounds totally cheesy, but I just had this like, "What would Janet do?"

Learn and Practice Skills to Manage Fear

Once we learn more about what we fear, we can learn and practice the strategies needed to tolerate and work through the fear. Those skills should be practiced repetitively until they become automatic or second nature, to manage it more effectively. West Point instructor Colonel Thomas Kolditz advises us to focus on our breath:

> Of all the autonomic responses to the adrenalin rush – including heart rate, respiration, skin conductivity, and muscle tension – the

one that we can best control consciously is respiration. Deep, controlled breathing is incompatible with the other elements of the fear response. Physical relaxation can get you to the point where mental relaxation, and therefore outward focus, can be re-established and maintained. (Kolditz 2010)

While most of us will not have experienced ejecting from an aircraft that is burning up around us, the "fear hierarchies" we mentioned earlier in this chapter are a good way to train ourselves to face fears – until the situations we fear become almost mundane. For example, many people are afraid of public speaking. To "face" this fear, they may decide to write out their speech, and practice repeatedly alone while recording themselves or in front of a mirror, then with one or two trusted people, then with a larger audience.

Through all that practice, the person learns that the fear response rises and falls with time. The "threat" triggering it, they learn, looms large in our imagination but not in real life. They are then well equipped to face the high-stakes situation (like a class presentation). One of us (Jon) clearly remembers his first academic talk in graduate school – shaking knees, sweating palms, and a trembling voice – not a picture of confidence. But he didn't give up. Each talk after that became a little easier, even eventually interviews on national news.

Face Fear with Friends or Colleagues

Most people find it easier to face fear in the company of other people, particularly those whom they know and trust. Confronting fear with others tends to help in many ways. Having someone there with you may increase your ability to see a scary situation realistically. It may also reduce physiological stress responses, such as elevated heart rate and blood pressure, hyperventilation, and stomach "butterflies." As Dr. Mohanraj shared with us, even the mental image of a trusted friend or colleague can be enormously helpful.

One pioneering study in the field of social neuroscience found that women who received painful stimulation while in a fMRI had diminished brain responses to that pain if they held the hand of their romantic partner (Coan *et al.* 2006). Relationship satisfaction mattered – those with lower satisfaction had a greater brain response to pain. These researchers also found that there was still a protective effect, but a smaller one, when women held the hands of a stranger.

With supportive friends or colleagues by their side, people tend to feel more confident and are better able to cope with problems by finding constructive solutions rather than by avoidance. It is much easier to jump out of a plane, rappel down the face of a cliff, go to the hospital for a cancer biopsy, attend a divorce hearing, begin the first day of college, or risk arrest while demonstrating against political injustice when you are not alone. We saw this in our own research on how our healthcare workers coped with the impact of COVID-19. Those participants who said they felt supported by their leaders were less likely to report problems with depression, anxiety, or PTSD during the first wave of the pandemic, in early 2020 (Feingold *et al.* 2021). We will talk more about the importance of social support for resilience in Chapter 6.

Face Fear with Spiritual Support

Religious or spiritual support can also provide the perspective and strength needed to face one's fears. In the practice of mindfulness, emotions and fear are faced head-on. Mindfulness involves observing one's thoughts and emotions without judging them. In his book *Mindfulness in Plain English*, the Buddhist monk Bhante

H. Gunaratana notes that mindfulness and meditation require attention to reality and leaning toward the fear: "In order to observe our fear, we must accept the fact that we are afraid. We can't examine our own depression without accepting it fully. The same is true for irritation and agitation, frustration and all those other uncomfortable emotional states. You can't examine something fully if you are busy rejecting its existence" (Gunaratana 2002, p. 139).

Thich Nhat Hanh, a well-known Buddhist monk who was nominated for the Nobel Peace Prize in 1970 for his role in the Vietnam War Paris Peace Talks, recognized that all of us are afraid. However, he also understood that hiding from fear is not the answer. He wrote:

> If you try to run away, instead of confronting or embracing your ill-being, you will not look deeply into its nature and will never have the chance to see a way out. That is why you should hold your suffering tenderly and closely, looking directly into it, to discover its true nature and find a way out. (Hanh 2000, p. 84)

> The Buddha advised us to invite these fears to the upper level of our consciousness, recognize them and smile at them ... Every time your fear is invited up, every time you recognize it and smile at it, your fear will lose some of its strength. When it returns to the depth of your consciousness, it returns as a smaller seed. That is why the practice should be done every day, especially when you are feeling mentally and physically strong. (Hanh 2003, p. 148)

We will talk about the role of faith and spirituality in supporting resilience in Chapter 5. For now, we end this section with the words of one of our Mount Sinai nurses, Simone Murray, RN, who used her deep faith and prayer to get her through the early parts of the pandemic:

> "Lord Jesus, thank you for today. Help me to stay calm. Help me to show kindness. Help me to do the right thing. Help me, Lord, to

protect myself so I can protect my family at home." You have to pray. You have to ask God to take away the fear from you. Because if you go to work with that fear, you're going to make a mistake. And once you make that mistake, you potentially expose yourself to the coronavirus. You potentially might do harm to your patient because you're not focused anymore.

Get Someone to Push You

But facing fear is never easy, even with the help of friends, colleagues, or an inspiring leader. Organizations that specialize in overcoming fear, such as the military, have developed a host of methods to "coax" or "encourage" their members. Sometimes the "jump master" literally gives a push out of the plane to hesitating parachutists! Tim Cooper says that special forces training is designed to overcome fear:

> Just about every course will have something that bothers somebody at some time. And they'll try to push you through that. They'll be screaming, yelling in your face ... calling you all types of names ... They don't give you any space to retreat. It's all designed to get you to force yourself past the fear. Then once you go through it, they'll congratulate you and pat you on the back and tell you, "Good boy." And once you go over the edge and you're doing fine, you look back and say, "You know, it wasn't a problem."

The military designs its training to strengthen members and foster growth by pushing members beyond their current level of comfort, and numerous civilian organizations do the same. Examples include Outward Bound wilderness expeditions, police and fire academy training, high school and college athletic teams, and challenging educational programs. Medical students are "nudged" by their supervising residents, and residents, by their attendings.

Conclusion

Fear motivates us to stay safe, by helping us to avoid situations that could bring us harm. But at times, we fear things – ideas, situations, new opportunities, objects – that can't hurt us. What is the best way to deal with it when it is holding us back? The bottom line: The best way around fear is through it. *Avoid avoiding.* That is what resilient people do.

4

· · · · ·

Moral Compass

On January 6, 2021, alt-right protesters attending the Stop the Steal rally stormed the United States Capitol, vandalizing offices, assaulting law enforcement officers, and terrorizing elected officials, their staff, and families. Rioters were convinced that the 2020 election was fraudulent and were trying to force Congress to overturn the results. They thought they were right and just in their actions, encouraged by politicians and commentators, with violence necessary to ensure their end goal. As the nation looked on, the news media captured horrific scenes but also indisputable moments of bravery. US Capitol Police Officer Eugene Goodman in a now iconic photo bravely stands alone in a hallway, hand on his holster, ready to defend the building and those inside it from a violent crowd. The impact of this event in the US continues to reverberate.

On February 24, 2022, Russia invaded Ukraine. NATO member countries refused to get directly involved, concerned that they would be pulled into an unstoppable escalation of the conflict. The world watched as Ukrainian men and women made Molotov cocktails and learned how to operate machine guns to defend their homes; citizens who were outside the country returned to take part in the national defense, rather than staying back in safety. Civilian areas were bombarded, at times with weapons banned for their gruesome and indiscriminate effects.

These events and others make it seem like morality is simply a matter of perspective, that what is right depends entirely on who you ask. Treaties laying out basic human rights can be abandoned when convenient; and deeply held beliefs, so-called "sacred values," can be used to fuel violence (Ginges 2019). Yet, at the same time, we also see actions of people like Officer Goodman on January

6th – exemplifying altruism and courage in the face of extreme threat. Moments like those happen every day and give us hope that our moral compasses can find true north.

We want to acknowledge that morality and ethics are complex topics; they have been debated for more than 2,000 years by philosophers and religious leaders. We are certainly not proposing to compete with such authorities. However, we have found that many resilient individuals hold a core set of moral principles and strive to adhere to them when tested. In this chapter, we argue that actively identifying your core values, constantly checking how you are living by these values, and challenging yourself to adopt a higher standard can strengthen character and build resilience.

As you read this chapter, we encourage you to keep in mind this description of morality by the Rabbi Jonathan Sacks: "Morality, at its core, is about strengthening the bonds between us, helping others, engaging in reciprocal altruism, and understanding the demands of group loyalty" (Sacks 2020, p. 33).

Epictetus at the Hanoi Hilton

James Bond Stockdale, the independent candidate for vice president of the United States in 1992, was a highly decorated veteran. Midway through his naval career, in the spring of 1960, Stockdale received orders to enroll in a master's degree program in international relations at Stanford University. There he took a philosophy course called "The Nature of Good and Evil." His professor was a military veteran himself, and on the last day of the course he gave Stockdale a gift: a copy of *Enchiridion*, written nearly 2,000 years ago by the Greek philosopher Epictetus. The professor explained to Stockdale, "I think you might find this useful."

Stockdale was puzzled by the gift. Trusting in the wisdom of his professor, he kept the copy of *Enchiridion* by his bedside as he advanced through different postings. He read and reread it, all the while trying to live according to its messages about discipline, self-control, endurance and perseverance, virtue and moral character, courage, toughness tempered by compassion, and dignity in the face of deprivation and suffering. Stockdale did not fully appreciate its value until the day his plane was shot down over Vietnam.

Entering the World of Epictetus

Ejecting from his damaged A-4 Skyhawk fighter plane, Stockdale struck the ground with enough force to fracture a bone in his back and severely injure his leg. Through searing pain, he drew strength and inspiration from Epictetus:

> When I ejected … I left my world of technology and entered into the world of Epictetus. I was alone and crippled; self-reliance was the basis for daily life. The system of values I carried with me into this realm was to be tested by my captors. The payoff was my self-respect. I would keep it or it would be torn from me and used as leverage against my senses of purpose and stability. (Stockdale 1984, p. 4)

For the first four years as a prisoner, Stockdale lived in solitary confinement because the North Vietnamese knew that he was a commanding officer and they wanted to prevent him from giving orders to the other prisoners. Stockdale was rarely isolated, however, because his cell shared walls with those of other POWs. Prisoners communicated using the Tap Code, whereby they tapped out messages on the walls. In Chapter 6 we will talk more about the Tap Code and even show you how to learn it yourself.

As the senior-ranking officer, Stockdale knew that it was his duty to provide the others with leadership, inspiration, and military orders. At first, he turned for guidance to the Military Code of Conduct, which states that the American chain of command will remain in effect for those who are captured or imprisoned; that captured soldiers will divulge only name, rank, serial number, and date of birth; that they will resist by any means; and that they will make every effort to escape.

Some POWs supported adherence to a strict interpretation of the Code of Conduct, advocating death before giving up classified information. Stockdale did so as well until he was forced to face reality – the North Vietnamese began to use torture during their interrogations. Stockdale faced a major dilemma that was to preoccupy him for the remainder of his imprisonment. As a Navy officer, he was bound by military law to uphold the Code and to order his men to obey it. But after hearing graphic details of torture inflicted on his men, Stockdale knew that the Code would be impossible to follow; every POW, no matter how tough, had a breaking point. What guidelines should he provide his fellow POWs? Stockdale turned to Epictetus and Stoicism.

Key Lessons from Stoic Philosophy

Stoic philosophy is focused on personal control, reducing vulnerability, and living by a set of time-honored standards that promote dignity, even under the harshest of conditions. At the core of personal control is the ability to differentiate that which is within your control from that which is beyond it. Unsurprisingly, cognitive behavioral therapy, mentioned elsewhere in this book, has its roots in Stoic philosophy. Stockdale writes that

> a Stoic always keeps separate files in his mind for (A) those things that are "up to him" and (B) those things that are "not up to him." Another way of saying it is (A) those things that are "within his power" and (B) those things that are "beyond his power." … In short, what the Stoics say is "Work with what you have control of and you'll have your hands full." (Stockdale (1995, p. 190)

For Stockdale, many difficult situations belong in category B because often we have little or no control over them and often cannot predict when they will happen. One moment, Stockdale recalls, he was "on top," the admired commander of more than a thousand service members, but within minutes of being shot down he became "an object of contempt" and a "criminal" in the eyes of the North Vietnamese. In a matter of minutes, your station in life "can be changed from that of a dignified and competent gentleman of culture to that of a panic-stricken, sobbing, self-loathing wreck." (Stockdale 1995, p. 228)

Over the course of his four years in solitary, Stockdale himself was brutally interrogated on fifteen occasions. After one extended round of torture, he became so depressed that he attempted suicide by cutting his wrists with a shard of broken glass.

His own experience with torture taught him to avoid creating unrealistic expectations. Even when a POW resisted admirably and provided only information that was of little value, he typically felt ashamed, believing that he had betrayed himself, his fellow prisoners, and his country. Stockdale wrote that "a shoulder broken, a bone in my back broken, a leg broken twice were peanuts by comparison ... Shame is heavy, a heavier burden than any physical wounds" (Stockdale 1995, p. 199). In the lowest of moments, Stockdale looked to Stoic philosophy to offer support, compassion, and forgiveness to his men.

Rebuilding a Moral Compass

With Epictetus as his guide, Stockdale gradually developed a set of rules that incorporated many of the basic values of Stoicism and balanced the realities of prison life. These kept his men focused on a common mission. His rules formed the acronym BACK US:

- B = Bowing. Prisoners should never voluntarily bow in public. Refusing to do so would show the world that American prisoners had not been defeated, and if prisoners were forced to bow, any observer would see that they were being mistreated.
- A = Air. Refuse radio interviews ("on the air"), tape-recorded messages, or confessions.
- C = Crime. Never admit to committing a crime against the North Vietnamese people.

K = Don't kiss 'em goodbye. When the time comes to be released, never give the impression that the North Vietnamese were civilized in their treatment of prisoners and never show gratitude.

US = Unity over self. Stick together.

The BACK US rules provided much-needed structure, guidance, and comfort. While these rules are not exactly ones you can apply to your everyday life, the lesson we want you to take away from this is: in even the most brutal conditions, having a code to live by can prove invaluable – even lifesaving.

Morality Requires Courage

Living and standing firm with one's most deeply held values require courage. Taking his guidance from the Greek philosophers Plato and Aristotle, Stockdale defined courage as "endurance of the soul" (Stockdale 1995, p. 16). It is "the measure of a man's ability to handle fear" (Stockdale 1978, p. 2) and it must "be exercised in the presence of fear" (Stockdale 2013, p. 56). Without fear, there can be no courage. Stockdale understood this, and while he respected the courage of soldiers who march into battle or pilots who land on aircraft carriers in stormy seas, he was most impressed by what philosophers have called "moral courage."

Rushworth M. Kidder, who directed the Institute of Global Ethics, defines moral courage as "standing up for values ... the willingness to take a tough stand for right in the face of danger ... the courage to do the right thing ... the quality of mind and spirit that enables one to face up to ethical challenges firmly and confidently without flinching or retreating" (Kidder 2005). Taking a stand for what is right can fuel our well-being. For example, in a pre-pandemic study of nurses in Iran, researchers found that those with greater moral courage had greater self-reported resilience (Abdollahi *et al.* 2021).

How is moral courage developed? First, we must believe in and commit to a core set of moral values and principles. Second, we must know that by standing up for these principles we are likely to face danger. The danger may take many forms: physical injury, loss, rejection, or disappointment. Third, to be morally courageous we must be willing to bear these consequences (Kidder 2005).

Altruism

Helping others helps you, too. Research has shown that many kinds of altruism are associated with resilience, positive mental health, and well-being. One study of 6,944 older adults (age 64 to an incredible 107!) found that those who volunteered more had a greater sense of control over their lives and felt more socially capable and less lonely (Lee 2021). Examples of altruism, from donating time or money to charity to risking one's life to save others, are all around us. Even in the darkest times, we see humble people who are motivated by a desire to help. They ask themselves, If not me, then who?

In mid-March 2022, when the world was shaken by the invasion of Ukraine, messages of support for their citizens flooded social media, and many donation drives were organized. For Mount Sinai cardiologist Dr. Preethi Pirlamarla and her medical school classmate Dr. Danielle Belardo, this was not enough. They dropped everything to spend nearly a week in an underresourced medical relief effort in Poland, assisting a flood of individuals fleeing Ukraine for their lives.

Dr. Pirlarmarla's Story

Dr. Pirlarmarla shared her story of helping in the relief effort near the Poland-Ukraine border.

I was horrified and I just felt so much for what was going on to the people of Ukraine, and my friend and I had been talking about what we can do to help, to be involved – whether it was, you know, collecting or drives to collect donations to send there [or] increase awareness on social media … But we really, her and I really got to speaking that we really wanted to do that, but also see what we could do to help directly even if it meant to going there and helping in some way … So we just started to look for organizations that would potentially be there … By complete happenstance, one of her [Danielle's] friends … on social media had posted that she was with this organization, Medico … So she was put in touch with one of the organization members who was there and they essentially said, how soon can you get here? So we essentially got on the first plane we could and flew out.

They rented a car and drove to a set of GPS coordinates, not knowing what to expect or much at all about where they were going. They ended up at an impromptu relief camp set up on the Poland–Ukraine border.

Whatever they had on hand [in the camp] was purely by donation. So it was basically people who had driven across various European borders to come to that location. And they had just unloaded their cars or trucks with whatever donations they were able to get from hospitals, clinics, et cetera with all sorts of medications.

Dr. Pirlamarla told us about many people she aided there. She continues to think about one older woman she met:

I had another woman who was much older. She was very frail and weak, and she was tired, and you could tell that she was exhausted, and she actually fell or almost fell. I caught her, and I had to rush her back into the medical tent.

So, we had brought all these energy gels that we generally use for running. And we made her eat one, she had never seen a gel before, and I think it was probably some very odd flavor.

So she ate it and then she started crying and then, you know, we hugged her and we said, and we had a Ukrainian translator on the phone and we told her: "You're very strong, you are going to get through this." And she kept saying that "I am very strong, I am very strong." And then she left and then five minutes later, she came back, and she tapped us on the shoulder, and she had a small box of chocolates that she wanted us to have … And it was her way of saying, thank you … It was just such an emotional moment.

When we spoke with Dr. Pirlamarla, she attributed her call to action to a huge role model in her life – her mother, a trailblazing Indian American anesthesiologist who passed away early in the pandemic. She told us: "When I decided to go, my thought was how would she react? She probably would've grabbed her stuff, the [stetho]scope, and said, I'm coming too."

Selfless action is clear in the stories of other individuals we have had the great fortune to meet. Margaret Pastuszko, the president of the Mount Sinai Health System, who we will profile later on, donated a kidney to her critically ill daughter amid the pandemic. In December 2021, John Cruz, a parking services worker at Mount Sinai, received a call that there was someone unconscious on the roof of one of our campus parking structures. Immediately noticing that the man was trapped in a car that was engulfed in flames and filling with smoke, John worked with two others to break out the windows and complete the rescue, all at the risk of their own lives.

As we shared at the start of this section, there are many ways to be altruistic that do not involve risking your life. Everyday acts of kindness show altruism and love.

A Pastor Shines Light on Altruism

Reverend Dr. Thomas Johnson of Canaan Baptist Church of Christ in New York City shared with us the everyday altruism he observed as a child in the 1970s.

Everybody was a part in our block of a Christian community, and there were clear mandates then, not as visible today – if your neighbor needs you, you go help. And when they would find out about it, which it didn't take long for word to get out of that – let's say, if my grandmother was sick, couldn't cook, then you'd have four or five dishes show up at dinnertime from somebody else's house.

[I]f a mother was going to have a baby ... well, that left her children and her husband – and of course, men weren't cooking at all ... So the women of the community, you'd see them crossing the street with steaming pots, and you could smell bread and chicken fry – well, the neighborhood always

smelled of food. In the morning, you always smelled baking sausage or whatever. And around five, six o'clock, then you could just take your pick of several items that might be on someone's stove, but it always smelled of food at all times.

This altruism left an impression, fueling his later life of service. Toward the end of our interview with him, Dr. Johnson told us the principle that guides his life: *Love thy neighbor as thyself.*

Sometimes There Are No Good Choices

Sometimes we realize that there is no "good" or "right" option or that what is right is impossible. The potentially devastating emotional impact of these situations has been called "moral distress." It hurts – bringing about feelings of sadness and guilt, and very negative changes in how we view ourselves and others.

The COVID-19 pandemic posed a conflict in values for many healthcare workers – often confronted with situations that had no "good" options. In our work with frontline healthcare workers (HCWs) at Mount Sinai Hospital in New York, we found overwhelming reports of moral distress during the first wave of the pandemic. HCWs frequently endorsed fear of infecting their family with the virus and being torn between their duty to take care of patients and being with their family (Norman *et al.* 2021). Especially in the first weeks, few medical options existed for the most critically ill. In many settings, healthcare workers were forced to do "battlefield triage," giving limited resources to those patients with the greatest chance of survival.

Like the Vietnam POWs who "broke" under torture, healthcare workers responding to a pandemic may be haunted by memories and questions of What else could I have done?, even when there were no viable alternatives. In our study of HCWs, those who reported making tough decisions about prioritizing care and thinking that they were not able to do enough for patients were more likely to have symptoms of post-traumatic stress disorder (Norman *et al.* 2021).

"Moral injury" can be understood as a more extreme form of moral distress; it is the psychological harm that comes from failing to stop or participating in events that violate one's moral code. One common example of a morally injurious event is soldiers directly participating in the killing of civilians or not stopping it, events that occurred for example during the Vietnam War and the post-9/11 wars in Iraq and Afghanistan.

Research has found remarkably similar levels of potential moral injury in post-9/11 combat veterans and US healthcare workers surveyed during the first wave of the pandemic. Both groups were asked about whether they were troubled by witnessing others' immoral actions, or if they acted in ways that violated their own values. Being troubled by the actions of others was most common in both groups – reported by an astonishing 46 percent of veterans and 51 percent of HCWs. Across both groups, those who endorsed either distressing event scored higher on measures of depression and PTSD; for HCWs, those saying yes to either of these items had greater professional burnout (Nieuwsma *et al.* 2022).

Moral injury can also have life-threatening effects if left unaddressed. In Chinese HCWs surveyed one year after the first wave there, those workers experiencing moral injury were twice as likely to have suicidal thoughts or behaviors, like making a suicide attempt (Ma *et al.* 2022).

Recovery from these challenging experiences can take time and professional support. In psychotherapy, a person might learn to see the "bigger picture" of aspects of the situation beyond their control and work through self-forgiveness for their actual part in the events, if any. People may seek the comfort and guidance of spiritual leaders; and in fact, work is currently underway training chaplains in a structured treatment for moral distress and PTSD symptoms in US combat veterans (Ames *et al.* 2021).

The Neuroscience of a Moral Compass

As we have discussed earlier in the chapter, altruism provided a guiding light for many of the people we interviewed. What do we know about the neuroscience of altruism? Research studies frequently involve games in which a participant can choose to give money to another person or a charity, with no expectation of getting something in return. This work shows consistently greater activation of the brain's reward center, the nucleus accumbens, when people act altruistically instead of "selfishly" (Cutler & Campbell-Meiklejohn 2019).

What about people who have engaged in significant acts of altruism in their own lives? Abigail Marsh and her colleagues studied "costly altruists" – individuals who had donated a kidney to a stranger. These researchers wanted to know if there was evidence in the brain that donors were more sensitive to the pain of others – in other words, did their extraordinary empathy drive them to donate? Participants completed an experiment where they first viewed a stranger in pain and then experienced pain themselves. Compared to non-donors, the donors showed greater overlap in activity in an area of the brain involved in pain processing (the insula) when viewing pain in others and receiving pain (Brethel-Haurwitz *et al.* 2018).

What do both imaging studies tell us about altruism? For most people, increased activation of the reward center would drive them to continue to act in the interest of others over their own – it feels good. For some, like kidney donors, others' distress rather than reward may be driving them to act.

TRAINING YOUR MORAL COMPASS

If you want to develop moral courage, where do you begin? In his book *Moral Courage*, Rushworth Kidder outlines a three-step process (Kidder 2005):

TRAINING YOUR MORAL COMPASS *CONTINUED*

- *Look inward.* We all have core values and beliefs. What are yours? Which is most important to you? Are you living by these principles and values? If not, where are you falling short? Do you have the courage to change?

- *Talk about it.* Kidder recommends that you discuss these questions with highly principled people you admire. These discussions can help you recognize the numerous situations in life where your actions have moral implications, and honestly evaluate the risks in defending your values.

- *Put values into practice.* Act according to your values. Remain vigilant because it is easy to make compromises and take shortcuts. By repeatedly doing what you know to be right, and by taking a stand, you strengthen your moral compass. As Aristotle wrote in *Nicomachean Ethics:* "We become just by doing just acts, temperate by doing temperate acts, brave by doing brave acts" (Aristotle 1926, p. 73)

We offer an additional piece of advice, applicable to our challenging times:

- *Check your assumptions about how different others' values are from your own.*

Researchers at an organization called Beyond Conflict (2020) show that even now, the actual differences between political parties may be exaggerated. They surveyed Democrats and Republicans in the United States about their beliefs, how they viewed members of the opposing party, and how they thought members of that party felt about them. They found that Democrats and Republicans vastly overestimated how much the "other side" disliked them and how far apart they were on key social issues. With this in mind, we encourage you to have conversations with people whose views differ from your own. Be curious and do not immediately get defensive.

Conclusion

We also know that there is usually no need to search for situations that require moral courage: opportunities are all around us and we can start small. In her book, *The Life Heroic* (2019), Elizabeth

Svoboda points out that small daily acts of kindness will build up a habit of helping others and prepare us to act heroically. In addition, we can practice heroism by imagining situations in which we would need to act, learning from role models, and using the lessons we have learned from difficult life experiences to help others.

Adherence to our moral compass anchors us as individuals and can bring us together in a common purpose in difficult times. According to Rabbi Jonathan Sacks,

> [the] availability of collective strength that we find in strong communities held together by moral bonds is an important source of resilience that we will need as we face the kind of uncertainty that seems to be the mark of the twenty-first century thus far. It is easier to face the future without fear when we know we do not do so alone. (Sacks 2020, p. 32)

We can become more faithful to our moral compass by taking an inventory of our most closely held beliefs and values, by learning from the writings and examples of others, and discussing our beliefs with people whose values we respect. When we most need to do the right thing, we will be ready.

5

. . . . .

Religion and Spirituality

5

Religion and Spirituality

Many people turn to religion or spirituality to cope with hardships or trauma. Some find solace in formal religious services and prayer when times get tough; while others may turn to meditation, walks in nature, tai chi, or yoga.

What do we mean by religion and spirituality? There are many different definitions. Spirituality is often seen as a sense of connection to something beyond and bigger than yourself like a supreme being or deity, and a sense of inner strength and wisdom. Unconditional love for others is one important part of spirituality for many people. Religion on the other hand, is comprised of traditional values, beliefs, and practices shared by a group of people; and often involves connection to one or more deities. Spirituality is deeply personal, and religion is this personal experience given a structure shared by others (Paul Victor & Treschuk 2020). In other words, religion can be seen as one way of connecting to spirituality.

Do you identify as spiritual, religious, both, or neither? You might not be surprised to learn that a 2015 survey by the Pew Research Center found that 84 percent of the world's population identified with a religion and that this is estimated to increase to 87 percent by 2060 (Pew 2017). But we also know that religion and spirituality do not always overlap. For example, another Pew poll done in 2017 found that 48 percent of surveyed US adults described themselves as both religious and spiritual and 27 percent as spiritual but not religious (Lipka & Gecewicz 2017). Young adults in the US are increasingly likely to identify as spiritual but not religious. Maybe you've not thought recently about spiritual dimensions and how they could fit into your life, or maybe this is something you devote a lot of time to every day.

In this chapter, we share the stories of several people who have turned to a power greater than themselves in life's darkest moments. We will hear from a hospital chaplain responding to the COVID-19 pandemic, Vietnam War POWs experiencing ongoing torture and other abuses, and the religious persecution faced by the Southwick family. We will also share the story of Elizabeth Ebaugh, who connected to her spirituality more broadly following a brutal assault.

Dr. Apolinary Ngirwa's Story

Over the course of the pandemic, Mount Sinai healthcare chaplains provided thousands of hours of support to families, patients, and staff. We interviewed Chaplain Dr. Apolinary Ngirwa, who described his experiences.

> My immediate fear was not about death or being infected. My fear was more of the foreknowledge of the upheaval the COVID-19 pandemic was going to bring along. This reawakened my experience and witness[ing] of HIV/AIDS and even the recent outbreak of Ebola infection. Both HIV/AIDs and Ebola, sadly, have shown that the first reaction is entrenched "blame game"-discrimination, as a result victimizing the persons who are already victims of social inequality.

He made a conscious choice to commit to his work, even under many unknowns and ongoing risk to himself and his family, strengthened by his faith.

> At the peak of the pandemic, many voices were coming from all over, exacerbating fear and confusion. In silence and during my meditation in the Chapel I made a moral choice to remain in the hospital and to continue to offer spiritual support to patients, families and staff.

As with other hospital chaplains, Dr. Ngirwa was on the front line, providing prayers at the end of life while in full personal protective equipment (PPE), often with family members connecting over video calls.

> I was called to the Emergency Department [ED] to be with a patient's family. The patient was in the process of being transferred to a unit, and the family was not allowed to go ... [with her] ... As the patient reached the unit she coded, the medical team tried to resuscitate her. The doctor emerged from the room, handed me a mask and asked me to [go in] the room. The patient was declared dead. The daughter was in total shock and intense grief, as she described her mother coming to the ED talking and seemingly okay ... Calmly I listened to her, and at her request we prayed at the bedside for her deceased mother .... Later on that day, I encountered the same doctor who had given me the mask. We were racing to another emergency. I was called to the Palliative Care Unit to offer prayers for a Catholic patient who was dying. The patient's wife wanted to participate in the ritual and prayer via [video]. Such incidents later became a norm of the day ...
>
> [Another day] a nurse of Mount Sinai had her father in the COVID Unit and requested that I offer a prayer for him. We visited her father at the bedside and arranged for the priest to offer virtual sacraments. When the patient passed away the nurse notified me, and expressed profound gratitude, noting that the prayer and my presence consoled the family.

Dr. Ngirwa was emotionally affected by the weight of the mounting losses. However, he turned to his faith, social support, structure, and physical exercise to help ride out the storm.

> These incidents above, and others kept me awake during the night ... I made intentional efforts to narrow the focus of my feelings, things I listen to, and I balance my inner struggle with prayer, physical exercises, listening to staff in the units – especially their fear, frustrations and hopes. I made a concerted effort to be with my family during dinnertime and even cooking from time to time.

Dr. Ngirwa derived immense meaning from the work and was moved by small moments of grace in the medical teams amid tremendous suffering.

The experience of the COVID-19 pandemic and working here at Mount Sinai for more than twenty years has shown me how people care for one another. The sacrifice of the medical staff and all related staff was phenomenal. Yes, every day I go back home exhausted, still feeling really satisfied [by] how people came together to care for a dying patient, and their loved ones. In the end it is how one cared [for] patient, families, and one another.

Prior to joining Mout Sinai, Dr. Ngirwa led an HIV/AIDS ministry in Tanzania in the 1990s, when little was known about the illness and there was tremendous stigma. Together with his wife, he continues to raise money for health centers in Tanzania, which provide vital services there.

The Southwick Family: Risking Their Lives for Religion

As Americans, we have the luxury of freedom of religion – a freedom only dreamed of by people in other places. When one of us (Steve Southwick) learned about his own family history, he found that religious convictions caused his ancestors, Lawrence and Cassandra Southwick, to put their lives on the line. This information came to Steve's attention after his father spent most of a decade researching and writing a book titled *Southwick Pioneers in Nebraska* (Southwick & Southwick 2005).

Lawrence Southwick sailed across the Atlantic Ocean with several hundred other settlers and arrived in the New World in the late 1620s. He lived in Salem, Massachusetts for a year or so before returning to England. Three years later he sailed back to Salem with his wife, Cassandra, and their four children. A glassmaker by trade, he was given land by the town of Salem on which to build a company.

Like the other residents of Salem, Lawrence and his family joined a Puritan church. Over time, though, they gravitated toward a small but emerging faith-based movement known as the Society of Friends, or Quakers. Quakers are typically known to be peace-loving and modest but determined seekers of the truth. They believe that all individuals possess the light of God within them, and that inspiration and revelation emanate from that inner light.

The egalitarian and personal nature of the Quaker tradition threatened the established Puritan Church, with its close ties to politics, social hierarchy, rules of conduct, and rigid doctrine. The Commonwealth of Massachusetts passed laws that punished colonists who identified as Quakers and who failed to attend Puritan church services. When Lawrence and Cassandra stopped attending services at the First Puritan Church and hosted two Quakers in their home, they faced harsh punishments: they were arrested, fined, publicly whipped, and eventually jailed, starved, and forced into hard labor.

Upset by how their parents had been treated, the Southwick children also stopped attending Puritan church services. One son, Joshua, was punished by being tied to an ox cart, stripped to the waist, and paraded through several towns where he was mocked and brutally whipped. Yet, it is said, a defiant Joshua, with his flesh torn and mutilated, called out to his torturers, "Here is my body. If you want a further testimony to the truth I profess, take it and tear it in pieces; your sentence is no more terrifying to me than if you had taken a feather and blown it in the air."

Two other children, a son named Daniel and a daughter named Provided, were ordered by a court to be sold as slaves in Barbados. However, captains sailing south from New England refused to transport them; one captain was reputed to have said he would rather sink his ship than "bear this child away."

While the elder Southwicks were in prison, a new law was enacted calling for the banishment or death of Quakers. As a result, upon their release, they were banished from the Massachusetts colony. Then in their late fifties, their land and possessions taken by the colonial authorities, they bought a small boat with the little money they had, said goodbye to their children, and sailed away in search of a home. Eventually, they made their way to Shelter Island in Long Island Sound, where they survived the frigid winter but eventually died of exposure and starvation. In 1884, a monument was erected on Shelter Island. It reads:

LAWRENCE AND CASSANDRA SOUTHWICK,
Despoiled – Imprisoned – Starved – Whipped – Banished, Who fled here to die.

Lawrence and Cassandra knew that they would be released from prison and restored to their previous position in the community if only they renounced their Quaker faith and returned to the Puritan Church. But they chose not to do so. A deep faith in God and profound moral courage provided the strength and resilience they needed to defend their unshakable belief in religious freedom.

Turning to Faith in the Acute Aftermath of Trauma

Elizabeth Ebaugh, a clinical social worker, had ample professional experience helping clients who had been affected by traumas. For years, she had volunteered as a counselor for a child abuse and crisis telephone hotline. But this professional experience was very different than going through a life-and-death situation herself. (Please note the next three paragraphs include details of abduction and physical and sexual assault.)

It was 9 p.m. on a cold January night in 1986 when Elizabeth, who was returning home from work, stopped at a supermarket to buy groceries. When she got back to her car with supplies in hand, she noticed a man sitting in a pickup truck in the parking space next to hers. Unsettled, she hurried along, trying to focus on getting into her car and driving away. But when she put her bag on the front passenger seat and turned to close the car door, there he was: crouching beside her, holding a hunting knife, ready to take the wheel.

Elizabeth began to bargain with her assailant by suggesting that the two of them drive to an ATM where she would withdraw cash and he would let her go. He agreed at first. He drove her car to the bank, she got money from the ATM, and they headed back to the parking lot. However, as they approached the supermarket, her captor had a change of heart. He drove to a hotel, where he raped her. After several hours in the motel room, he dragged her back into the car and headed back toward town. Ultimately, he stopped at a bridge, and forced her to get out. He pointed to the bridge. "He wanted me to jump off. That's when I fainted."

Elizabeth woke up when she hit the icy water forty feet below. He had thrown her off the bridge and left her to die. Upon landing, she felt no pain, just the shock of the freezing water. Rather than panicking, Elizabeth felt an immediate burst of hope. She was an accomplished swimmer, and now she had a chance to get out of this alive. Using only her legs, she rolled onto her back and began to kick toward shore, nearly 100 yards away. Each time she began to sink beneath the surface, she kicked faster and harder. Miraculously she reached the shore. Inch by inch, she scaled the slick bank of mud, and then crawled to a nearby road. After being ignored by several passing cars, she successfully flagged down a UPS truck. The driver took her to the nearest convenience store and called the police.

Not surprisingly, Elizabeth developed symptoms of PTSD. Like many individuals who have gone through such a horrific event, she felt haunted by memories of her ordeal and lived day in and day out with an overwhelming sense of terror. Even though she knew that her abductor had been arrested, she felt so frightened that she could not be alone in her house for more than fifteen minutes at a time. She moved in with a close friend. When she felt ready to return to work, she got a ride from friends because she felt uneasy driving herself. Her boss allowed her a flexible schedule; some days she could work, some days she simply couldn't handle it.

Elizabeth believes that her background in spiritual practices strengthened and helped to protect her during the horrific ordeal and played an enormous role in her recovery. When she regained enough emotional equilibrium to reach out, she looked for spiritual leaders and healers. She meditated, chanted Sanskrit mantras, and studied breathing and movement therapy. She was relentless in her pursuit of healing and inner peace.

Finding Meaning after Trauma

Despite living with debilitating stress which plagued her for years, Elizabeth believes that her abduction forced her to evaluate her life and gradually change it for the better. She credits her ability to move forward after her abduction to many resilience factors, but most importantly her dedication to spirituality. Her path to healing led to a radical change in her world view. Before her ordeal, even though she wasn't a stranger to trauma, she had lived with the belief that it wouldn't happen to her. Now she had to grapple with the truth: Life is fragile and can be taken from us in an instant. She shared:

I believe that the only way to find closure is within yourself. It's not about what's happening outside. I could never go back to feeling that it wouldn't happen to me – it did.

Studying spiritual philosophy and practicing meditation and chanting helped me experience the spiritual field, or field of awareness, and the inter-connectedness of all that is. I am more completely present in my current reality and yet I feel a deep knowing that I am part of something much greater.

When something bad happens, instead of asking how I can fix it or make sure it doesn't happen again, I recognize that suffering and pain can be a part of life. However, I am not stuck in the experience of pain. The experience of pain dissolves, and I can feel completely alive in the face of all that is. This helps me to have faith that every experience, no matter how traumatic, can bring me closer to the essential, to the awakened awareness. This doesn't

*rule out any reaction of anger that I was raped; however, those moments
are only part of the journey to the experience of the essential self.*

Elizabeth believes that for survivors of trauma, there is a bridge between
victimhood and returning to the world. She believes that she crossed that
bridge by turning to spirituality and by deepening her connection with a
larger view of reality and with a power greater than herself.

Turning to Spiritual Practices in the POW Camp

Former Vietnam POWs also described drawing strength from their
spirituality. In fact, in *Honor Bound*, the classic account of American
prisoners in Vietnam, Stuart Rochester and Frederick Kiley made
the following observation: "There is virtually no personal account
in the Vietnam POW literature that does not contain some reference to a transforming spiritual episode." They wrote:

> In solitary especially, PWs [prisoners of war] rediscovered religious
> connections that had either lapsed or become too casual: Charlie
> Plumb devoted two hours to meditation and prayer in the morning
> and again in the evening; Howie Rutledge painstakingly struggled
> to recall verses of scripture and hymns from his childhood ... They
> closed tapped conversations with the sign-off GBU for "God bless
> you," hid and secretly exchanged makeshift crosses and Bibles, and
> said grace over the scraps that passed for meals. (Rochester & Kiley
> 1998, p. 609)

Ritual and ceremony are central elements in most religious and
spiritual practices. Even when formal ceremonies are forbidden,
people of faith somehow find a way to worship together. As we
mentioned in previous chapters, the North Vietnamese centralized
their prison system by housing large numbers of American POWs in
one facility, nicknamed the Hanoi Hilton. In 1970, the North
Vietnamese brought many more prisoners to Hanoi from outlying
locations. Soon dozens of prisoners, against prison rules, held a

formal religious service. Men from all over the prison heard the singing and joined in. Even though the organizers of what was later called the "church riot" knew that the North Vietnamese would punish them severely, they proceeded because they believed that this collective expression of faith would improve morale. After the service, North Vietnamese guards shackled the organizers for thirty-eight days.

Bob Shumaker, one of the most respected senior officers at the Hanoi Hilton, believes in God but does not see himself as devout. However, as a seasoned prisoner, he offered the following advice when a new POW arrived in the cell next to his: "The first thing you need around here, old buddy, is faith. I'm not a preacher. I'm not gonna try to convert you. I'm just gonna tell you the truth. If you can't tap into a source of strength and power greater than yourself, you're probably not gonna last."

Some of the POWs we interviewed told us that although they embraced religion and prayed frequently during their imprisonment, they had not considered themselves to be religious before their capture. Being subjected to conditions in which suffering was all around them and death never far away, motivated them to focus on God and to pray far more than they had at any other time in their life. The authenticity of this so-called "foxhole religion" has been questioned by some religious figures, but for many POWs and other trauma survivors, religion and spirituality, whether long-standing or newfound, played an essential role in their survival.

What Does the Research Say?

Studies have linked religiosity and spirituality to lower levels of depression and suicidal ideation – it seems to protect people from developing symptoms in the first place and may help them recover if they do become affected. In a large study of over 89,000 nurses, those who attended religious services at least once a week had a fivefold lower suicide rate compared to other nurses (VanderWeele *et al.* 2016). Early in the COVID-19 pandemic, one study found that adults under quarantine who had greater spirituality (along with other factors, such as greater social support) had lower levels of depression (Schmitt *et al.* 2021). Even for adults hospitalized for treatment of depression, religious service attendance and spirituality seem to be associated with a lower risk of having thoughts of suicide. This study also showed that service attendance was associated with remission from depression when patients were resurveyed six months later (Mosqueiro *et al.* 2021).

As we described earlier in this chapter, religion and spirituality have often been studied in soldiers. In a study of over 3,000 US military veterans, those with higher scores on a measure of spirituality and religious belief were at lower risk of developing lifetime PTSD and alcohol use problems. High scores on this scale were also associated with greater dispositional gratitude, purpose in life, and post-traumatic growth (Sharma *et al.* 2017).

It is also important to know that religious coping is not always associated with well-being or resilience. Some researchers have distinguished between positive and negative patterns of religious coping (Pargament *et al.* 1998; Pargament & Lomax 2013). Individuals who see their God as punitive and judgmental may feel that they "deserve" their troubles, and that their fate is controlled by an unsympathetic all-powerful being leaving them with little sense of personal control. "Negative religious coping," as it has been called, has been associated with greater anxiety, depression, and worry, including in older adults (O'Brien *et al.* 2019).

How does religious practice enhance resilience? Regular attendance at religious services may foster resilience factors including social support, optimism, altruism, and a search for meaning and purpose. In addition, as a member of a religious congregation, parishioners routinely interact with positive and resilient role models who encourage them to adopt meaningful social roles through acts of generosity. Religious faith may also protect against misusing substances because it values and promotes self-regulation.

Our Mount Sinai colleagues, including Dr. Deborah B. Marin and Dr. Zorina Costello, have developed partnerships with faith-based organizations, to provide timely health information and facilitate access to care. We recently built on this program to teach faith leaders in New York City about many of the factors mentioned in this book. The leaders then provided resilience-building workshops, adapted to include relevant passages from Scripture and prayer, to their congregants (DePierro *et al.* 2021). Over the year-long pilot of this program, we partnered with nine organizations and completed sixty-three workshops. With the success of both these programs, we saw how faith and community can fuel recovery and growth.

More broadly, we also know that spiritual practices support well-being. A recent study compared once-weekly yoga to a health education and walking program in veterans and civilians with PTSD. The yoga group had greater changes in PTSD symptoms at the end of the intervention, though these improvements did not last when participants were reassessed seven months later (Davis *et al.* 2020). We suggest that encouragement to continue yoga practice may have been helpful in sustaining gains. Similarly, tai chi, an ancient Chinese mind–body exercise and martial art, may be effective in reducing anxiety and perceived stress. These practices incorporate multiple elements known to help manage our stress response and enhance performance, including physical fitness, meditation, and breathing techniques (Zheng *et al.* 2018).

Practical Suggestions: Bringing Spirituality into Your Life

There are clearly many ways to explore the spiritual dimensions of your life and to build a spiritual practice. Prayer and meditation are some of the most common practices and are part of most world religions. These practices have been used for thousands of years to quiet and discipline the mind.

Let's start with a few words about prayer. Father James Martin, a Jesuit priest, in his book, *Learning to Pray: A Guide for Everyone*, shares that, for him, prayer is a "conscious conversation with God" (Martin 2022, p. 58). He also emphasizes that prayer takes many forms: it can involve words passed down from faith traditions, a specific request for help, or quiet reflection on the beauty of the present moment. For him, and many other theologians, there is no "right" way to pray. Not surprisingly, prayer has been a source of immense comfort and strength during the pandemic for many people (Killgore *et al.* 2020).

Are prayer and meditation different? Most people would say yes, though some would also say that one can pray while meditating and vice versa. Meditation takes a variety of forms. Some are based on mindfulness, which teaches the practitioner to live consciously "in the moment" and to be "fully present" for what is happening right now. With practice, a person who meditates learns to become a "participant-observer" who watches their mind as it automatically and repetitively follows the familiar paths of old conditioned responses. One monk explained that, while meditating, we can observe our mind going off on a tangent, and gently bring it back as we would correct a child who has wandered from a path.

Learning to use the mind, as opposed to having the mind use you, is one of life's most challenging tasks. As the *Bhagavad Gita*, the Hindu scripture, warns, "The mind is restless, turbulent, powerful, violent" and trying to control it "is like trying to control the wind." However, many meditative traditions teach that such efforts can increase personal freedom, springing out of an enlarged capacity to modify thoughts and feelings and change behaviors.

CONNECTING WITH YOUR SPIRITUAL SIDE

Whatever your individual circumstances, here are a few specific recommendations that may be helpful to connect to your spiritual side:

- Set aside time for prayer or meditation as part of your daily routine. This is often first thing in the morning, last thing at night, or both. There are many ways to think about prayer: it can be an important religious text read aloud or recited from memory, a conversation with a higher power, or as actions out in the world that are consistent with your beliefs and values.

- If you have a faith tradition, make a regular habit of turning to scripture, sacred texts, or other writings for wisdom and guidance. You may also benefit from exploring writings from faith traditions other than your own.

- Practice a physically active form of spirituality such as walking prayer, yoga, martial arts, or dance.

- Practice a creative form of spirituality such as chanting; singing, or playing sacred music; painting or drawing with the goal of expressing sacred ideals; or writing spiritually inspired poetry.

- Become part of a group that worships or practices together, such as a congregation, a scripture study group, or a prayer or a meditation circle. This community may come together in person or online.

- An essential part of a spiritual life is feeling connected to something greater than yourself. You can connect to this feeling in many ways, including taking walks through nature, joining a group with a common purpose (e.g., volunteerism), and fully pausing to appreciate the present moment with all five senses.

We also encourage you to consider a major component of many faith traditions – forgiveness. Anger and self-blame can haunt people years after a traumatic event, and to forgive a specific person, organization, or society that has intentionally caused great harm may be next to impossible for many of us. However, when left unattended, these emotions can be emotionally draining and contribute to depression and PTSD. For returning war veterans, for example, spiritually based programs often address the guilt that many veterans carry, consciously or unconsciously. In their work with soldiers, Everett Worthington Jr. and Diane Langberg observe that "being in the military ... can create opportunities for self-condemnation" and therefore "soldiers need the skills of self-forgiveness" (Worthington Jr. & Langberg 2012, p. 274).

Why should you work on forgiveness? Let's look further at the research. In one study of over 50,000 registered nurses, researchers asked participants how much they agree with the following statement: "Because of my spiritual or religious beliefs, I have forgiven those who hurt me." Nurses who forgave more frequently had better social functioning, lower psychological distress, and more positive emotions approximately eight years later (Long *et al.* 2020). In such a large sample, we see compelling evidence that letting go of anger toward those who have harmed you can be one pathway toward improved well-being.

Conclusion

Perhaps more than any of the other resilience factors described in this book, religion and spirituality are deeply personal matters about which people tend to have strong feelings. As a potential source of strength and resilience, religion, spirituality, mindfulness, and meditation are available to billions of people on our planet. No matter how it is achieved, connecting to a sense of something greater than yourself can put your life challenges in perspective.

6

Social Support

To thrive in this world, we need other people. We all benefit from knowing that someone cares about our welfare and will catch us if we fall. Even better is having an entire network of family and close friends who will come to our aid at a moment's notice. It is also important for us to give of ourselves to help others. Forming relationships may not seem important when things are going well; we tend to take our friends and family for granted. However, close relationships built during good times protect us when we face danger.

Never was the importance of social support clearer than during the early parts of the COVID-19 pandemic. As quarantines were put in place globally, people reached out over video from the safety of their homes to give and get support from friends, relatives, and colleagues. In New York City, thousands of residents opened their windows twice a day to clap in appreciation of healthcare workers, some lining up outside hospitals to give thanks and support in person. Within the walls of hospitals, family visitation was stopped due to safety concerns, so healthcare workers stepped into that role, including in their patients' last moments.

Social Connection amid the Pandemic

Mount Sinai physician assistant, Cilin Philip, who was redeployed multiple times from his typical orthopedics role to critical care during the pandemic, shared the following in a 2020 interview for our Road to Resilience podcast:

The most prominent memories of working through COVID, other than the interactions with fellow co-workers and friends, were my interactions with patients. But not from a provider standpoint, just from a being-a-human standpoint. I remember I was in the ED (Emergency Department) and there

> was a patient kind of tucked away in one of the rooms in the corner. She
> was elderly. She was suffering from COVID. She wasn't going to make it, she
> was DNR/DNI (Do Not Resuscitate/Do Not Intubate). It was just a matter of
> time. And so, I just sat with her, and I just thought in my head, "If her family
> was here, what would they be doing? Maybe saying a prayer? Maybe just
> making sure she's comfortable?" I didn't save her. And this is not somebody
> that I had direct involvement in her medical care, but just to be able to sit
> there with her and just let her know, "Hey, you're not alone." I don't know. To
> me, that was probably the most significant thing that I was able to do in
> that entire pandemic. (Earle 2020)

There were many other examples we witnessed of human connection amid suffering. Dr. Mirna Mohanraj, a critical care physician, led a project to increase the human connection between providers and their patients who were unconscious and connected to breathing tubes and other life support equipment. Staff interviewed family members to learn about the important life milestones, hobbies, occupations, nicknames, and important relationships in their patients' lives. Then, this information was posted outside the patient rooms, so staff could learn more about who they were treating and connect on a new level. Throughout the health system, staff members of all roles held up tablets so family members could say goodbye and religious rites could be performed. Almost immediately, group-based support also emerged, with our behavioral health, employee assistance, and spiritual care teams providing spaces for our healthcare workers to heal in person and virtually.

Learning from Vietnam War POWs: The Tap Code

Former POW Admiral Robert Shumaker intuitively knew the importance of social networks. During his eight years in North Vietnamese prisons, Shumaker helped develop an ingenious method of communication known as the Tap Code. This code, based on a strategy used years before by Korean War POWs, provided a critical lifeline that allowed scores of prisoners to connect with one another. In the Tap Code, letters of the alphabet are organized in five numbered rows and columns:

	1	2	3	4	5
1	A	B	C	D	E
2	F	G	H	I	J
3	L	M	N	O	P
4	Q	R	S	T	U
5	V	W	X	Y	Z

To understand how the code works, readers will find it helpful to know that the sender taps to indicate the row first, then the column. For example, to send the letter "H," which is in the second row and third column, one would tap twice, pause slightly, and then tap three times. To form a symmetrical grid, the letter "K" is omitted from the matrix; "K" is represented by "CC."

Shumaker and his three cellmates memorized the code; when they were eventually separated, each one spread it to new cellmates in the camp. Then, whenever one of them was transferred from the Hanoi Hilton to a different prison, he would teach the code to a whole new group of prisoners.

By tapping with their knuckles and listening with their water cups against the wall, the POWs began relaying messages to each other. Within months, the Tap Code formed the backbone of the prisoners' communication network and resistance efforts. Sometimes, instead of tapping on the wall, prisoners used other noises to send messages. If someone was in solitary and did not share a common wall with another prisoner, he would use coughs or sweeps of a broom to signal numbers. All the prisoners knew that a sniff was 1, a cough 2, clearing the throat 3, a hack 4, and a spit 5.

Shumaker understood that the Tap Code was an essential tool not only for passing on information and organizing resistance but also for preserving sanity. Supportive communication was especially important whenever a prisoner returned from being interrogated and tortured. Using the Tap Code, a POW could get support and unburden himself of the guilt and shame of having divulged any sensitive or confidential information. Telling comrades what he had revealed during the interrogation also helped other prisoners keep their stories straight.

Steve Long's Story

Steve Long believes that the Tap Code saved his life. During the Vietnam War, both American and North Vietnamese combat and supply missions spilled over into Laos, even though Laos was not officially involved in the war. When soldiers were captured there, both sides kept the information secret. Prisoners captured in Laos were kept separate, held incognito and always listed as missing in action. For Steve and the others caught in Laos, this was a living nightmare. How could he reassure anyone back home that he was still alive?

> There was no media, there were no letters home, there was nothing for us. We realized that we needed to communicate with them [the "regular" prisoners] so that if one of them got released, they could get our names out ... So we communicated extensively, probably more than a lot of the other prisoners, because we felt the need for our own safety, for our own lives.

Steve's hunch proved to be correct. When the Vietnam War ended, the Paris Peace Talks called for an exchange of prisoners. Waves of relief and joy spread throughout the prisons of North Vietnam, but for him the exhilaration was short-lived. When a North Vietnamese soldier came to their cell, he asked, "What do you think?" Steve told us in our interview with him: "We thought, This is great. We're going home. He said, 'No. The Vietnam War is over. The Vietnam prisoners go home. When the Laotian

War is over, the Laotian prisoners go home.'" He added, "It took the wind right out of your sails. We would not be released."

As anticipated, one week after the peace accords were signed, the first cohort of American prisoners was released. They immediately met with intelligence debriefers, who asked for the names of all known American POWs. Because of the Tap Code, Steve and the other POWs who were released knew precisely who was left behind in their camps. Steve told us:

> Well, the intelligence community gave that to the State Department, and the State Department went back to Paris and said, "Hey, look … we know that Long, Stischer, Bedinger and Brace are in North Vietnam and if you do not release them, then we will resume bombing North Vietnam with B-52s." … So it did pay off that we communicated as much as we did.

Strong Ties Save Lives

It is not surprising that Vietnam POWs found ways to bond with each other despite solitary confinement, because the military strongly emphasizes fostering and sustaining strong personal relationships. Soldiers belong to units: squads, platoons, companies, battalions, and divisions. No one operates in isolation. Groups, not individuals, solve most problems. This *esprit de corps* is conveyed symbolically from the first day of training, when new service members are issued fatigues and have their hair trimmed to be within regulation. The preferences of the individual give way to the needs of the group.

As we saw in Chapter 4, Admiral James Stockdale developed the BACK US principle of resistance. Stockdale insisted that after a torture session, prisoners never be left alone to worry. As soon as a prisoner returned, he was to be greeted with supportive messages that fellow prisoners whispered or tapped on the walls of his cell.

Lessons in Altruism and Connection from the Military

Admiral Stockdale recognized that humans, like other animals, are biologically "wired" for survival. When confronted with stressful and dangerous situations, a person naturally focuses on his or her own welfare. It is normal to protect oneself and to fight for resources. However, like so many of the literary and philosophical writers he admired, he believed that true resilience and courage were measured by acts of generosity, compassion, and altruism. As he wrote in *A Vietnam Experience*:

> *When you are alone and afraid and feel that your culture is slipping away, even though you are hanging onto your memories … hanging on with your fingernails as best you can … you suddenly know the truth that we all can become animals when cast adrift and tormented for a mere matter of months. It is then that you start having some very warm thoughts about the only life-preserver within reach – that human mind, that human heart next door … [When people ask] "What kept you going? What was your highest value?" my answer is: "The man next door." (Stockdale 1984, p. 110)*

Strong connections among soldiers motivate military service members more powerfully than do abstractions such as patriotism, according to General Hugh Shelton. Shelton, who commanded US Special Operations before becoming chairman of the Joint Chiefs of Staff, told us:

> When you find a high-speed unit in today's Armed Forces, you find that its members are more concerned about the individual on the left and right than they are about themselves. Everybody is there to accomplish the mission of the team. The organizational and social structure recognizes team performance, not what one individual carries out. We know that's why people fight – we like to say people fight for the flag or they fight for the nation, but they really fight for the one on the left and right – their buddies.

The Special Operations Forces provides a strong example of how units foster close ties. For the twelve-man team of soldiers, the label "band of brothers" has real meaning. Most of the special forces instructors we interviewed told us they know they can count on former team members for the rest of their lives. Even members who have never met one another will wholeheartedly welcome fellow special forces members into their homes.

Social Connections Are a Key Part of Being Human

One need not be a special forces soldier or a POW to experience mutual support and helpfulness. Much of our behavior, whether we know it or not, is driven by the need to connect with others and to be understood. Social support makes us feel good and leads us to connect even more, as does anticipating getting money. Positive social cues like smiling faces activate the same reward centers of the brain as anticipating getting money (Gu *et al.* 2019). Conversely, social rejection activates some of the same brain areas that process physical pain and makes that pain feel more unpleasant (Landa *et al.* 2020).

We give and receive social support in countless ways throughout our lives. Most of us have "built-in" social connections in the form of family members, classmates, co-workers, and the like. Technology has also given us new opportunities to connect through electronic social networks. With today's technologies, people with disabilities who have difficulty leaving their homes can have richly rewarding social lives by participating in online communities. As we have seen, technology, where available, enabled people to maintain crucial social ties during the pandemic.

There are also voluntary organizations of all kinds that provide, among other benefits, the opportunity for social support. For example, the Boy and Girl Scouts organizations, although primarily designed for youth, value and encourage service and helping others. Many world religions view providing help and social support as part of their mission. These are just a few examples of groups that foster a sense of common cause and community.

Reaching out for Support

After trauma and loss, often (but not always) people can receive an outpouring of help and kindness. Many faith traditions have rituals around support that follow losses, gathering support around the surviving relatives for days to weeks after the death. But once the initial flurry of attention dies down, the real tests of love and friendship begin. Well-wishers typically return to their normal daily routines; and sometimes surviving family members, themselves, may react to even the best-intended approaches with coldness or even hostility.

Without caring professionals, steadfast friends, and a loving husband and family, Elizabeth Ebaugh believes that she would still be drowning in the psychological aftermath of her horrific ordeal, trapped in the haunting memory of her attack. "We can't do anything without support," she says. However, she also observes that "supporters need to know not to coddle – there's a difference between supporting and enabling. At some point, we all need somebody to say, 'It's time to get on with it.'"

Our friend Victor Daniels found the same was true after he lost his wife of forty-two years to cancer. Victor and his wife had no children, and family members were too busy with their own lives to spend much time with him. Several of his friends and neighbors had also lost their spouses, and most seemed to be trapped in grief for years after being widowed. He did not want the same thing to happen to him.

On a visit to his primary care doctor, Victor described feeling listless and having trouble getting out of bed in the morning. She recommended that he attend a weekly bereavement support group.

Victor took her advice and began attending the group, where he met other people who were working toward finding a "new normal" and establishing positive directions for their lives after losing a loved one. Victor began to look ahead, to reconsider how he wanted to spend the rest of his life, rather than dwelling on what he had lost. He made a list of goals he wanted to accomplish: Step one was to resume working part-time at a local golf course, which he did. This gave structure to his days and provided social contact with people who were actively enjoying life. Victor's energy and outlook gradually improved. Before long, social networking really paid off: Victor fell in love and remarried. His new wife was a widow whom he had met in the support group.

Finding support requires taking the initiative to seek help. It does not mean passively waiting and hoping for someone to rescue us. We will hear more about asking for help in Jake Levine's story in Chapter 8.

Social Support Helps Emotional and Physical Health

Strong social support has been linked to lower mental health symptoms after severe trauma and facilitates recovery in those who do develop symptoms (Fletcher *et al.* 2021; Wang *et al.* 2021). Studies of individuals with breast cancer, type 2 diabetes, and multiple sclerosis have found that greater perceived social support may protect against depression (Azmiardi *et al.* 2022; Ratajska *et al.* 2020; Zamanian *et al.* 2021). In a study of over 2,000 adults, greater perceived social support during the COVID-19 quarantine was associated with lower loneliness and depression, and better sleep (Grey *et al.* 2020). We saw the same result in our frontline healthcare workers at Mount Sinai; having greater emotional support and support from leaders predicted higher resilience (Pietrzak *et al.* 2020).

In contrast, a large body of research supports the finding that social isolation and low levels of social support are associated with high levels of stress, depression, and PTSD. In a study of over 4,000 older US veterans, those who reported that they often felt lonely were almost *twenty times* more likely to be currently depressed than those who rarely felt lonely, twelve times more likely to be struggling with suicidal thoughts, and three times more likely to have current PTSD (Straus *et al.* 2022). Isolation can also affect our physical health and how long we live. For example, greater social isolation and loneliness predicted new onset heart disease in a study of nearly 58,000 older women followed over eight years (Golaszewski *et al.* 2022).

Loneliness and social isolation are both well-established risk factors for shorter life spans in large epidemiological studies that carefully follow participants over time. In a study of over 21,000 adults in Denmark, being socially isolated was associated with a 60–70 percent greater likelihood of death over a seven-year period (Laugesen *et al.* 2018). These effects hold up over even longer stretches of time. In a study of 2,588 men in Finland, social isolation and loneliness predicted mortality over a period of approximately twenty-three years (Kraav *et al.* 2021). These findings are particularly striking given rates of loneliness, including in the United States: A 2021 survey by Cigna of US adults found that a stunning 58 percent reported feeling lonely (Cigna 2022).

There are many explanations for why having a larger and stronger social support network supports psychological and physical resilience. When people feel supported by family and friends, they tend to feel more confident and in better control; more motivated to adopt healthier and less risky behaviors, such as smoking and drinking alcohol; more inclined to use active coping strategies; and less likely to see negative or stressful events as being insurmountable. In many innovative projects across the globe, our colleague Dr. Valetin Fuster, a renowned cardiologist, has harnessed the power of community, school-, and family-based supports to change lifestyle habits and boost heart health in both children and adults (Fernandez *et al.* 2019; Vedanthan *et al.* 2021). Dr. Fuster has also served as the inspiration for Dr. Ruster, a *Sesame Street* character who encourages children to make healthy lifestyle choices.

Overall, social support can be life-saving. It is worth the time and effort. In fact, we would argue that it is one of the strongest drivers of resilience after traumatic events.

Giving Support Is Also Important

We already talked about the research on the health benefits of being emotionally supported by others, but we are beginning to understand how providing support can benefit mental health. One early but important study of older adults showed that providing social support to others, including a spouse, not getting support was associated with a lower risk of mortality over a five-year period (Brown *et al.* 2003). More recently, our colleagues (Na *et al.* 2022) found that over 60 percent of veterans they studied provided some type of support to others (such as being a confidant or through loving someone). They also showed that giving support significantly lowered veterans' personal risk for PTSD, depression, anxiety, and suicidal thinking. Veterans who both gave *and* received support had even better mental health.

We also see reference to the personal benefits of lending social support in literature. In E. B. White's novel *Charlotte's Web*, the beloved spider at the heart of the story tells the pig whose life she saved: "By helping you, perhaps I was trying to lift up my life a trifle. Heaven knows anyone's life can stand a little of that" (White 1952, p. 164).

Both befriending people and providing social support depend on our ability to be "fully present" for the friend. In a world rife with distractions, truly paying attention to someone, even for a few minutes, is easier said than done. A 2019 study by Asurion found that

US cellphone owners checked their devices on average 96 times per day, or once every ten minutes; and nearly one in five people in the same survey said that they frequently talk to others while looking at their phone (Asurion 2019). To engage in the practice of giving social support, it is crucial to turn off distractions and give the other person your full attention. By doing so you may help not only your friend but also yourself.

The Power of Love and Attachment

Close ties between friends and family members, and among community members, provide strength, motivation, and acceptance. Love in all its forms is a key component of many of the worlds' religions, foremost among virtues. To take an example, the Christian Bible says the following: *And now these three remain: faith, hope and love. But the greatest of these is love* (1 Corinthians 13:13 [New International Version]).

Most scientific research has focused on romantic love between couples, but we are beginning to understand more about "everyday" experiences of love. In one study, adults were asked by text message to answer the following question six times daily for a month: "How much do you feel loved right now?" The results indicated that those participants with higher ratings of daily love at the start of the study had greater psychological well-being – they felt happier. There was also an upward trend in the love ratings over the month, which might mean that simply asking about it made people notice the feelings more (Oravecz *et al.* 2020).

Parental love plays a key role in child development. The bonds between parents (or other close caregivers) and young children form the basis for how the child manages difficult emotions as they grow up, and how they sustain supportive relationships of their own. Babies who have a reliable and emotionally responsive caregiver are more likely to have "secure attachment." They develop strong self-esteem and effective emotion regulation and are more likely to try out new things knowing that their caregiver is close by.

Anxious parents who do not allow their children to take measured risks, or those on the more extreme end who are abusive or neglectful, can contribute to "insecure" or "disorganized" attachment in their children. As adults, these children may avoid close relationships or form bonds too quickly, to the detriment of their emotional well-being. For them, negative emotions are more likely to be overwhelming.

Attachment "styles" are mostly consistent from childhood through adulthood, but can change with new experiences, including psychotherapy. As you might expect, recent research supports the idea that secure attachment is associated with psychological resilience (Darling Rasmussen *et al.* 2019). We will talk more about what we know about resilience parents and families in Chapter 12.

The Neuroscience of Close Relationships

The field of social neuroscience investigates how during times of need, various brain regions, neurotransmitters, and hormones help to bind people together – parents with their children, romantic partners with one another, friends with friends.

We have already mentioned how social and monetary rewards engage similar brain regions (Gu *et al.* 2019) – and may be equally motivating. Social neuroscientists have also found that the hormone oxytocin plays a key role in our relationships with others. Oxytocin improves a person's ability to recognize a familiar face, to identify a facial expression as either positive or negative, and to accurately infer the mental state of another person. Scientists believe that these actions of oxytocin may enhance prosocial behavior by promoting social recognition, trust, and social approach (Sippel *et al.* 2017). Research shows that it helps recovery from stressful situations and may even sharpen cognitive abilities. For example, one study found that women with higher baseline oxytocin did better on a challenging task that required them to ignore certain emotional cues while providing fast and accurate responses (Young Kuchenbecker *et al.* 2021).

In summary, we know that oxytocin is released during social situations where it appears to facilitate interpretation of social signals, enhance recognition, increase feelings of affiliation, and promote social connection. Oxytocin's actions in reducing amygdala activation may help to explain why positive support from others can reduce stress, and through those means, how it could impact cognitive abilities. We are more "clear-headed" when our stress level is under control.

Building Ties That Bind

Clinicians and researchers, including ourselves, have not always fully appreciated the importance of social support. In the past, we focused most of our attention on trying to improve one-on-one psychotherapy techniques and searching for medications to reduce painful symptoms. We did not spend much time thinking about the social networks of our patients. But that has changed. We are now convinced that social networks have the power to protect and strengthen us.

So, how can you see how strong your network is, and build it up if needed? First, take stock. Social scientists have developed ways to measure social networks. They may ask the extent to which you agree with various statements, such as whether you have "someone available to love you and make you feel wanted" or if you are "someone that others could confide in or talk to about their problems" (Amstadter *et al.* 2010; Na *et al.* 2022). We recommend you answer for yourself.

The resilient people we interviewed invest effort in giving and receiving social support. For instance, Tim Cooper calls upon his extensive national network of fellow special forces members for help with problems, no matter how large or small. Many groups have formed in recent years to provide social support for veterans of the Iraq and Afghanistan wars.

As General Hugh Shelton noted, the resilience-enhancing effects of a strong, supportive, and trustworthy social network are by no means restricted to the military. We all can find strength by reaching out and connecting with friends, colleagues, mentors, and family.

BUILDING YOUR CYCLE

There are many ways to broaden and strengthen the extent and strength of your relationships. Gaining and giving social support is a process, not an event; it does not happen overnight. Nevertheless, even if you feel friendless or isolated, it is important to start somewhere.

- *Be fully present.* Do not check your phone or do many other things when supporting someone or getting support from them.

- *Be curious and ask follow-up questions.* Avoid asking questions that can be answered with "yes" or "no." Effective social support reaches beyond the superficial. Anne Milek and her team (Milek *et al.* 2018) analyzed data from four different studies totaling 486 adults who agreed to wear a recording device that captured 5–10 percent of sound snippets from their daily life. When the clips were rated by the research team, they found that those participants who had more substantive, as opposed to trivial or "small talk," conversations in their day were happier.

- *Notice who is in your day-to-day life.* You might make a habit of smiling and saying hello to the neighbor at the elevator or the co-worker who sits near you; and at a basic level, learn the names of the people you run into daily at work or where you get your morning coffee.

- *Schedule time for social connection just like anything else in your life.* Start small. You might pick up the phone and call a family member

BUILDING YOUR CYCLE *CONTINUED*

who is lonely, send a social media message to a distant friend who has suffered a loss, or take the time to debrief with a classmate who has just done poorly on a test.

- *Take a risk and say yes to support when people reach out.* After stressful events in our lives, like a loss, we may feel the urge to withdraw. But continued withdrawal for weeks and months can fuel depression and post-traumatic stress symptoms can fuel depression and post-traumatic stress symptoms. Remember the key lesson from Chapter 3: avoid avoiding.

- *Be transparent and say what you want.* When in doubt, tell people explicitly the kind of support that you would find most helpful. If they do not know what you want, they may miss the mark by offering advice when you might just want to be "heard and seen."

Conclusion

In summary, those who know how to build strong positive social networks reap many benefits. Strong positive relationships are associated with better physical health, protection against depression and stress disorders such as PTSD, enhanced emotional well-being, and longer life. In our experience, most resilient individuals take advantage of the profound strengthening effects of positive social networks. In fact, special forces soldiers often deny having exceptional personal strength, sturdiness, or resilience. Instead, they believe their strength and courage come from their "family" of fellow soldiers – they never "go it alone." But, for most of us, our support network, even if it is extensive and strong, will not automatically reach out to embrace us when we are most in need. Rather, we would be wise to follow the example of the resilient individuals in this book by asking for help.

7

· · · · ·

Role Models

Role Models

One of the first psychologists to study resilience, Emmy Werner, observed that children who grew up through adversity were more likely to thrive as adults if they found at least one person who truly supported them and served as an admired role model (Werner 1993; Werner & Smith 1992). Our research has found a similar pattern: many of the resilient individuals we interviewed have role models whose beliefs, attitudes, and behaviors inspire them. They, in turn, have inspired us. In an interview in preparation for this new edition, one of us (Steve) said:

> It's been great because everybody we interview, they become a role model. They just flip through my mind when I'm beginning to kind of wimp out on something, or when I'm feeling sorry for myself or whatever, one of these wonderful people we've interviewed comes to mind and I said, oh come on, you can do this, so it's actually a joy.

Reverend Dr. Thomas Johnson, who we encountered in Chapter 4, shared with us how his mother and grandmother were role models to him as he grew up in the United States in Springfield, Ohio. In turn, he would go on to become a role model for others many decades later – at a time when lives were at stake. Amid the first year of the pandemic, he saw many people in his predominately Black congregation decline the first round of vaccines. He knew this was partly because of the broken trust between communities of color and the medical system; it was also due to the rampant misinformation about the virus and the vaccines. He had to do something: "There was a fear that the injections were intended somehow to harm you ... Pastors were sought out more than anyone else to affirm certain things and give hope ... once Canaan saw ... a picture of *me* getting my shot ... they started pouring in to get theirs."

Many other faith leaders around New York City did the same. Knowing how much faith leaders are turned to as trusted role models, Dr. Johnson and many other pastors collaborated with our team at Mount Sinai on several projects that have helped them share high-quality information about mental and physical health with their congregations.

Reverend Dr. Thomas Johnson's Story

As you might expect, parents, grandparents, and older siblings are often our first role models. Here is what Reverend Dr. Thomas Johnson told us.

The community we lived in, the neighborhood, even though we were very much low-income, my mother ... never relied on public service even though she was always eligible. But having grown up in the sharecropping period – that was the ethic; you worked. And so if times got really tough, she would go to the Social Services and maybe get some food stamps and then after things [worked] out, she go back down there and take herself off ... their survival skills are just unbelievable when it comes to making sure there's shelter and food ... And so shelter was provided, modest but sufficient.

There was no way ... the resources that were generated in the house were going to be sufficient for four people, five people ... but I don't remember them ever being in a state of panic about it. It was, we'll make this work, and they knew how to make it work because in the Jim Crow era, that's what you did every day. And they knew – they knew how to live off the earth and they knew how to sew so that when your socks were wearing out, you mend them, you didn't throw them or toss them – or if I had a tear in my jeans, even though that's fashionable now, they knew how to patch it.

Who Else Can Be a Role Model?

In addition to parents, role models can include other relatives, teachers, coaches, or clergy. They may be older or one's own age; they may be friends, siblings, colleagues at work, or military buddies. Role models can even be children – and not necessarily our own children.

Dorinne Naughton, who worked with us for years, was not only a dedicated administrative officer but also a good friend. She was shocked when she learned that she had cancer. In the year leading up to her diagnosis, her fiancé, mother, and father had all died of cancer. Five days a week for more than a month, Dorinne received radiation treatment at a National Institutes of Health facility. There, she found an unexpected role model.

> Every day I saw a little boy there in the waiting room. His name was David and he was 5 years old ... He and I would play checkers or tic-tac-toe while we were waiting. Seeing that little boy made me realize that I was pretty lucky to go through fifty years without ever being sick. He had a brain tumor and had been through surgery, but he was the happiest little kid, not scared a bit. He used to bounce in and say hello to me. He once said, "I'm going to teach you tic-tac-toe so you can beat all of your friends."

In Chapter 2, we told the story of Deborah Gruen, the Yale University graduate and Paralympic swimmer born with spina bifida. She sees Franklin Delano Roosevelt as one of her role models:

> Franklin Roosevelt really exemplifies what it's like to be a person with a disability in an able-bodied world. I mean, you don't understand how hard this guy had to work just to walk. When he gave speeches and he was standing up, he grabbed the podium so hard to keep himself steady. He hid the fact that he had a disability, but at the same time it was always with him. And I think having polio really changed him. I feel like that's me, too.

In some families, resilient role models span multiple generations. Thich Nhat Hanh, one of the world's great Buddhist teachers, points out that we are each a continuation of our ancestors from both a genetic and a behavioral perspective. You already have those ancestors within you. Resilient grandparents and parents beget hardy sons and daughters, who, in turn, raise their own resilient children.

Perhaps it was coming to understand this that motivated one of us (Steve) to look back at his own family heritage from the standpoint of resilience. He was struck by the account of his seventeenth-century ancestors Lawrence and Cassandra Southwick and the persecution they and their children endured after embracing the Quaker religion. Steve kept their story in mind when facing adversity and gained strength from it.

But what about people who do not have access to a family history with such detail? We can consider all of humanity that has gone before us as "ancestors" from whom we can draw inspiration and strength. If we think about the hardships of life in past generations, we might say that just about anyone who lived 200 or even 100 years ago was resilient by today's standards, and we are part of that human continuum.

Lew Meyer, one of the POWs we interviewed, remembers three adults who guided him through a difficult childhood. The first was his truant officer, Ed Rowe, whose job was to catch Lew and bring him back to school whenever he climbed out of the classroom window. Lew and his best friend Dave made a habit of escaping whenever the teacher stepped out of the room.

Second Chances

Although Officer Rowe pursued and reprimanded Lew and Dave, he also looked out for them. Once, when the boys had no sponsor for their neighborhood baseball team, they stole baseball gear from a well-equipped rival team.

> Our baseball team all of a sudden showed up with catching paraphernalia and bats and balls … Officer Rowe, instead of catching us, talked to us and told us if we could find the guys who did it and tell them to return it, then he would get us a sponsor … So we went through the fence and under the bleachers and into the lockers and returned the stuff. Then the police sponsored our team, and we went to our games in police cars and everything. The local patrols would stop to watch us while we were playing. I think that's how he started turning us around.

Lew Meyer's second role model was Captain Herman Shawver, the strict but patient local fire captain. Shawver took a liking to Lew, caring enough about him to intentionally break firehouse rules by allowing the boy to hang around the station. Lew stuck close to the captain, watching how he ran the firehouse, how he inspired his men, and marched into flames without hesitation. Lew Meyer followed in Captain Shawver's footsteps and eventually became a fire chief himself.

Lew also told us about the football coach he had when he was in his late teens and playing for a military team. His coach never let him take the "easy path" despite being the smallest player on the squad. Beaten and bruised during a game with a rugged team, Lew went to the sidelines to catch his breath. "They're killing me in there," he said to his coach. He never forgot his coach's reply: "I know it. Now get back in there."

Looking to Peers

As we have seen, role models do not necessarily have to be older and wiser. Sometimes our peers can guide, inspire, and motivate us. Air Force pilot Steve Long was 25 years old when, on a flight out of Thailand, he was shot down over Laos. Throughout his imprisonment, he drew inspiration from his fellow POWs.

> [T]he role models we had were just fantastic. People referred to us as heroes, and I don't think any of us considered ourselves as a hero. But those guys are my heroes, the ones who got us through these ordeals. You'd hear stories, sometimes you'd hear some guy being beaten down the cell block from you and just resisting. And you felt really bad for him, but it pumped you up to know that you were just proud to be serving in the same military with a guy like that. There was always somebody there to set a standard.

At the top of Steve's list was Ernie Brace, a civilian pilot whose plane was shot down over Laos in 1965. Steve describes how Brace spent the next three years in the jungle on the side of a mountain, strapped inside a bamboo cage.

Talk about solitary confinement! Three and a half years in a bamboo cage! He escaped three times and was beaten horribly. The last time he escaped, they buried him in a hole for a week. He lost all control of his body from his chest down. When they pulled him out, he couldn't walk … So he got around dragging his body by his elbows. And I guess out in the jungle, he got to the point where he could sit up. They brought him into Hanoi and put him in one of the cells next to John McCain. But Ernie was able to crawl over to the corner and by holding on to two walls, he could stand up. And eventually, he regained the ability to walk … And you know what, Ernie was one of those guys who never complained.

Jerry White, who we will talk more about in Chapter 10, never served in the military. As an 18-year-old foreign exchange student to Israel from the United States, Jerry was hiking in the Golan Heights when he stepped on a landmine. Grievously injured, he was taken to a hospital in Tel Aviv, where he became depressed and discouraged. There, one of his role models was a wounded Israeli soldier.

The guy in the next bed wanted to die after losing both legs. I needed to distance myself from that. Then an Israeli soldier came for a peer visit. He walked up to my bed and said, "I stepped on a landmine, too. Can you tell which leg I lost?" He had a perfect gait. I said I couldn't tell and he said, "That's the point. The battle isn't down there." He pointed to his legs. "It's up here." He pointed to his heart. When he found out that I still had my knee, which meant that I wasn't that bad off, he said, "What you have is a nose cold. You'll get over it."

The Negative Role Model

Although we think of role models as providing positive examples to admire and emulate, sometimes a person stands out by embodying traits we emphatically do not want to adopt. We can think of such a person as a negative role model.

Dr. Laurie Harkness, a clinical professor of psychiatry at the Yale University School of Medicine and a national leader in psychiatric rehabilitation for the US Department of Veterans Affairs, was in her early fifties when she was diagnosed with leukemia. While undergoing treatment, she encountered many other cancer patients, one of whom seemed to be "giving up," resigning himself to the idea that he would never get better. Laurie clearly remembers the moment she thought, I will not be like that. Whenever she felt discouraged, she would remember this "negative role model" and use that memory as a motivation to fight the disease and strive for a positive outlook. And that is exactly what she did. Despite feeling weak and nauseated for weeks at a time, Laurie never gave up. If anything, she picked up the pace. Following her diagnosis, she worked tirelessly to develop vocational and housing opportunities for individuals and families who are homeless or who are at risk of homelessness, raising substantial federal and private funding.

There is ample evidence of the impact of negative role models in the workplace. For example, one study found that leaders who showed up to work even though they were feeling sick (known as "presenteeism") had employees who were more likely to do the same (Dietz *et al.* 2020). But that's not the end of the story. Those employees who had greater presenteeism also went on to take more sick leave, potentially due to the emotional and physical strain of working when ill. What is unclear from the study is whether loyalty to the leader or company, or fear of negative consequences, motivated the employees to work when sick.

In our clinical work, we have often encountered people who were mistreated in childhood by one or both parents. Such individuals are often fiercely determined to live a life different from that of their abusers. Rather than imitate the negative behavior, they make a great effort to learn new, more positive behaviors. Like Dr. Harkness, they use the example of the abuser as a guidepost for what not to do and what not to become. This becomes a mission that they carry out as they develop relationships and raise their own families.

Everybody Needs Resilient Role Models, Especially Children

Abundant research shows that parents and other adult mentors can help a young person develop the ability to handle trauma and to overcome adversity. Parents often ask, How can I be a strong role model for my child or teenager? One answer is to practice the resilient behaviors that we outline in this book, and to give your child many opportunities to do the same. Children who are resilient and well adjusted typically receive support and encouragement from committed mentors and resilient role models. Even one person can make a dramatic difference.

Ideally, mentors help to foster resilience through both words and actions: words that teach and actions that demonstrate how to live well. Good mentors inspire, motivate, provide reliable support, and foster self-esteem. By imitating their mentors, children and adolescents learn right from wrong, how to handle challenging situations, and when and how to control their impulses, delay gratification, and soothe themselves. They learn about moral and ethical integrity and about courage. They begin to take responsibility for their actions and their lives. Physical health benefits from having role models, too. For example, having more physically active teachers seems to inspire greater activity in young children (Cheung 2020).

Research has shown that teens with dedicated mentors have more positive attitudes toward school, better grades and attendance, greater maturity, and less depression and anxiety. They also are less likely than teens without mentors to begin drinking alcohol and misusing substances. This is particularly true of young people whose mentors come from their natural social environment – that is, relatives, neighbors, teachers, and coaches. These kinds of mentors tend to be more effective than volunteers who come from outside the child's natural social network. Especially effective are non-parental relatives, such as grandparents or uncles and aunts, who know and understand the child's story and his or her personal, family, and cultural history.

Volunteer mentors from outside the child's natural social network tend to be less effective because often they limit their investment of time and energy and because they tend to have only a superficial understanding of family and cultural issues. This does not mean, however, that volunteer mentors cannot be helpful. The mentoring program Big Brothers Big Sisters (BBBS), for example, has experienced impressive success over the years. One study of the BBBS of Canada program found that greater mentorship support predicted increases in children's sense of self-efficacy, positive attitudes about school, and coping skills over time (Larose *et al.* 2018).

Of course, modeling continues to be an important form of learning well into adulthood and even old age. We are never too old to learn from the example of others.

How Role Modeling Works

Imitation is a powerful form of learning, and it shapes human behavior. Throughout our lives, each of us learns by imitating the attitudes, values, skills, and patterns of thought and behavior of those around us, even though we are often unaware that we are doing so. How do we learn from a role model?

It depends, in part, on observational learning: learning that takes place not because someone teaches us, but simply because we watch what someone is doing. According to a Buddhist proverb, "A child learns more from his mother's back than from her face." Thus, without intending to teach her child, the mother is providing opportunities for observational learning all day long simply by being where the child can watch her.

Even as adults, we benefit from observing others. For instance, if we were traveling in a foreign country for the first time, we might be unfamiliar with subtleties of the local culture, such as the way in which people wait for a table in a restaurant, summon a taxi, or greet one another. Rather than asking a native how to go about these behaviors, we could simply observe and then "do as the Romans do." In this case, we would learn by observing. Medicine has its own saying: "See one, do one, teach one."

Albert Bandura, who was one of the most influential psychologists of the twentieth century, believed that learning from a model often involves more than simple imitation (Bandura & Walters 1977). Instead, it involves learning rules of behavior that can guide future action. For example, the traveler might absorb and then apply the rules for how to greet people in each culture: by shaking hands, by kissing, or by nodding or bowing. Through trial and error, over time they take these rules and put their own spin on them, mixing the observations with their own personality.

Being a Mentor Can Give a Sense of Purpose

In addition to recognizing and benefiting from the role models in our lives, we can also try to serve as a role model for others. For Dr. Lisa Satlin, being a role model to others adds meaning to her daily life.

> What I love most is mentorship. It is why I agreed to take the chairmanship [of pediatrics] in the first place. I love the idea of encouraging young people and trying to help them figure out their strengths. How can I help them build on their strengths so that they can enjoy a more fulfilling life? So this is my purpose: helping, in whatever way I can, to guide the next generation of pediatric clinical researchers.

> The young people I have been privileged to mentor – they are my extended family in a way. I just like looking out for them, whether it's writing a letter of support for someone's promotion or grant application or helping someone think through a career decision. For me it's so much fun to stay

connected with people who I really care about all over the world. It's fabulous. I am so lucky.

And what do students learn from Dr. Satlin? They learn about the science and art of pediatric medicine, how to care for children and their families, how to design and carry out innovative medical research. They also learn about many of the resilience factors described in this book by watching how Dr. Satlin negotiates her way through life; by embracing the attitude, I am just going to do it.

The Neuroscience of Learning from Role Models

The ability to imitate others plays an essential role in acquiring behaviors, skills, mannerisms, social bonds, empathy, morality, cultural traditions, and even language. While many developmental psychologists argue that babies are born with the ability to imitate others' facial expressions, the results of research studies do not always support this idea (Slaughter 2021). Whether we are born imitators or learn this skill over time, it is vital to our development.

Advances in neuroscience illuminated potential brain mechanisms that underlie imitation. In the mid-1990s, researchers from the University of Parma in Italy discovered "mirror neurons" in monkeys, in areas of the brain that control movement. Later research with humans has implicated a far broader network of neurons involved in processing movement, perception, emotions, and language. Researchers found that when humans observe the behavior of another person, the observers activate many of the same brain regions that are being activated in the person who they are observing. Thus, it appears that some of the same brain regions that fire when we catch a Frisbee also fire when we watch someone else catch one. Perhaps we can understand and, in a sense, vicariously experience the movements and actions of others because we have our own neuronal template for similar movements and actions.

In addition to simulating movement and action, some evidence suggests that mirror neurons may help us to understand and empathize with the emotions of another person. In *Mirroring People: The New Science of How We Connect with Others* (2009), the neuroscientist Marco Iacoboni describes how, when we observe the facial expression of another person, our own analogous facial muscle mirror neurons become activated. These cortical mirror neurons then send signals to the emotion center of the brain, causing us to experience the emotion that we are observing in the other person.

Research into the nature and role of mirror neurons is ongoing. After their discovery, they became the focus of heaps of news coverage and scientific interest (Heyes & Catmur 2022). They were thought to provide some "key" to the human experience, and to be an essential pathway to healing from trauma. With careful study, their role is now understood to be humbler than the initial hype suggested. Over the years, we have seen that they do play a significant role in motor, speech, and emotional processes. We hope it is clear to the reader by now, though, that no one set of brain neurons or circuits holds the key to resilience.

Like imitation, collaboration can also be an important aspect of learning from role models; many of the people we interviewed had the privilege to work side by side with their resilient mentors for years. Innovative research techniques, involving simultaneous brain imaging of two or more people, shed light on the neuroscience of collaboration. Recently, researchers (Xie *et al.* 2020) had groups of three people play a collaborative drawing game, all while each person was undergoing functional neuroimaging (fMRI). They found that active collaboration on drawings activated in a brain region that is important for "theory of mind" – understanding the thoughts and feelings of others. Trios who had synchronized brain activity in this area did a better job of collaborating. They learned from one another, adapted quickly in real time, and effectively "got on the same page."

Using Role Models to Become More Resilient

Modeling our behavior on that of a resilient person can increase our own resilience. During his POW experience, Rod Knutson preserved his integrity while enduring torture sessions by emulating the moral strength and discipline of his father; while struggling to find his identity as a young man, Lew Meyer looked to the leadership of Fire Captain Herman Shawver; during his forty-nine months in a North Vietnam prison, Steve Long turned to his peers to find inspiration and to observe how they resisted the enemy. And after losing his leg to a landmine, Jerry White emulated the no-nonsense approach of an Israeli amputee in order to "get on with it."

Tangible Reminders of Resilient Role Models

Sometimes it's helpful to have a physical reminder of our resilient role models. You might even have these around you right now – photographs, armed forces medals or other accomplishments, or a piece of furniture passed down for generations. Dr. Lisa Satlin surrounds herself with physical reminders of her mother and grandparents.

> In my bedroom, I have a couple of my mother's favorite paintings. To me they are absolutely beautiful. When I wake up in the morning, I look at them. Then I make coffee and there are a few more of her canvases in the kitchen … I look at those canvases and every time I imagine both of them painting. … [My mother and my grandmother] put everything into those paintings, their feelings and emotions.

Walking into Dr. Satlin's living room, the first thing a visitor notices is a massive antique samovar – an ornate metal urn traditionally used to boil water – that does not fit with the style of the room's other furniture. "It's completely not 'me,'" Lisa explains, "but I placed it in the most prominent spot in the apartment because it's part of my life. I hang all sorts of little things on it, and I look at it every morning." When Lisa and her sister were young girls, their grandparents took them on a trip to what was then the Soviet Union. They purchased the bulky antique there and lugged it all the way home, paying for an extra seat for it on the flight back. For Lisa, these objects are reminders of her family role models.

> *I still feel like my mother and grandmother are always here with me, even though they are not alive. There's not a day goes by that I don't think about them. They are part of my fabric. People ask me if I go to the cemetery to see them, but that doesn't make sense to me. Physically, what's remaining? There's so much more. They are part of me.*

Reverend Thomas Johnson keeps one of his mothers' paychecks from when he was a child as a reminder of her struggle and persistence – in the early 1970s she supported her family with $58.38 a week.

Another way to benefit from role models, as mentioned earlier in this chapter, is to learn from a particularly resilient friend. Perhaps you notice that during times of high stress, they not only ask for help from others but they also make every effort to eat well, get enough sleep, and exercise. That gives you a good starting place. Maybe you don't really know how they do it. Ask them and see what you can learn.

LEARNING FROM ROLE MODELS STEP BY STEP

Over the years, researchers have learned a lot about how best to learn from role models. Here are a few helpful steps:

- Observe the skill as many times as you can in different situations.

- Break the skill into smaller pieces and focus on one step at a time. If you try to learn something complex all at once, you will likely be bombarded with too much information, make many errors, and have great difficulty mastering that skill. Be patient and give it your full focus.

- Practice: you will find it helpful to practice in between observations. You may do this by imagining yourself acting or thinking a certain way (e.g., "mental rehearsal") or pushing yourself to actually act or

LEARNING FROM ROLE MODELS STEP BY STEP
CONTINUED

think that way. Both forms of practice are helpful, although practicing in real life is ultimately needed.

- Obtain feedback on how you are doing. Whenever possible, ask an expert or someone with a trained eye to point out similarities and differences in your behavior and the behavior that you are attempting to emulate. They can recommend tweaks along the way and encourage you.

Obviously, most people are less than scientific in the way they benefit from seeing how others behave. It is entirely possible to learn from role models without even being aware of it.

Conclusion

As we have seen from the examples in this chapter, most people typically have more than one role model. This makes good sense, because it is rare, if not impossible, for anyone to be exemplary in every area of life. We are all human, with our own strengths and weaknesses. Thich Nhat Hanh suggests that each of us try to internalize the best qualities of family members who came before us, even those whom we have never met. For example, if your mother is depressed *and* courageous, then you can imitate her courage. If your father is dedicated *and* punitive, then you can imitate his dedication. As the landmine survivor Jerry White might say, "Search for resilient role models, imitate their best qualities and then play to your best self." By emulating what is best in multiple hardy role models, we can weave for ourselves a resilient tapestry.

139

8

. . . . .

Mind Your Body

There are indisputable links between mental and physical health. Good sleep, diet, and exercise lowers one's vulnerability to the effects of stress. Many of the people we have interviewed have formed regular habits of exercising and have shared how being physically fit has helped them during traumatic situations and as they recovered. For some, climbing Mount Everest or K2 was their personal goal; for others, it was building up strength and balance to ride a horse or even walk around the block following devastating injuries. Athletics taught them perseverance, recovery from "failure," communication and collaboration, and confidence in their own abilities.

Surviving with Military Exercise Regimens

Korean War veteran Lew Meyer, who we met in the previous chapter, was a civilian firefighter working for the military in South Vietnam when his post in Hue was overrun by North Vietnamese soldiers during the 1968 Tet Offensive. After three days of fighting, Lew and twelve others were captured and forced to march through the jungle for an arduous five months. He was imprisoned in a dark eight-by-four-foot cell, where he remained alone for the next twenty-two months. By the time of his release, on March 27, 1973, he had spent more than five years as a POW.

Lew exercised in prison whenever possible, even when he felt tired or weak. Sometimes he jogged in tiny circles around his cell and sometimes he did isometric exercises, but at other times it was as many sets as possible of the Air Force five basic exercises (5BX),

Army "daily dozen," or "JFKs" (exercises recommended by President John F. Kennedy's Council on Physical Fitness). These widely known routines contain a variety of exercises such as sit-ups, push-ups, squat jumps, and jumping jacks. His cell was so small that his fingernails would strike the wall, leaving scratch marks when he did jumping jacks. Lew continued to exercise even while shackled:

> In the morning, I asked them to take my legs out of the locks. I wanted to do my JFKs, my exercises. But they didn't listen. So I started doing sit-ups. Then they pushed me back, yanked my leg locks off, removed them from the cell, and never put the leg locks on me again because the locks helped me do more sit-ups.

When he was transferred to a larger cell with roommates, Lew increased the intensity of his workout routine and encouraged others to join. They started with one repetition of each exercise and then progressed to two, three, and four repetitions. Devotion was matched with creativity: the routine often included "weight-lifting," using the smallest prisoner as a weight. Repetition paid off.

One year into his captivity, Lew got a new cellmate named Jim Thompson, a Green Beret who had been held in camps in the mountains of South Vietnam and Laos for five years, where he was starved, brutally tortured, and subjected to years of solitary confinement. When they first met, Jim weighed less than 100 pounds. Mike O'Connor, a fellow POW, couldn't believe what he saw when Thompson first arrived.

> He was standing right next to me. This guy is dead, I thought. As part of some cruel joke, I thought, they had stuck a corpse up against the door. Then I realized he was moving. He looked like something out of Auschwitz ... I didn't know how he stood up, how he breathed, how he did anything. His features were so distorted ... I could literally see his entire skeleton and the balls of his joints around his knees and elbows ... His stomach was completely wrapped under his rib cage ... It took him half an hour to stand ... Talk about a gutsy guy. (Philpott 2012)

On their first morning together, Lew began the day with his customary exercise routine. When he got to push-ups, Jim tried to join him but was so weak that his arms gave way, and his face struck the concrete floor. He couldn't do a single push-up. Lew began to coach Jim back to health. At first, Jim could tolerate only deep breathing exercises and gradually some bending and stretching. Every day, Lew would patiently coach his cellmate, and within six months, Jim could complete the daily dozen. That was just the beginning.

With time, Jim's health improved enough that the two men devised an escape plan. Success would depend on preparation. For over a year, they planned and trained for the extreme physical demands that lay ahead. Their exercise routine became increasingly challenging. They stacked their beds on top of one another and ran laps around their tiny cell, first in their rubber-tire sandals, and eventually barefoot to build up calluses. At the height of their training, they ran laps for twenty-four and fifteen hours, respectively. Lew could do sixty-four one-armed push-ups.

Like Lew Meyer, fellow prisoner Rod Knutson believes that rigorous exercise fosters physical and psychological resilience.

I worked hard to stay in shape. In 1969, when I lived in a cell with seven guys, we had – I forget what we called it – an Iron Man Contest or something. It involved sit-ups and push-ups, and they had to be regulation style push-ups, regulation style sit-ups. A guy by the name of Cole Black won the push-up contest at 501 push-ups. I won the sit-up contest at 1,615. I was in bad shape after I did that, because I wore all the hide off my tailbone, and I got boils.

Most of us did keep an exercise regimen. And it depended on the cell block you lived in, because sometimes you couldn't exercise. I lived in one cell block without floor space. All there was were the two pallets. And so if you wanted to walk, it was two paces to the end of your pallet, a turn, and then two paces back to the other end of your pallet. But there was always room to do sit-ups or push-ups or deep-knee bends, or something like that.

Another thing. We had a guy who loved to walk on his hands, so he would teach us to walk on our hands. I frequently did handstand push-ups or walked on my hands. When I got to the States, to a hospital in Oakland, the morning coffee show was to watch me come out of my room walking on my hands, walk down to the coffee urn and get a cup of coffee, and then come back.

For these POWs, rigorous exercise in prison was not a hobby or a way to pass the time; it was a necessity. Exercise gave structure and purpose to their days and provided them with a routine that enhanced confidence. Because American POWs had been through boot camp and many other advanced military training exercises, they were accustomed to physical challenges. They understood the value of making the effort to stay fit, even under adverse conditions.

Perspectives of a Navy SEAL

Scott Moore is a former commander of Navy SEALs. The son of a decorated pilot who died in Vietnam, and a great nephew of an Army Air Corp Pilot killed in the Pacific during World War II who has an Air Force base named after him, you might imagine that Scott had a clear path to military service. For Scott, though, it was a twisting road, full of misadventures in the Boy Scouts and a stint framing houses in Colorado.

Ultimately he attended the United States Air Force Academy, transferring afterwards to the Navy to begin SEAL training, which would become his career. Of all the turning points in his life, Scott said it was Outward Bound that had the biggest impact:

I'm thinking it's a climbing school, which is why I wanted to go. It's not a climbing school. It's something way more impactful in life – it's an outdoor leadership school. At the end of the thirty days, it was like … drinking a gallon of self-esteem straight.

One of the last things you do, after three weeks backpacking daily and sleeping under the stars in the Colorado Rockies, is what's called "solo," three days alone in the woods with no one else. In our case, you walk as a group up a valley in the San Juan mountains, also called "the Switzerland of the Rockies," and the instructor drops off one person at a time far enough apart, so no one can even see each other. You have three days. You have a sleeping pad, a water bottle with iodine tablets, a raincoat, a flashlight, a pocket-knife, and a diary. You have no food … At night there's these animals, you're not sure what they are, wolves, coyotes, they start howling and they get closer. All night, for three nights.

They tell you it's the only time ever in your life you'll be alone, without another human. And you do it for three days. It's an absolute remarkable builder of confidence.

From this physically and mentally taxing experience, Scott learned to face his fears and embrace uncertainty. All of this served him well later in his military career.

The Outward Bound program was founded in 1962. In their book, *Leadership the Outward Bound Way*, the organization describes their purpose as follows;

The term "outward bound" signifies the moment that a ship leaves the safety of the harbor and commits itself to the unknown challenges, hazards and rewards of the open sea … In the process of undertaking difficult tasks in unfamiliar situations with relative strangers, Outward Bound participants learn to draw on reserves of strength that they didn't know they had, learning that *plus est en vous* [you have more in you than you think]. (Raynolds 2007, p. 25)

Physical Fitness Can Boost Recovery

Jake Levine became involved in team sports from an early age. Being an athlete became a major part of his identity, a source of joy and where he made lifelong friends. However, these contact sports came with risks. Over ten years, from early high school through medical school, Jake sustained eight concussions. All these injuries eventually triggered awful symptoms. At the Class of 2022 Icahn School of Medicine Commencement, Jake told his story.

Life throws unexpected hurdles at each of us. I spent most of the first two years of medical school battling fairly debilitating post-concussive symptoms from a series of sports injuries. It hurt my head to look at a computer screen. The sound of a piece of silverware landing on a table was at times too much to bear. I was running on fumes, as I battled my post-concussion reality, barely staying afloat academically, physically, and emotionally, "pushing through" as though I had no other choice. But this approach was not sustainable or healthy. I ultimately came to understand that I needed to pause and search for a path to healing and recovery.

Desperate to recover and willing to try anything, I made my way to a sports neurology clinic in Michigan that had helped many athletes with lingering post-concussive symptoms. The clinic's primary emphasis was to return to high-intensity non-contact exercise to achieve concussion recovery. At the beginning of the week, I was asking the nurse to turn the lights off in the exam room because my head couldn't bear it. I was unable to jog on the treadmill without my head spinning. By the end of the week, the doctors and trainers had me riding a moving surfboard while returning ping-pong balls and reporting hockey highlights from a projector screen across the table. All of which I was able to do without a headache.

I left Michigan with an exercise regimen I could rely on, a headache medication that worked for me, and a lot of hope and determination. I was able to finish the year of classes and head off to Japan for an extraordinary global health opportunity through Sinai to study, fittingly, resilience and post-traumatic growth.

While in Japan, Jake conducted research on how medical students in Fukushima, Japan, coped with the 2011 "Triple Disaster" – the combination of earthquake, tsunami, and nuclear meltdown that left 20,000 people dead and over 300,000 displaced (Kaye-Kauderer *et al.* 2020, 2019). While there, however, he faced another life-threatening situation.

While in Japan, I had a dose of bad luck, contracting myocarditis, [which is] very rare in an otherwise healthy young person. Unclear what had caused it, over seventy-two hours my heart slowed to a crawl and my body started to shut down. Luckily, I received great care in Japan and departed my week-long ICU stay in Fukushima with great optimism that my heart would fully recover, but with the caveat that I would need to stop exercising for a few months while my heart rested. With the elimination of exercise, my head symptoms returned.

Jake is tough – undoubtably so. Yet, these experiences forced him to question his understanding of "resilience."

Sometimes simply "pushing through" and "toughing it out" isn't the smartest or safest path. I now appreciate the importance of listening to one's body and slowing down to ask for help ... Resilience is not necessarily continuing to try something that isn't working. Pausing and trying a different approach is not quitting ... Resilience can mean having the humility and confidence to be okay retracing your steps and trying something new. It is, perhaps, finding a new lens to look through.

Jake is now starting his medical residency in physical medicine and rehabilitation at Mount Sinai, where he will help others who have experienced sports-related injuries and life-altering medical conditions recover and adapt.

Exercise Improves Physical and Mental Health

The Physical Activity Guidelines for Americans describes how exercise lowers the risk of many health conditions, including multiple forms of cancer, depression and anxiety, stroke, type 2 diabetes, high blood pressure, and high "bad cholesterol" (Piercy *et al.* 2018). Indeed, there is solid evidence that exercise routines boost long-term physical health. In a study of about 80,000 adults in the United Kingdom followed over fourteen years, doing *any* strength training reduced the likelihood of dying of any cause, including cancer.

Strength training was defined as going to the gym, using an exercise bike, doing sit-ups or push-ups, or lifting weights for at least fifteen minutes in the past month. Participants who did the recommended weekly aerobic exercise – activities like swimming or running that elevate breathing and heart rate – also had lower risk of all-cause and heart-rate deaths (Stamatakis *et al.* 2018). We will talk more later about specific recommendations around aerobic exercise, but it's fair to say that most people should be able to meet and far exceed the fifteen minutes a month goal by building habits.

Many studies have linked exercise to increased resilience to common mental health problems, including depression and anxiety:

- In a study of over 35,000 adults in Sweden, those who reported exercising one to two times or more per week had lower likelihood of elevated symptoms of depression and anxiety (Hallgren *et al.* 2020).
- In 22,000 Norwegian adults followed over eleven years, those who reported at least one hour of weekly exercise at the start of the study had a lower risk of depression over time (Harvey *et al.* 2018).
- In a study involving almost 400,000 Swedish adults, those who did a 30–90 km (19–56 mile) ski race were at lower risk of developing anxiety disorders than non-skiers (Svensson *et al.* 2021).

These results suggest that a little bit of work each week (even spread over many days), potentially working up to a "big" goal, can go a long way to protect one's mental health.

Deborah Uses Swimming to Build Her Resilience

Deborah Gruen, born with spina bifida, began team swimming when she was 6 years old because her sister Michele swam, and it looked like fun.

The coaches treated me like I wasn't anyone different. I didn't kick as well as everyone else, and I was slower than kids in my own age group. But, every once in a while in a swim meet, I do beat able-bodied kids, and if you've never swum before I'll totally blow you away; it's not even close.

I've always been really comfortable in the water; I had a disability that impaired my walking, but I always found that water leveled the playing field a little bit. I could keep up with everyone else. I really liked that and plus I didn't need to use any sort of helping device to help me swim. I could just do it on my own … I could master the full turns, I could play on kickboards, I could swim across the pool; I could keep up with other kids during games.

As a member of the US Paralympic Team, Deborah practiced eight times a week, swimming an average of 26 miles. By pushing herself far beyond her own initial expectations and the expectations of others, Deborah has discovered an inner reservoir of power that carries over into other areas of her life. Swimming has also helped her understand the fortifying effects of support from others, including coaches and teammates.

We're all on the same boat. It's January and it's like zero degrees outside, the pool is cold, it's dark, and your coach is there and he doesn't want to be there either and I'm going, "Oh, this is really bad." But then you come together and realize we have two hours, we're clearly not going home, and you just get in and you do it. That's when it really helps, when you have support from other people. When you have to go it alone, that's when it becomes really difficult.

Finally, like many people, she came to see swimming as a good prescription for reducing stress. A student in high school when we first interviewed her, she told us:

I don't worry because I have a disability. I worry about whether my term paper is going to be late, is my paper good enough? I swim it out. Swimming is so good for that. Really gets your mind off it. That's why I love sports. I think everybody should learn to compete. It just takes out all the stress.

Physical Resilience Requires Recovery

Rose Long believes that competitive cycling contributes to her resilience in everyday life.

Endurance training is essential for the stamina and perseverance required for a Ph.D. and pursuing a research career … The methodical building of power and endurance through training gives me a structure to follow in my professional career where grants aren't won and papers aren't written overnight, but instead through years of careful and methodical research.

But Dr. Long also recognizes the importance of recovery. As she puts it, "You can experience a pathological state of stress if you train too hard ... Physical recovery is really important." Dr. Long's observation is strongly supported by exercise physiologists who emphasize that we do not build strength, agility, and coordination only by exercising. Instead, we need to alternate periods of exercise with periods of rest. This is true both for an individual workout and in the longer view of a weekly fitness routine, so you should give your body more challenges on some days than others. Without the opportunity to recover, the body becomes worn down.

Most experts in nutrition and diet recommend a diet composed of a variety of fruits, vegetables, and whole grains. The guidelines call for modest amounts of lean meat, legumes, and low-fat dairy products and sparing use of fats and sugars. USDA daily calorie recommendations range from 1,600 to 2,400 for adult women and 2,000 to 3,000 for men. Still, the more physically active you are, the more calories you need to maintain your weight. A healthy diet also involves limiting intake of alcohol – for some people, abstaining altogether – and avoiding tobacco, and many other substances.

Sleep is another component of recovery, one that is essential to good health and well-being. For most adults, this means seven to eight hours of sleep every night. It has become increasingly clear that the benefits of sleep go far beyond just feeling alert and rested.

As you might expect, there is a two-way relationship between sleep and mental health. In a study that involved two years of follow-up, teenagers who had greater sleep disturbance were found to be less resilient to stress, and in turn, lower resilience predicted sleep problems (Wang *et al.* 2020). Sleep problems are a risk factor for depression, for example, and depression is associated with increasingly worsening sleep quality. Studies have shown improved sleep is associated with reductions in stress, anxiety, worry, and depression (Scott *et al.* 2021). Inadequate sleep has been shown to impair performance. Getting less than four to five hours of sleep in one day, or less than ten to twelve hours over two days, has been associated with increased risk of accidents and impairments comparable to driving while intoxicated (Dawson *et al.* 2021).

For people who are healthy and busy, getting enough sleep is easier said than done, given our hectic schedules and the rapid pace of our society. Getting sufficient sleep is still more problematic for people who suffer from insomnia, sleep apnea, or other sleep disorders. Although diagnosing and treating sleep disorders is beyond the scope of this book, there are many useful resources for sleep "hygiene." What we wish to emphasize here is that the right amount of sleep enhances recovery, physical and emotional health, and resilience.

As noted in Chapter 1, the parasympathetic nervous system (PNS) has almost the opposite effect of the SNS. Rather than activate the body, the PNS tends to calm and slow down our stress response systems. As such, it plays an important role in our capacity to recover and bounce back from adversity and challenges. One of the easiest ways to increase PNS activity is through voluntary regulated breathing. For thousands of years, breathing practices have been a fundamental component of meditative and spiritual practices.

The notion that resilience and recovery go hand in hand has been strongly supported by the research of the late Rockefeller University professor Bruce McEwen and Stanford University researcher Robert Sapolsky. Problems regulating our stress response can damage our body and brain. For example, stress that is chronic and inadequately regulated can lead to damage to neurons located in the amygdala, the hippocampus, and the prefrontal cortex. These changes may be accompanied by anxiety, memory impairment, increased sensitivity to alcohol and drugs, diminished mental flexibility, and depressed mood (McEwen 2017).

Exercise, Resilience, and the Brain

Abundant scientific evidence shows that physical exercise can also improve brain function and cognition, which includes thinking and memory. One recent study used smartphones and activity trackers to look at how physical activity may improve cognition. The researchers asked ninety adults with a range of different health conditions to complete cognitive tests on their phones twice a day for two weeks while maintaining their usual level of activity. Greater daily physical activity was associated with better executive functioning – a set of skills including the ability to rapidly shift attention and act flexibly (Zlatar *et al.* 2022). Among older individuals with cognitive decline or dementia, exercise may slow cognitive decline, particularly changes in working memory, the ability to keep information actively in mind for a few moments (Law *et al.* 2020).

Most of us want to do whatever we can to remain mentally sharp as we age, and to reduce our risk of developing age-related memory loss and dementia. Yet the fact is that the hippocampus, a key brain area associated with memory, shrinks an average of 1–2 percent each year in healthy older adults, likely beginning around the mid fifties. Exercise may help here too. Older adults, on average 77 years old, who participated in a group-based exercise program for one year (twice weekly for twelve weeks then once weekly) were found to have no change in volume of their left hippocampus following the program, relative to a control group who received a few sessions of health-focused education (Demnitz *et al.* 2021). This study suggests that exercise may have prevented or slowed loss of brain volume, though certainly more follow-up work is needed.

A few different neurobiological mechanisms may help to explain the antidepressant, antianxiety, and cognitive-enhancing effects of exercise. First, exercise has been shown to increase concentrations of chemicals that are known to improve mood (e.g., endorphins) and that lessen depression (e.g., serotonin and dopamine).

Regular exercise helps to protect against the hormonal effects of chronic stress. During stress, the HPA axis releases high levels of the stress hormone cortisol, which over time can damage neurons in the hippocampus. The good news is that this response may be dampened in exercise-trained individuals. Dampening of the HPA axis would most likely lead to lower cortisol production, less brain exposure to cortisol, and therefore less damage to neurons in the hippocampus.

The beneficial effects of physical fitness on brain function, cognition, and learning are also well documented in children. A randomized controlled trial of over 2,000 fourth-grade students in Mongolia compared high-intensity interval training or HIIT (three minutes of training twice weekly for ten weeks) to children's typical physical education. The HIIT group had significantly greater standardized test scores on a national math and language examination (Takehara *et al.* 2021). Physical activity also probably helps children sit still and pay attention in school or at home, with salutary effects on academic performance.

Building Physical Health Habits

For most of human history, people have spent their waking hours engaged in the physical demands of daily life. The human body evolved for living as gatherers, scavengers, toolmakers, hunters, and artisans. Like our hunter-gatherer ancestors, we as modern humans evolved with physical activity and the capacity to respond rapidly to relatively short bursts of physical stress. However, over the past few centuries, with the advent of the industrial revolution and advances in technology, we have adopted a dangerously sedentary lifestyle. In developed countries, relatively few people engage in physically demanding work, and many of us sit for hours in front of computer screens. We are more likely to drive, or ride a bus or train, than to walk.

While many Americans do exercise with some regularity, building resilience typically goes beyond "routine maintenance" exercise; to become more resilient, we need to push ourselves. Growth and change won't occur unless you push past your comfort zone, but pushing too hard increases the likelihood that you will give up.

Cliff Welch, a special forces instructor, describes it this way: "If you do things in incremental steps, you know, harder and harder, the person will get better. They'll get stronger and they'll get harder. And that starts from day one of basic training, and it never really ends the whole time you're in the service."

Of course, most people reading this book are not aspiring to become world-class athletes or elite soldiers. But how much exercise is enough to enhance resilience? And what type of exercise is best for your physical health? How about for your mental health? Is it best to exercise alone or with others? Should you consider hiring a trainer to teach you proper exercise techniques? What about cross-training? These are complex questions that we will not cover in this book. However, bookstores and libraries are filled with excellent books that outline sensible and scientifically sound exercise programs geared toward maintaining good health.

A note of caution is also in order: the recommendations we do make are not intended to take the place of medical advice. Before beginning any exercise program, it is always wise to check with your doctor, who can assess any conditions you may have that would limit the amount and types of exercise that are appropriate for you.

While many types and intensities of exercise have medical and psychological benefits, to enhance physical and emotional resilience, we recommend an exercise regimen that is manageable but challenging. The Centers for Disease Control and Prevention currently recommends 1 hour and 30 minutes of moderate-intensity aerobic exercise (e.g., walking fast or pushing a lawn mower) or 1 hour and 15 minutes of intense aerobic activity (e.g., jogging or swimming laps), together with two sessions of muscle-strengthening activity (e.g., weightlifting), each week. In general, exceeding those basic guidelines provides even greater health benefits.

WORKING ON PHYSICAL FITNESS

We believe that such a regimen should incorporate the following elements:

- Consult your healthcare provider before beginning a physical fitness program.
- Try different forms of exercise. Cross-training has many benefits.
- Develop a set of clear goals for your physical exercise regimen. Record the details of your workouts to ensure that you are achieving them.
- Build on social support by working out with a friend, colleague, or trainer.
- Reward yourself as you meet your goals.
- Gradually increase the intensity of training. Repeating the same comfortable routine each time you exercise may help to ward off some medical illnesses. However, it will not do as much to enhance your physical resilience as exercising out of your comfort zone (though not to the point of injury).
- Face setbacks head-on. Setting big goals means that sometimes you fail. For retired Rear Admiral Scott Moore, learning from failure has been a key part of his personal and professional growth:

  I'm a big advocate of doing occasional "gut checks," a physical event that totally kicks butt and humbles the hell out of you. I've done long challenge century rides in the mountains, or long ocean swims. This

WORKING ON PHYSICAL FITNESS *CONTINUED*

"humbling" is so powerful because it puts your ego in check, you stop thinking about yourself so much, and just keep going to finish. It clears your brain big time. All you are looking for is your best "you."

- Take steps to practice healthy eating. A full review of nutrition is beyond the scope of this book, and we acknowledge that there are many "food deserts" in underserved neighborhoods where healthier choices are either unavailable or unaffordable to residents. Regardless of where you are located, educating yourself about the food choices available to you is a good start. For example, research shows that parents who are provided with information about the health impact of sugary drinks are less likely to buy them (Hall *et al.* 2022).

- Take sleep seriously. To improve sleep, many people find it helpful to control their "sleep environment" by avoiding watching TV, using a laptop or phone, or eating in bed. For some people with sleep problems, it can be helpful to get out of bed and do something else if they find themselves lying awake for 15–20 minutes.

- Savor the feelings that come from a good workout or meeting personal goals. Fully attend to the positive feelings and greater sense of self-esteem and mental toughness that typically accompany increases in physical resilience.

- Aim for the point at which being physically fit becomes integral to your sense of self – a part of who you are. It eventually becomes a routine that does not require a second thought.

Conclusion

Researchers are continually seeking more answers about how best to exercise, and more to the point, how to get maximum benefits from the least possible expenditure of time and energy. As we all know, there is no easy way to become physically fit and resilient. It takes planning, desire, drive, consistency, perseverance, and the willingness to live with discomfort. But the benefits are many and may very well be life-saving.

9

. . . . .

Challenge Your Mind

Challenge Your Mind

In challenging situations, it helps to be mentally sharp, curious, and humble. Those attributes allow us to focus on the problem, make wise and creative decisions, "course correct" when needed, admit when we don't know something and need help, and learn new information. These skills also are closely tied to our emotional health and our ability to manage difficult emotions rather than be controlled by them. In our experience, resilient people tend to be lifelong learners, continually seeking opportunities to become more mentally fit.

The capabilities of the human brain are indeed remarkable. In a world full of distractions, many of us tend to rush through our lives, not really focusing on details and rarely being "fully present" in the moment. When we give our full attention, on purpose, to the present moment, we can notice the rich details of life around us and gain control over our racing thoughts and difficult emotions. Many of the POWs we interviewed learned to appreciate the scope and power of the brain during months or years in solitary confinement, when few outside distractions intruded.

POW Paul Galanti recalled, "When I was in solitary my memories would go way back ... I started going through algebra and calculus ... I remembered the periodic table and started chemical equations in my head." Bob Shumaker spent twelve to fourteen hours a day building a house:

> I built a house in my mind. I would buy all the lumber and materials and everything for it. I knew how many bricks were in it; how much it weighed; the square footage ... So, it kept me busy, but I think even more than that it kept me hopeful, you know, that someday I would actually build this house ... Which I did.

These accomplishments are minor when compared to those of a young Navy apprentice seaman, Douglas Hegdahl. The self-effacing 19-year-old South Dakotan was in the Navy less than six months when he was captured in the predawn hours of April 6, 1967. During a night of bombardment, he had gone topside on the guided missile cruiser USS *Canberra* without authorization and been knocked overboard by the concussion of the ship's giant guns. After staying afloat for six hours, he was picked up by a fisherman, turned over to the North Vietnamese army, and forcibly marched to the Hanoi Hilton.

Most of the POWs were offered early release, but they refused because of their Code of Conduct and the strength of their unity. However, the senior-ranking officers selected Hegdahl to accept the offer of early release. Why? Because Hegdahl had been able to memorize the first, middle, and last names of 256 POWs along with each person's capture date, method of capture, and other personal information. He was also able to recite the names of their next of kin, their hometowns, and telephone numbers. How did he do it? He memorized all the information to the tune of "Old MacDonald Had a Farm"!

When Hegdahl was released from the Hanoi Hilton after over two years in captivity, the first thing he did was travel around the United States, from west coast to east coast, north to south. He visited each hometown whose name he had memorized, spoke to each prisoner's relatives, and told them that their loved one was alive.

Miracle on the Hudson

On the afternoon of January 15, 2009, US Airways pilot Chesley "Sully" Sullenberger was captain of a flight departing from New York's LaGuardia Airport when, just seconds after takeoff, the plane collided with a large flock of geese. The collision disabled both engines. Suddenly the 150,000-pound aircraft was coasting like a glider over one of the most densely populated areas in the nation. Sullenberger quickly realized that his best option was to attempt a water landing on the Hudson River. Seconds later, he and copilot Jeffrey Skiles succeeded in making the emergency landing – an extremely difficult maneuver that required the plane to touch down on the water at a precise angle and speed. Not only did the pilots narrowly miss hitting the George Washington Bridge and successfully land on the river without crashing, but the aircraft continued to float long enough for all aboard to evacuate. Not a single person died, and no one suffered serious injuries.

As Sullenberger describes in his book *Highest Duty*, "What I focused on, extremely quickly, was that this situation was dire. This wasn't just a few small birds hitting the windshield … I heard the noise of the engines chewing themselves up inside as the rapidly spinning, finely balanced machinery was being ruined, with broken blades coming loose" (Sullenberger *et al.* 2009, p. 209). He credits his own training and that of the crew for their successful emergency landing. He reflects, "I did not think I was going to die. Based on my experience, I was confident that I could make an emergency water landing that was survivable. That confidence was stronger than any fear" (ibid., p. 237).

Sullenberger displayed the power to disengage his attention from the emotions of the moment (anxiety and fear: "Can I do this?" "What if I crash the plane and we all die?") and focus it on the task at hand.

Although few of us will ever face circumstances as grueling as those of a POW or a pilot of a damaged passenger aircraft, we can all challenge our brains and increase our mental fitness so that we are prepared for the challenges our lives present us with.

Brain Plasticity: A Possible Key to Brain Fitness

One of the most exciting findings of brain research over the past decade has been the observation that the brain is not an unchanging 3-pound ball of neurons; the size, connections among, and number of brain cells respond to our experiences. What we do, what we experience (happy, traumatic, or mundane), and what we practice all change the brain. Neurons that are actively used tend to make more connections with other cells and transmit their messages more efficiently. This process is called *neuroplasticity*, and you might recall that we talked about it earlier, in Chapter 1.

Elite sports, requiring years of intense focus and discipline, have provided a window on how the brain can change based on experience. A recent study of twenty-one professional basketball players, and a matched group of adults who were not professional athletes, found that these elite players had large-scale differences in their brain networks – particularly in pathways relevant to attention, self-reflection, and visual perception. Those players who practiced more had more pronounced changes – their brains became more efficient "computers," likely helping them on and off the courts (Pi *et al.* 2019). Similar positive effects have been seen in elite ice skaters (Zhang *et al.* 2021).

For individuals who have suffered a bodily or brain injury, brain plasticity is especially good news because it allows the brain to reorganize and regenerate itself to a degree. The brain can compensate for brain injury or damage, such that other areas may take over some of the injured area's functions.

Mental Exercises to Enhance Brain Function: Do They Work?

All of us would like our brains to work more effectively. Commercial products, or "brain games," have been developed that claim to improve cognitive performance. These approaches are based on neuroplasticity and the idea that repeated "exercise" of brain systems involved in learning and memory will be beneficial. The mental exercises in these products include mathematical challenges such as calculations, verbal challenges including word lists, and spatial challenges such as mazes.

The available evidence on cognitive training is increasingly controversial. Research clearly suggests that when a person practices mental tasks, performance improves on those specific tasks. However, the appeal of "brain games" is based on the hope that such skills will "generalize" – carry over to their lives and help them when cognitive demands are high – and persist over time. What does the research show? A recent study of over 1,000 adults who used some kind of "brain training" product for up to five years found no relationship between using brain training and improvements in cognitive function – across many areas, including memory, attention, reasoning, and planning. Surprisingly, in this study, participants who thought brain training worked tended to fare *worse* on cognitive tests (Stojanoski *et al.* 2021). Some other work has supported limited benefits of training for older adults (Bonnechère *et al.* 2020).

Do training tasks benefit individuals with mental health conditions for which we have a reasonable idea of the brain circuits to target? Our team at the Icahn School of Medicine at Mount Sinai worked with patients suffering from major depression and asked them to complete a challenging computerized task that combined recognizing emotions and keeping information in mind for a short time (working memory). By having participants practice this task repeatedly over eight weeks, the intervention was intended to change activity in the many brain regions associated with depression – and ultimately help make them feel better. That's exactly what we found. Participants who received this intervention had a significantly greater reduction in depressive symptoms than those who did another, less complex task (Iacoviello *et al.* 2014, 2018). Cognitive training tasks are not likely to be a stand-alone treatment for any mental health condition, but they may be a useful companion to medications or psychotherapy. We should also not forget the healing power of human connection with a trusted provider.

So, what can we recommend at this point? You may be equally able to boost your cognitive fitness and resilience by learning new things on your own as by spending money on a brain fitness product. You are also never too old to learn new things and to develop new skills.

Training the Emotional Brain

The ability to regulate emotions is an essential life skill that takes years to develop. As children develop, their first role models are often their parents or caretakers. Tantrums happen (even as adults); and we take cues from people in our lives about what to do to recover. Emotions coming from tough situations, like the death of a relative, should be named out loud rather than stuffed away. Some of us need a boost to get more resources to name, express, and manage emotions in a way that works for us. This is where many forms of psychotherapy can be helpful.

Is there a "right" way to feel about something? No – it really depends on the situation. If we underreact emotionally to something, we may devote too little energy to solving the problem we face. People may experience us as cold or checked out. Similarly, having an overreaction might also disrupt our ability to process information and make good decisions, and we may unintentionally push people away who could otherwise support us. By learning to recognize our emotions, and their intensity, we are more able to face problems flexibly – seeing many paths forward rather than getting stuck in the mud.

One effective technique that can help regulate emotions is the practice of mindfulness, which we discussed earlier, in Chapter 5. Jon Kabat-Zinn, who has done a lot of work to make mindfulness "trendy," defines it as "paying attention in a particular way: on purpose, in the present moment, and non-judgmentally" (Kabat-Zinn 2009).

Benefits of mindfulness practices include learning to develop calm and accepting awareness of thoughts, emotions, perceptions, and bodily sensations and functions such as breathing. People may also find that they can tolerate negative emotions better without impulsively acting upon them. Just as with the brain training platforms mentioned above, mindfulness training apps and websites are increasingly available to consumers; we will discuss these in more detail later in this chapter.

As you can see in Kabat-Zinn's definition, participating fully in the present moment is one aspect of mindfulness. "Sully" Sullenberger focused most of his attention outwardly on the technical procedures needed to land his plane safely on the Hudson River in 2009. However, even though he appeared calm to others, he later described the emotional reaction that hit him when the engines went silent: "It was shocking and startling … I knew that this was the worst aviation challenge I'd ever faced. It was the most sickening, pit-of-your-stomach, falling-through-the-floor feeling I had ever experienced" (Sullenberger *et al.* 2009). This is a powerful example of observing one's emotions but not allowing them to interfere. Sullenberger felt the emotion but did not become the emotion. He did this by inwardly observing his emotions as well as by focusing on the precise behavioral tasks needed to land his plane safely.

A Kayaking Adventure

Several years ago, we (Steve and Dennis) decided to compete in a 90-mile, three-day kayak race in the Adirondacks. For a competition of this length, it is vital to train for many months in advance. But one of us (Steve) didn't start training until about five or six weeks before the race:

The day before the race, I realized I wasn't in good enough shape to do it justice. I almost called Dennis to tell him that I needed to back out, but I just couldn't do it. Here we were writing a book about resilience and I was about to quit before we had even started. Not good. Not possible. Fortunately, perhaps as a desperate attempt to reframe the upcoming race, I began to think about mindfulness, a discipline that I had been practicing for several years. I remember thinking, This will be great. I can turn the race into a self-experiment in mindfulness and resilience.

When we got to the race, there were about 500 competitors. The course covered the last 90 miles of an old Native American trade route through the lakes and rivers of the Adirondacks. I was a little nervous at first, but when the starting pistol fired, I began to paddle furiously. I immediately forgot all about my mindfulness experiment and within minutes was gasping for air, wondering how I would ever make it through the first day. No one else looked like they were breathing that hard. In fact, to me they looked relaxed and comfortable.

Soon my neck began to hurt. An almost unbearable pain gripped the right side of my neck from my ear all the way down to my shoulder blade. You complete idiot, I thought. You've got 85 miles left and you're already in excruciating pain. What were you thinking? What are you trying to prove? You're not in shape. Now you're gonna have to quit and look like a real jerk.

But then, thankfully, I remembered my intention to turn the race into an experiment in mindfulness. For most of the next 85 miles, to my amazement, I thoroughly enjoyed the race, and I paddled faster than I had anticipated. Somehow … I was able to remain in the "present moment" and observe my thoughts and emotions without constantly judging them. I even spent time marveling at the beauty of the Adirondacks and feeling invigorated by nature. It was pouring with rain on the second day, but I didn't care.

I should disclose that by the end of the race my shoulders were so inflamed that I could not touch them; I was unable to kayak for six weeks afterwards.

Our kayaking adventures remind us of another line of research – the benefits of spending time in nature. One study of over 2,500 children aged 9 to 15 years and living in London found that those who had more daily exposure to woodlands had 7 percent greater "executive functioning" (such as better working memory and attention skills) and 16 percent lower risk of mental health problems over a two-year period. They also found that more time in natural environments that were further away from home and school conferred the largest benefit for cognition and psychological well-being (Maes *et al.* 2021). Another study found that children who participated in outdoor activities during the early parts of the COVID-19 pandemic may have been more protected from its emotional impact (Jackson *et al.* 2021). Brain imaging studies have also shown us that brief walks in nature can help calm stress reactions; perhaps unsurprisingly, these benefits are not seen for walks in urban settings (Sudimac *et al.* 2022). Certainly, we, the authors, can attest to the many benefits of time spent in nature for our own personal growth.

Attention, Emotion, and the Brain

The neurobiology of attentiveness and emotion regulation is extraordinarily complex. In this section, we are going to focus on two emotion regulation interventions: mindfulness meditation and neurofeedback.

Many studies have examined how mindfulness practices may have long-term benefits for mental health, and, within people who developed depression and anxiety, may help foster recovery. Research suggests that mindfulness meditation practices have helped people cope with the stress and unpredictability of the COVID-19 pandemic, potentially protecting against the development of anxiety and depression (Zhu *et al.* 2021). Mindfulness meditation has also been associated with improved ability to focus, sustain, and shift attention (Verhaeghen 2021).

As we said earlier in this chapter, mindfulness meditation is closely related to emotion regulation. Many studies have reported an association between mindfulness meditation and increased activation of the PFC along with decreased activation of the amygdala. With mindfulness training, the PFC (which you can think of as the brain's "stop switch") may be more able to quiet the amygdala in times of great stress.

Another promising approach, real-time neurofeedback, involves training yourself to increase or decrease activity in various brain regions. The advent of real-time fMRI makes it possible to observe the biology of one's own brain while thinking, feeling, and acting. In these studies, people can learn to control activation in parts of their brain by observing information from their own brain while inside the magnet.

In a 2022 neurofeedback study, researchers asked fifteen individuals diagnosed with PTSD and fifteen "healthy controls" without a mental health condition to make a list of words relevant to traumatic or stressful events in their lives. Then, while in the MRI, the participants saw a "thermometer" readout that reflected the *real-time* activity of a brain area called the posterior cingulate cortex, which is related to emotion regulation and is often overactive in individuals with PTSD. In the experiment, they were asked to do whatever worked for them in the moment to bring the "thermometer" reading lower when they saw the upsetting words on a screen. Both individuals with and without PTSD were able to do this effectively; and in those with PTSD, this neurofeedback work seemed to be associated with a temporary decrease in emotional distress (Nicholson *et al.* 2022). These tools may provide a powerful platform for people to learn to better regulate difficult emotions, but it remains unclear how long these changes last.

What about if you don't happen to have a multimillion-dollar brain imager in your backyard? We talked about brain training apps or computer programs earlier, and how they may or may not show benefit for cognitive functioning. There has also been a multibillion-dollar investment in apps to improve emotional well-being, especially during the pandemic. Part of the rationale for company after company entering this space is that the need for preventative care and psychotherapy overshadows the availability of trained providers, particularly during the pandemic. Most, though not all these apps, focus on mindfulness training, which we mentioned earlier in this chapter.

Do they work as advertised? Maybe not. A recent review by Harvard-based digital mental health expert John Torous found that *most* apps, specifically those that involve self-help activities, lack rigorous evidence to show that they actually work in terms of reliably improving wellbeing or managing symptoms (Goldberg *et al.* 2022). Several free apps developed by the National Center for PTSD and the US Department of Veterans Affairs – including PTSD Coach – do seem to help people to manage trauma-related symptoms (Voth *et al.* 2022). Based on what we know now, we would advocate for you to do your own research on a given mental health app, especially if you are considering paying for it. Be wary of claims that apps – especially ones that don't involve any human interaction – cure depression or anxiety. Many apps are also not so clear about if and to whom they share your personal information.

BUILDING BRAIN FITNESS

Here are a few recommendations you can try on your own:

- *Start with one new thing.* Set aside time to listen to a podcast or audiobook. Many libraries lend audiobooks. If it's not too distracting, you can listen during a commute or while doing daily chores. You are not going to become an expert overnight – and trying to learn too many things at once will just be overwhelming. Start small.

- *Try learning a game that requires skill.* Even if games do not lead to huge changes in brain functioning, many board games (ranging from chess to ones involving elaborate adventures or mysteries) require your full focus – and have the added benefit of bringing people together to play them. It trains you to connect, have a routine, and do one thing at a time. We are strong advocates of board-game night.

- *Try mindfulness activities.* Mindfulness practices have been addressed in many books over the past few decades and there are many ways

BUILDING BRAIN FITNESS *CONTINUED*

to be *mindful*. As we mentioned, mindfulness has been defined as being fully *present* in the moment, without judging yourself or others, and doing one thing at a time. How often can you say you do that? So frequently we are multitasking – not doing any one thing effectively. Try a simple activity to start – if you are eating breakfast or dinner, just eat. Notice the tastes and textures. We miss this experience entirely if we eat while answering emails or watching TV, because our attention is elsewhere.

• *Be humble.* Some of the most talented scientists and physicians, physically fit and mentally agile soldiers, and effective leaders that we met were humble. They are not show-offs; they rarely talk about their personal accomplishments, and often attribute their success to a combination of hard work and support from others. Being humble about the limits of your knowledge also pushes you to learn more and actively listen to others, rather than think you know best.

Conclusion

As we have argued throughout the book, change requires dedicated mental and/or physical activity. You cannot become physically stronger simply by wishing for larger muscles. Similarly, you can't really develop or enhance mental skills by allowing your mind to wander randomly from one thought to the next. Instead, you need focus, discipline, and curiosity. Invite others to join in your creativity and challenge; and to the extent possible, do one thing at a time and be fully present when you are doing it.

10

. . . . .

Cognitive and
Emotional Flexibility

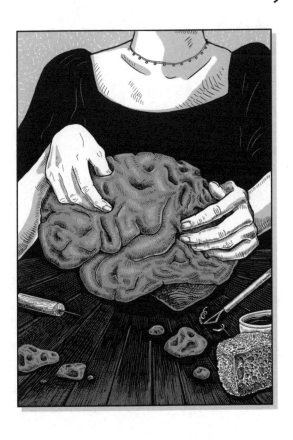

10

Cognitive and
Emotional Flexibility

People who are resilient tend to be flexible – flexible in the way they think about challenges and in the way they react emotionally to stress. They are not wedded to a specific style of coping. Instead, they shift from one coping strategy to another depending on the circumstances. Many can accept what they cannot change; they can learn from failure, use emotions like grief and anger to fuel compassion and courage, and search for opportunity and meaning in adversity. They come up with new solutions to challenges they face. They have usually learned these skills from role models such as parents, relatives, teachers and mentors, or faith leaders.

Researchers have studied how cognitive flexibility may protect against the impact of severe traumas. In one interesting study, a research team in Israel closely followed up with people who came to an emergency room after experiencing a life-threatening event like a serious accident or assault. These participants were interviewed about mental health symptoms and completed computerized tests of attention, memory, and cognitive flexibility, among other skills. For the test of cognitive flexibility, participants had to quickly jump between letters and numbers in the right order without making a mistake (not as easy as it sounds!). These researchers found that participants with greater cognitive flexibility one month after their trauma had lower symptoms of PTSD when they were reassessed more than a year later. In a second part of the study, participants who completed games intended to improve cognitive flexibility also had lower PTSD symptoms over time compared to people who played other types of games (Ben-Zion *et al.* 2018).

There are many other ways that we can practice cognitive flexibility, which we will cover in the rest of the chapter.

When Life Blows Up

Let's return to the story of Jerry White, who we introduced in Chapter 7. As a young man, Jerry attended Brown University, where he majored in Judaic Studies. Jerry was raised in the Catholic Church and was particularly interested in the teachings of Jesus Christ. He wanted to walk in the footsteps of the prophets, so during his junior year at Brown he chose to study in Israel.

When school in Israel closed for Passover, Jerry and his friends Fritz and David went camping and hiking in the Golan Heights.

> We wanted to get away from people, off the beaten track. We found a primo camping spot, where we could see the valleys of Syria and Jordan. An old bunker from the Six Day War seemed like the perfect shelter. It was a beautiful sunny day, April 12, 1984. I was walking out ahead of my friends, with a song in my heart. I like being the leader, the one out in front. Then, BOOM! A huge explosion. The whole earth seemed to be exploding under me. I thought we were under terrorist attack. I thought someone was shooting at us.

The explosion knocked Jerry off his feet. Stunned and lying face down, he screamed for help. When he tried to crawl, he immediately collapsed. Within seconds, David knew that Jerry had stepped on a landmine. David jumped to safety onto the nearest rock and commanded Fritz to do the same. But as Jerry lay immobile, pleading for help, his friends stepped off their rocks and came to his aid. Blood poured from Jerry's leg, the skin was shredded and charred, and splinters of bone were covered with dirt and blood. Small toe bones, as if shot from an arrow, impaled his calf.

"I have no foot! I have no foot!" Jerry screamed repeatedly. Slipping in and out of consciousness, imagining the fluids draining out his body, Jerry yearned for a cool jug of water. And then, as David and Fritz flipped him onto his back, Jerry was touched by a profound presence:

I felt something touch me, like God's hand, telling me to shut up. Later, I asked my friends if they told me to shut up and they didn't. It seemed like something forceful saying, "Quiet, listen." I stopped screaming ... And then I focused and felt a sense of peace and purpose. I knew I didn't die. This is not how the story ends. I don't die here. And there's a purpose in the Middle East. This focused my brain, like someone gave me a pill that said, "Focus, and be calm."

While Jerry lay in a state of surreal calm, David removed his own shirt, wrapped it over Jerry's stump, and tied a makeshift tourniquet around the injured leg. Once the tourniquet began to slow the bleeding, David and Fritz took a hard look at the situation. Their good friend Jerry was bleeding to death, they were many miles from a hospital, and they were standing in the middle of a minefield.

As David and Fritz maneuvered their way through the minefield, Jerry's body became entangled in the thick underbrush and briar patches. They dropped him three times, and each time Jerry hit the ground, he flashed back to the explosion, waited for another blast, and imagined he would die. It took them an hour to reach the edge of the minefield, which was enclosed by a fence with a sign reading "Muqshim" – *mines*.

Residents at a nearby Kibbutz came to their aid, helping to get Jerry immediate medical attention. For seven days, Jerry stayed in a small hospital in Safed, where a surgeon saved as much of the leg as he could. The surgeon performed a risky operation called the Symes Procedure. Unfortunately, gangrene set in several weeks later, forcing Jerry to undergo a second surgery in which more of the leg was amputated. Jerry was transferred to the Tel Hashomer rehabilitation hospital outside Tel Aviv.

Even though many friends visited him, Jerry felt afraid, isolated, and self-conscious:

It felt like *One Flew Over the Cuckoo's Nest*, and I suddenly felt sad and alone. I thought that I might be crazy. People were trying to introduce themselves, but they were all missing arms, legs, eyes, or they were burn victims. I felt sick and afraid, and all of these people were like ghosts. And I remember this older guy who was doing rehab and he had this new above-the-knee prosthesis and he said, "You're gonna get one of these, too," and he took it off and I saw his stump and his leg, and he was making light of it. And I remember feeling that I hated him, that I hated his stump, that I hated his prosthesis.

When Jerry did go home to Boston, he worried about his friends. Would they feel uncomfortable around him? Would they treat him differently?

Some of my closest friends drove up to see me, and I remember how afraid they were. I had been living with this for six months but no one else had; they had only heard the awful news. Was I changed? Was I the same Jerry? How should they act? Should they look really glum and sad? I probably overcompensated by trying to make people feel comfortable. Like asking them if they wanted to see my stump or making fun of it and treating my stump like a puppet and making it bark. I even had a pet name for it – Dino.

Jerry White went back to college and completed his studies, then moved to Washington, DC, where he served for a time as assistant director of the Wisconsin Project on Nuclear Arms Control, an affiliate of the University of Wisconsin Law School. Jerry had grown accustomed to his disability and learned to compensate for the inconvenience. He had moved on.

In 1995, Jerry got a phone call from a stranger named Ken Rutherford, who had met one of his college friends at a party. Although Rutherford knew that Jerry was an amputee, he did not know how much the two of them had in common. Jerry recalls:

He [Rutherford] thought that he was perhaps the only American civilian amputee who had lost a leg to a landmine. Actually, Rutherford lost both of his legs in Somalia. And he was like, "I can't believe it, a landmine survivor, and with your work! Don't you know that landmines are called weapons of mass destruction in slow motion? They've killed more people than nuclear chemicals and biological weapons combined. So with your work experience in nonproliferation and weapons of mass destruction and your personal experience losing a leg to a landmine, you could really be effective."

White had read several articles about landmines in arms control magazines but had never made the conscious connection between the two types of weapons. Once he did, he was hooked. Three months later, he and Rutherford attended the UN-sponsored First International Conference on Landmines in Vienna. There, each man told his story for the first time in public.

> I saw immediately how this could tap into my passion for a cause and also how powerful the voices of survivors were in this movement. They were living evidence – the lifeblood of the campaign to end landmines. Vienna was a turning point for me, a philosophical turning point that set me on fire for the advocacy issue.

White left his job, cashed out his retirement plan, and set up an office in his basement. It was a risky move, to put it mildly. But he was committed to the cause. He spent day and night fundraising. Even after the group had achieved a great deal, Jerry was willing to acknowledge that he might not succeed.

> All along I felt that, even if it doesn't work, even if I fail, it's not failure because, look, we will have helped change the world, drafted a treaty to ban landmines, saved millions of lives, helped thousands of survivors. So, if I fail as a director of a nonprofit organization because I'm not a good enough fundraiser or I don't know how to build properly as an entrepreneur, then I still succeeded. The failure would still be glorious.

Twenty years after losing his foot in Israel, Jerry White, along with his friend and colleague Ken Rutherford, accepted the Nobel Peace Prize, which honored the work of the International Landmine Survivors Network. The group has since been renamed Survivor Corps.

Applying Cognitive Flexibility in Your Own Life

As we saw from his story already, Jerry White is a master at approaching problems flexibly. In his 2008 book *I Will Not Be Broken*, he outlines five general steps to overcoming a life crisis:

- Face facts: accept what has happened.
- Choose life: live for the future, not in the past.
- Reach out: connect with others who are going through similar situations.
- Get moving: set goals and act.
- Give back: service and acts of kindness empower the person to shift perspectives.

Acceptance

A vital component of cognitive flexibility is accepting the reality of our situation, even if that situation is frightening or painful. To cope effectively, we must keep our eyes "wide open" and acknowledge, rather than ignore, potential roadblocks. We are called upon to accept, rather than try to push away or avoid, difficult emotions like anger, fear, sadness, or grief. Avoidance and denial are usually counterproductive mechanisms that may help people cope for a while, but that ultimately stand in the way of growth and the ability to actively solve problems.

Sometimes acceptance involves not only acknowledging the reality of one's situation but also assessing what can and cannot be changed, abandoning goals that no longer seem feasible, and intentionally redirecting efforts toward that which can be changed. Thus, acceptance is different from resignation and does not involve giving up or quitting. Instead, it is based on realistic appraisal and active decision-making.

Many of the resilient individuals we interviewed cited acceptance as critical in their ability to thrive under conditions of high stress and trauma. Somehow, they learned how to focus their attention and energies on problems that they believed they could solve, and they rarely wasted time and energy "banging their head against the wall," fighting battles that they could not win. In other words, they were realistic and pragmatic.

Perhaps our most graphic example of acceptance involves a Vietnam POW who, after fifteen months in solitary confinement, sensed that he was about to "lose his mind." Each day he struggled to understand how and why his life had taken such a dramatic turn. Less than two years earlier, as a Navy aircraft carrier pilot, he had reached the top of his game. He was highly respected, had the "best job in the world," and was happily married with two children. Now, starved and emaciated, he lay shackled in a rat- and mosquito-infested windowless concrete prison cell, refusing to believe or accept that his life had been reduced to mere survival.

And then, one morning, he heard a loud and distinct voice, which startled him: "This is your life." And it was true. This was his life, not a dream, not his imagination. There was no denying it, no wishing it away. This was real.

> When I heard that voice, things changed. I don't know where it came from. It was pretty loud. I'm sure I heard it. I know it sounds weird but it wasn't my voice. It's almost like it lifted this weight off my shoulders, 'cause the voice was right. I was in this cell and I wasn't going anywhere. So I guess when I really admitted it to myself, I just kind of stopped fighting and things got a lot better. I mean, I always knew I was in prison, but after that voice, it just changed. I just wasn't as miserable anymore, and I started to take care of business, you know. I started to exercise as much as I could, and I tried to stay in touch with some of the guys ... After that voice, I felt a lot better.

These experiences echo the essence of the well-known Serenity Prayer: "God grant me the serenity to accept the things I cannot change, the courage to change the things I can, and the wisdom to know the difference."

The Science of Acceptance

In scientific literature, acceptance has been cited as a key ingredient in the ability to tolerate highly stressful situations. Acceptance has also been associated with better psychological and physical health in many different groups of people. For example, in individuals with cancer, acceptance of the diagnosis has been linked to lower rates of emotional distress (Secinti *et al.* 2019). The most common scale to measure resilience, the Connor–Davidson Resilience Scale, includes a question about acceptance of change.

Elsewhere in this book, we have mentioned cognitive behavioral therapy to develop a more positive explanatory style, and to observe the world more realistically. A related therapy called acceptance and commitment therapy (ACT), developed by psychologist Stephen Hayes, takes acceptance as a starting place for addressing problems. Clinicians use a variety of different strategies to help their clients build psychological flexibility. One core component of ACT is "cognitive defusion" – learning to observe and be fully present with difficult thoughts, not push them away or think your way out of them, and to not see them as facts but simply as part of human experience (Hayes 2022).

Therapists have successfully used ACT to treat problems ranging from chronic pain to smoking cessation to eating disorders. A recent study combining data from 12,477 participants supported ACT's efficacy in addressing anxiety, depression, chronic pain, and substance misuse. ACT fared just as well as CBT when patients could have received either treatment (Gloster *et al.* 2020). ACT is often referred to as "third wave" cognitive therapy among an increasingly popular and scientifically grounded set of approaches which focus on the process of becoming well through building awareness, acceptance, and mindfulness, and by connecting to core values.

Cognitive Reappraisal

Many years ago, while conducting a study on the psychological and neurobiological consequences of the Holocaust, a colleague asked an elderly Holocaust survivor if she had ever dreamed about her experiences in the camps.

"Oh yes," the woman replied. "I've never stopped dreaming about those times. I had a dream just the other night. Mostly it's the same horrifying one. It wakes me up in the middle of the night. I'm in a panic. I'm sweating, and it's hard to breathe. Yes, I still dream about the camps."

At that point, our colleague replied, "My goodness, it must be horrible to still have those nightmares after all these years."

"Oh no," the woman said. "It's OK. It's OK because when I awaken, I know that I'm here and not there."

Positive reappraisal requires us to find alternative positive or more helpful meaning for negative events, situations, and/or beliefs. While this remarkable woman suffered profoundly from her Holocaust experiences, she somehow found a way to reappraise her nightmares. Although she was unable to control the nightmares, she was able to view them as powerful reminders that she was lucky to have survived and was privileged to wake up each morning to a new day.

Numerous researchers have found that the capacity to positively reframe and extract meaning from adversity is an important part of stress resilience: resilient individuals often find that trauma has forced them to learn something new or to grow as a person (Southwick *et al.* 2016). Cognitive reappraisal can be an especially important survival strategy for people who have had difficult childhoods. A 2020 study of nearly 500 adults compared the helpfulness of cognitive reappraisal and "expressive suppression," which is hiding one's emotional responses from others. Participants answered questions about the use of these strategies along with measures of current stress and a checklist of difficult childhood experiences. The results showed that cognitive reappraisal lessened the impact of childhood trauma on current stress levels while suppression exacerbated these effects (Kalia & Knauft 2020). One takeaway from this study is that even from the most challenging of starting places, emotional change and growth is possible.

Everyday failures also call upon us to use cognitive reframing – instead of being stuck in self-pity, focusing on what can be learned from the failure and trying again. In our experience, people who are resilient meet failure head-on and use it as an opportunity to learn and to self-correct.

A POW Reframes His Struggles

Vietnam War POW and Medal of Honor recipient Admiral James Stockdale used his knowledge of history and the Bible to reframe the challenges he faced.

> The only way I know how to handle failure is to gain historical perspective, to think about men who have successfully lived with failure in our religious and classical past. When we were in prison, we remembered the Book of Ecclesiastes: "I returned and saw that the race is not always to the swift nor the battle to the strong … but time and chance happeneth to them all." … Failure is not the end of everything, a man can always pick himself up off the canvas and fight one more round. To handle tragedy may, in fact, be the mark of an educated man, for one of the principal goals of education is to prepare us for failure. (Stockdale 1984, pp. 56, 73)

There's truth to the cliché, "It's not how many times you fall down that counts – it's how many times you get up." Failure can teach us to adjust, to improve, and to find new ways to overcome difficulties. Thomas Edison provided a classic example of reframing: "If I find 10,000 ways something won't work, I haven't failed," he said. "I am not discouraged, because every wrong attempt discarded is another step forward."

Sometimes cognitive reframing is slow and deliberate, built up like a muscle with repeated practice. It is taught to patients receiving CBT, as a way of challenging negative thoughts and seeing them with some perspective. But sometimes we are jolted into a new perspective. This was the case with Margaret Pastuszko, who we will profile later in the book, when she learned her young daughter had a life-altering medical diagnosis:

> I remember sitting there when my daughter was first diagnosed, and it was devastating. And I was sitting in Philly on a windowsill, thinking to myself, Oh, my God. My life has ended. And it was about me and I was like, I don't know how I can do this. It was all the typical I don't know. I'm not sure. How is this going to—

In that moment of despair, she was interrupted mid-thought by something – someone else – who captured her full attention.

> [Then] my 4-year-old son came up to me and said, "Mom, I'm hungry." ... I looked at him and I'm like, This isn't about me. It's not about me. It's about my daughter. It's about my son. I got to feed my son. I got to go into that hospital because she's more scared than I am. It's like, Since when is this about me? And that was kind of a pivotal moment for me to turn and say, "This is not about you. It's about somebody else. It's about doing what's in their best interest. It's about thinking about how you're going to be most effective for them." And you lead with that.

Gratitude

The old advice to "count your blessings" is a time-honored way of promoting a positive view of life. Even survivors of severe trauma can express a measure of gratitude, feeling that the ordeal has enriched their lives in some way. "First of all, it makes you very humble," says former Air Force pilot Steve Long when describing the effects of more than five years as a POW in Vietnam.

A lot of the old axioms that you hear – like, "You never really appreciate anything until you take it away" – those axioms exist because they're true. And I think anybody that goes through an experience like this, and even like the World Trade Center, the families that were associated with it, they all come to understand this sooner or later: Life is precious. Appreciate it while you can, while you have it, because it can be taken away very easily.

Steve has been invited to speak about his war experiences to many audiences, including high school and college students. For him, it provides a way to educate others about the importance of moral integrity, perseverance, learning from role models, and facing fear. It also reminds him what the experience taught him:

It keeps things fresh in my mind that I want to remember. I want to remember to appreciate the things that we have, the freedoms that were taken away from me. I want to remember to place my family first ... I swore that when I got home I'd never forget to be thankful for that piece of bacon, because that was one of the things that I thought about a lot. Just simple things in life.

In our work with US combat veterans, we found many benefits of gratitude on well-being. To measure gratitude, we asked veterans to rate how much they agreed with the following statement: "I have so much in life to be thankful for." First, what we found is that almost 80 percent of veterans strongly agreed with that statement. We called them the "high gratitude" group. The high gratitude group had lower risk of having PTSD, depression, social phobia, and suicide attempts over their lifetime, compared to those with lower gratitude. They were also less likely to be currently struggling with depression, anxiety, PTSD, or suicidal thoughts. Not surprisingly, our study showed that gratitude is close cousins with experiences such as optimism, curiosity, purpose in life, and spirituality (McGuire *et al.* 2021) – all topics we cover in this book.

Gratitude in the form of journal writing or intentional expressions has been used as an adjunct to psychotherapy in treatment for depression and other disorders. Such gratitude interventions show promise in improving well-being and positive affect and in reducing worry. Expressing gratitude may also improve physical health and foster healthy behaviors (Millstein *et al.* 2016).

The Science of Cognitive Reappraisal

Cognitive reappraisal is thought to play a key role in supporting resilience – it helps to manage negative emotions and opens the possibility of positive "spins" on challenging situations (Tabibnia 2020). Studies have shown that individuals who frequently use positive cognitive reappraisal to change their emotional reactions to stress report greater psychological well-being (McRae *et al.* 2012).

We can also take cues from those around us to help us interpret (or reinterpret) our own experiences in a more positive light. For example, in the workplace a manager or supervisor may point out the positive aspects of an adverse situation or event, providing employees with cognitive and emotional tools to view adversity as a challenge. Similarly, if a husband is upset about something a neighbor has done, then his wife might provide an alternative explanation for the neighbor's behavior that allows for a more constructive interpretation (Reeck *et al.* 2016).

Neuroscientists have found that reappraising an event as being more negative or more positive changes activation in brain regions associated with emotions. Studies often involve asking people to use a few different strategies to manage their emotional reactions to upsetting pictures they see while in the scanner. As an example, one study asked participants to simply look at the pictures without changing their emotional responses, or to use cognitive reframing. For reframing, they were taught that they could imagine (1) the situation not being as bad as it seems, (2) the situation getting better with time, or (3) seeing with distance as a scene from a movie, not a real-life situation. They found that when participants "reframed," connections were activated between the ventromedial prefrontal cortex and the amygdala, effectively lessening negative emotions (Steward *et al.* 2021).

As we've talked about before, the prefrontal cortex is the "executive" region of the brain, involved in planning, directing, and inhibiting; and the amygdala is the "alarm center," where the brain processes emotion and fear outside of conscious awareness. This study, and many others, suggests that conscious efforts to positively reframe or reappraise a painful situation activates the brain's executive region (the prefrontal cortex) and inhibits its emotion center (the amygdala).

Humor: A Form of Cognitive Reappraisal

In his classic book *Man's Search for Meaning*, Viktor Frankl refers to humor as "another of the soul's weapons in the fight for self-preservation. It is well known that humor, more than anything else in human makeup, can afford an aloofness and an ability to rise above any situation, even if only for a few seconds" (Frankl 1963, p. 63). For Frankl, humor provided a healthy means to gain perspective.

Like other positive emotions, humor tends to broaden one's focus of attention and fosters exploration, creativity, and flexibility in thinking. Humor provides distance and perspective but does so without denying pain or fear. It manages to present the positive and negative wrapped into one package. As the noted Viktor Frankl scholar Ann Graber puts it, humor combines "optimism with a realistic look at the tragic." Without Pollyanna-like optimism, humor can actively confront, proactively reframe, and at times transform the tragic. Consider screenwriter and director Woody Allen musing on mortality: "I don't want to achieve immortality through my work. I want to achieve it by not dying."

Of course, we have all known people who use humor as a form of avoidance, making jokes even when circumstances call for seriousness. This is not what we are recommending. However, while it may sometimes appear incongruous, humor can be a creative way to confront and cope with what we fear or find painful.

In this way, humor may be viewed as a user-friendly and creative form of "exposure." As we talked about in Chapter 3, exposure therapy is a kind of treatment for anxiety disorders and PTSD that involves facing, not avoiding, the feared situation or memory to gain more mastery and control. Humor tends to be a safe platform for facing fear because it incorporates what's feared or painful in a new way, taking away its power. It is no surprise, then, that health-care workers, exposed to extreme human suffering day after day, are often known for their "dark humor," which helps them process their experiences together.

Jerry White used humor when he endorsed Timberland boots and gave a nickname to his stump. In addition, he recalls: "I have always said that humor is everything in recovery, so I'll gravitate to whoever laughs the most. No matter what it's about, even if it is dark humor, it just sort of helps."

Most of the POWs we interviewed also cited humor as an essential tool in their ability to survive and resist. For example, when Rod Knutson could no longer withstand another day of brutal torture, he "succumbed" to the demands of the North Vietnamese to provide them with information about his personal life. "I told them my dad had a chicken farm and he raised three chickens. I told them that I went to school at Farm District Number One and the only job I ever had was selling peanuts to basketball players."

Humor and the Brain

Substantial evidence exists for the effectiveness of humor as a coping mechanism. In patients with depression, humor can sometimes diminish depressive symptoms by reducing tension and psychological discomfort, attracting support from others, and creating a positive perspective on difficult circumstances.

In a recent study, researchers (Wu *et al.* 2021) had participants focus on one of three interpretations while looking at upsetting pictures: (1) a humorous spin (stories about the pictures made up by professional comedians), (2) a "plain" cognitive reappraisal (e.g., thinking of a neutral or positive take on the picture or a story about it), or (3) an objective description. Interconnected regions of the brain involved in problem solving, emotional processing, generating laughter, memory, and learning were activated as the participant used humor to cope. Interestingly, when participants were asked to rate their emotional responses to the same pictures three days after the scan, humorous coping was associated with greater positive and lower negative emotional reactions compared to the two other strategies.

As many people we interviewed would say, humor is a powerful tool with lasting effects. Humorous situations, such as responding to harmless jokes, also activate the "pleasure center" of the brain – the nucleus accumbens (Chan *et al.* 2018).

BUILDING FLEXIBILITY

Let's look at some more specific ways to build your coping toolbox.

Reappraisal Whether working with a therapist or practicing self-help, asking questions of your thoughts can help to get you out of our own narrow view of a situation and open new possibilities. Here are some questions you can ask yourself:

BUILDING FLEXIBILITY *CONTINUED*

1. Is there another way of looking at this situation?

2. Will this situation or worry matter in a month or in five years?

3. What would I tell a friend going through the same situation?

4. Am I holding myself to unrealistic standards?

5. Is there a way I can push myself to test if my assumptions or judgments are accurate?

Acceptance Many faith traditions embrace acceptance as a core tenet. Holding emotions, thoughts, or memories "too tightly" can cause suffering. The more you ask Why me? questions or try to push thoughts away, the stronger negative emotions can become. One common exercise is imaging thoughts or feelings that spring up in you as "leaves on a stream"– wandering in and out of awareness – if you let them.

Gratitude As we mentioned above, embracing gratitude can be a powerful way to boost your well-being and build relationships. *The Little Book of Gratitude* by Robert Emmons (2016) is a great resource to learn more about building gratitude. Based on Dr. Emmons' work, here are a few activities you can try:

1. For one week, spend fifteen minutes each day writing about every possible thing or person for which you are grateful.

2. Think of a time when a loved one benefited from the kindness of a friend or stranger. How did you show you were thankful?

3. Think about a time when you were down on your luck or going through some other challenging situation that made you grateful for what you have – that made you "count your blessings."

Conclusion

Recent research on coping has shown that successful adaptation to life's challenges depends less on which specific strategies you adopt and more on whether you apply coping strategies flexibly depending on the nature of the stressor. Sometimes it is wise to accept and tolerate a situation while at other times it is best to change it. Emotion researchers have been clear that no one strategy is the "best"; what helps people cope is having the flexibility to express or suppress emotions to match the demands of a given situation. All these skills can be cultivated with patience and practice.

11

Meaning, Purpose, and Growth

11

Meaning, Purpose, and Growth

Meaning can give us strength and courage. During your own life, when called upon to defend a cherished idea, stand up for a worthy cause, or protect a loved one, you may have been surprised by the reservoir of strength and resilience that lies within. In that moment, you might have felt or thought of a "what for" – a higher purpose – that kept you going. Undoubtedly the best known and most influential advocate for finding meaning is Holocaust survivor Viktor Frankl, who we will refer to later in the chapter.

In our own work, we have looked for ways to help patients derive strength in the wake of their traumatic experiences. One of us (Steve) co-developed a treatment program for veterans with PTSD based largely on logotherapy, an intervention created by Frankl and several of his students (Southwick *et al.* 2006). The literal meaning of logotherapy is "healing through meaning." For years we had worked with veterans who expressed doubts about the meaning of their lives. Many of them had experienced the darkest side of human nature and were plagued by painful memories and feelings of aimlessness and sometime guilt.

For us, a key component of this work was to find a way to make meaning out of the suffering. During the orientation to this group therapy, veterans were reminded that they were already experts in many respects: They are experts in fear and psychological trauma, experts in personal and spiritual pain, experts in loss and failure, experts in hopelessness and emptiness, experts in coping with a society that rejects its injured members, and experts in survival and resilience. We next posed the question, "What can you do and what will you do with your expertise?" (Southwick *et al.* 2006, p. 166). By engaging in community service work as part of the treatment, our patients often discovered a sense of purpose by giving to others.

Each veteran was assigned to a community service site that tapped into their special expertise. For example, if a veteran had been homeless, we recommended volunteering for Habitat for Humanity. Another veteran, who had spent years living alone, volunteered with Meals on Wheels, which delivers meals to elderly shut-ins. Like the veteran, the recipient of meals may have felt socially isolated and afraid. As a group, the veterans also initiated their own projects, including a toy drive and holiday party for children in the foster care system. Much of the impetus for the service work was suffering, guilt, and loss.

Most of the people we interviewed for this book found ways to exercise whatever freedom they had as they searched for meaning in the aftermath of trauma. For example, we saw this with Jerry White after he lost his leg to a landmine. Jerry says:

> There are three types of trauma victims: Those people who say why me, and the pity piece that goes with that. Then there's the other Christian martyr thing, why not me – with suffering all around, why do I deserve not to be in a wheelchair or maimed or burned or whatever? And the third type simply asks, "Why?" This is a healthy question. This question is a search for meaning. For years I never asked the why questions, like "Why did I step on that landmine?" Or, "Why were those minefields there in the first place? Who put them there? Why are minefields blowing up people during wars and even years after wars are over?" Now, twenty years later, with perspective and enough living, I understand that the better question is "Why?"

Survivor Mission: HEART 9/11

Bill Keegan was a lieutenant for the Port Authority Police Department (PAPD) when the World Trade Center was attacked on September 11, 2001. The PAPD, based in the Twin Towers, suffered the largest loss of law enforcement personnel in US history.

Thirty-seven officers died. Bill was suddenly thrust into the longest, most painful but rewarding journey of his life when he was assigned to be night commander of the World Trade Center rescue and recovery mission at Ground Zero.

Like most of his colleagues, Bill was afraid. He was unsure if he was up to the job because nothing in his life had fully prepared him for what lay ahead. For the first few hours, Bill simply took one step forward, any step, believing that he could learn whatever he needed to. He found himself thinking about courageous first responders who had answered the call, like PAPD Officer Christopher Amoroso who kept charging back into the inferno despite his own injuries and who died in the line of duty.

The Rescue and Recovery Effort

Responding to the horrors of 9/11, Bill found himself at a critical crossroads. He had experienced what he called the "bottom" at least once before in his life, following a family tragedy. As he put it:

> Nothing prepares you for the bottom. The bottom is a very personal place. At the bottom there is no reason for anything. At the bottom there is only choice. It is between hope and despair ... I chose hope and suddenly saw it was the only reason I needed; that I could decide to make things better; and that everything in life, including my daughter's tragic illness, had special meaning.

When the attacks were over, both 110-acre towers had fallen, leaving the immediate area piled high with smashed concrete and jagged steel hiding human remains. Workers waded through clouds of steam and smoke from the fires that burned at over 2,000 degrees Fahrenheit and inhaled toxic chemicals that would cause devastating illnesses years later. The recovery and cleanup effort lasted for eight months, ending in late May 2002.

On the last day of the World Trade Center rescue and recovery mission, Bill addressed his crew. These were his parting words.

> A lot of people talk about closure like it's something you're supposed to have – like pain just stops because you want it to. Like if you don't move on,

you're selfish or screwed up. Closure just means someone else is tired of dealing with your pain. But life isn't about forgetting what hurt you; its learning to live with it. It's getting up when you're at the bottom and you got nothing left. It's believing there's still a reason to try and make things better. If you forget that … call me.

The recovery process had changed 9/11 first responders. As Bill wrote in his 2007 book *Closure: The Untold Story of the Ground Zero Recovery Mission*:

The irony was that in the beginning we thought we would do anything to get to the end. Now, and it may be hard to understand, we dreaded the end. We were about to lose the certainty of purpose and the place we had found here. We felt a growing emptiness … the mission that began in chaos ended with grace. Many of the responders weren't prepared to let go. They suddenly "faced a void" in their personal and professional lives.

Although Bill continued his work as a lieutenant, he no longer felt the same excitement and enthusiasm for his job. Having gone to "the Mount Everest of police work," Bill now felt lost. In 2005, at the age of 50, with no plans for what he would do next, he retired from the PAPD, a job he had once loved. He became a stay-at-home dad while his wife Karen worked.

One day while walking his 6-year-old daughter to school, Bill was ordered to stop and wait on the street corner by a crossing guard. The irony did not escape him. What am I doing?, he asked himself. I'm just treading water. This isn't working for me. What do I do well? How can I use whatever experiences and skills I have to do something real, something that has meaning to me?

At that moment, he remembered the words and actions of his good friend Ed O'Sullivan, who had been awarded the Silver Star for bravery while serving as captain of a combat unit in Vietnam. As Bill explains in *Closure*, Ed made a crucial decision after Vietnam:

"I was going to take everything good that happened to me in Vietnam and everything bad that happened to me in Vietnam and

I was going to use it all in an effort to be good. I was going to look at what happened to me as an opportunity to become a much greater man than I ever could have been had I not been through it."

With toughness tempered by empathy and compassion, trauma-tested leadership skills, and a burning desire to follow a meaningful path again, Bill found a new mountain to climb. In July 2007 he founded HEART 9/11. HEART 9/11 is a team of volunteer first responders, FDNY, NYPD, PAPD, and the NYC Building Trades, who bonded in the aftermath of September 11, 2001. Since 2007, HEART 9/11 has deployed over 1,200 unique volunteers to forty-two disasters in four countries and thirteen US states. Members have rebuilt or modified 846 homes, deployed rapid-response teams to assist with emergency operations, and trained others to respond effectively to major disasters. More recently, in collaboration with the Benson-Henry Institute for Mind–Body Medicine at Mass General, and the Newtown Connecticut Police Department, it has begun training first responders in evidence-based strategies and techniques to manage stress and to build resilience.

There are countless other examples of individuals who have turned their misfortune into a survivor mission; they include:

- Candy Lightner, Cindy Lamb, and the other women who founded Mothers Against Drunk Driving after their children were injured or killed by drunk drivers.
- John Walsh, host of the TV show *America's Most Wanted*, who began his crusade to bring fugitives to justice and to help find missing and exploited children after the 1981 abduction and murder of his 6-year-old son, Adam.
- Jennifer Breen Feist and J. Corey Feist, the sister and brother-in-law, respectively, of Dr. Lorna Breen. They founded the Lorna Breen Heroes Foundation after the death by suicide of Dr. Breen, a New York City emergency medicine physician, in April 2020 – right at the beginning

of the COVID-19 pandemic. The Lorna Breen Heroes Foundation advocates for issues around healthcare worker well-being and burnout, including reducing stigma and barriers around seeking help.

In Chapter 12, we will provide two more examples of individuals who undertook a "survivor mission" and derived a strong sense of meaning and purpose from that work.

Finding Meaning in Parenting an Extraordinary Child

Margaret Pastuszko was born in Poland and spent most of her early life there. In 1983, rejecting Communist rule in her homeland, her mother, a biochemist, decided to move to the United States. The family often moved from apartment to apartment over the years in Philadelphia, and Margaret remembers learning English from watching old television repeats. This was clearly a difficult change for her family, but Margaret learned many important lessons from her mother along the way:

> You do everything you have to for your children, and she found a constructive way to do it. To give us a new life in a time when there was so much uncertainty and political unsettlement in Poland. And this was an opportunity for her to create a different path for her two kids and she took it. And she didn't look back and she never questioned it. And I was beyond proud.

Margaret drew on this strength when she became a parent. In 2002, Margaret and her husband welcomed a daughter, Milena. Soon after her birth, her health deteriorated, and she was diagnosed with an incurable metabolic disorder, a condition affecting the energy-producing parts of cells in her whole body. It was devastating, but out of this diagnosis came tremendous meaning.

Margaret was clear that parenting Milena changed her life and is convinced that she has changed the lives of so many people who have met her over the years. Margaret explains:

> Despite every challenge that's put in front of her, she wakes up every morning with a smile and finds everything possibly positive in this world ... If you have so many challenges, you would look from the outside and say, "Why? Why get up? Why do this? Why do that? This is too hard. I can't do this." And if she doesn't complain, how dare I, right?

Facing these challenges head-on, Margaret embraced what Frankl (1963) has described as "experiential" sources of meaning – including the beauty of nature. As she described in Chapter 2, she finds herself savoring the beauty of sunrises and blossoming flowers, which her daughter cannot see. Margaret and her family make the most of every moment, accommodating challenges and never missing opportunities for joy:

> My daughter and I learned how to play tennis when she was younger and when her eyesight started to give her problems and now, she pretty much can't see, tennis became obviously very much of a challenge. You would think. But we figured out a way, where I stand by her side and I tap her shoulder when she has to swing and she plays tennis ... Everybody just stops. And they know her now and they are just amazed. "Oh, my God." You have parents who are pushing their kids to play more and better and so on and here's a person who just does it for the joy of doing it. And her achievement is so much greater than winning a tournament.

When her daughter urgently needed a kidney transplant recently, Margaret did not hesitate:

> [T]he only thing I remember thinking because it all happened so fast, is, Please let me be a match. Please let me be a match. And it was like I couldn't wait to get it done. It's like, Please have it. I joked with her. I said, "I have a few more organs left. I don't have kidneys, but you can have a piece of my liver and you can have lung."

Margaret Pastuszko joined Mount Sinai in 2000, quickly ascending through many leadership positions, including chief strategy officer, chief operating officer, and executive vice president. In September 2021, she was appointed president of the Mount Sinai Health System.

Meaning at the End of Life

One of Viktor Frankl's observations is that meaning may be found even in the most ominous circumstances:

> We must never forget that we may also find meaning in life even when confronted with a hopeless situation ... For what then matters is to bear witness to the uniquely human potential at its best, which is to transform a personal tragedy into a triumph, to turn one's predicament into a human achievement. *When we are no longer able to change a situation – just think of an incurable disease such as inoperable cancer: We are challenged to change ourselves.* (Frankl 1963, p. 116)

Frankl referred to the capacity for finding meaning in adversity as "tragic optimism," optimism in the face of human suffering, guilt, and even certain death. Tragic optimism encompasses the human potential to transform suffering into human achievement and guilt into meaningful action.

Connecting to meaning considers life's limitations. For example, a terminally ill patient may be incapacitated to the point of depending upon others even for basic daily activities like eating and bathing. Accepting one's own imminent death, or that of a loved one, may be one of the most difficult tasks that we face as humans. In her book on death and dying, *The Journey Home*, Ann Graber writes,

> As a first step when hospice is invited into the treatment team, the illusion that recovery will be forthcoming has to be given up.

Denial of approaching death can no longer be sustained ... Those who can accept this inevitability, in spite of the anguish it may cause, are preparing for a harmonious parting of ways on their journey home ... The transformative process – inherent in unavoidable suffering – makes us realize that tragedy often contains the seeds of grace: We can become more than we were before, by facing the challenges life presents to us.

(Graber 2009, pp. 31–32)

Since our work almost two decades ago with veterans who had PTSD, logotherapy has gone on to inform the development of meaning-centered psychotherapy (MCP) by a team based at Memorial Sloan Kettering Cancer Center in New York (Breitbart *et al.* 2010). MCP, which focuses on ways to connect to and make a meaningful life even in suffering, has proven effective in managing end-of-life distress in individuals with cancer. One of us (Jon) participated in adapting MCP to support 9/11 responders fighting advanced cancer (Masterson-Duva *et al.* 2020); and this therapeutic approach influenced the recommendations we make at the end of the chapter for connecting to meaning in calm and challenging times alike.

Post-traumatic Growth

In the immediate aftermath of a trauma, survivors struggle to comprehend what has happened. They may have trouble believing and accepting that a loved one is gone forever or that they have lost all their possessions. Their long-standing assumption that the world is safe and predictable may be shaken, leaving them feeling vulnerable and lost, and they may repeatedly experience intrusive thoughts about the trauma. However, over time, many survivors find that their attempts to comprehend the trauma gradually shift; their new focus is then to create meaning out of the trauma.

Dr. Alin Gragossian's Story

Dr. Alin Gragossian, a critical care fellow at Mount Sinai, faced a sudden life-threatening illness in late 2019, just as she was finishing her residency.

I was having some shortness of breath and a cough, and it was persistent for a couple of weeks and of course ... I thought I would never get sick ... I was thirty and I had had no medical problems my whole life ... I went to the hospital and my heart basically stopped ... nobody knew what was going on until we did a whole bunch of tests, and I was told that I have end-stage heart failure with an ejection fraction of 5 percent, which is basically a barely functioning heart.

Within three weeks of my life, I went from a completely healthy, normal 30-year-old woman in residency, athletic, no medical problems, to a transplant recipient, which is a very difficult thing to go through and have and manage.

She distinctly remembers a swarm of doctors crowding around in the emergency room as they were first trying to diagnose her. As they were waiting for test results to come in, her heart rate plummeted and she needed to have a tube placed down her throat into her lungs to help her breath. She was in such severe heart failure that she made it to the top of the priority list to get a new heart.

After receiving a transplant, Dr. Gragossian quickly decided to use her experiences to support others, including her own critically ill patients:

Because of that I feel like I've learned a lot from the experience [the transplant] and I've tried to reassess my life and see what exactly is important and what shouldn't be prioritized or not as much as before ... honestly, in some ways I find myself thankful for what happened to me ... because I feel like not every physician has the same, I don't want to say another skillset, but I feel like I understand patients a different way, and that, in itself, is very rare ... Having that experience has [also] made me just a little more aware and mindful of the time that I have right now.

Days after her transplant, she started a blog about her illness and recovery. In addition to helping her make sense of her "new normal" and continued medical complications, this work has been a source of strength and inspiration for other young people facing severe illnesses. More recently, she started a podcast with another physician who was a transplant recipient, called Both Sides of the Stethoscope. Her courage and sense of meaning in her work as a critical care physician fueled her to do something else incredible – when physically able, she worked through the worst parts of the pandemic at no small risk to her own health.

How do we measure post-traumatic growth (PTG) in individuals like Dr. Gragossian? To evaluate the kinds of changes that people can experience after life-altering events, researchers often use a questionnaire called the Posttraumatic Growth Inventory (Tedeschi *et al.* 2017; Tedeschi & Calhoun 1996). The latest version of the scale measures growth in five areas: (1) better relationships with others, (2) increased sense of new possibilities in life, (3) increased sense of personal strength and abilities, (4) spiritual or existential changes, and (5) a new appreciation for life. Many other individuals we interviewed experienced these changes; and we saw them too in our research with healthcare workers responding to the pandemic.

We used the Posttraumatic Growth Inventory to better understand the experience of healthcare workers at Mount Sinai approximately eight months after the first cases in New York City. The results may surprise you. The majority (76.8%) of healthcare workers endorsed PTG in at least one part of their life; for example, many said they had an increased appreciation for life (67.0%) while some endorsed improved relationships (48.7%) and greater sense of personal strength (44.1%) (Feingold *et al.* 2022). Even amid horrible experiences and emotional strain, our colleagues became stronger in some key areas of their lives.

It is important to understand that intense psychological distress does not preclude post-traumatic growth. In fact, in our work, HCWs with PTSD symptoms early in the pandemic (April–May 2020) were more likely to endorse PTG eight months later (Nov.–Dec. 2020) (Feingold *et al.* 2022). In general, research shows that post-traumatic growth is most likely to develop when PTSD symptoms are moderate, but not when they are severe *or* low (Greenberg *et al.* 2021). To promote growth, a traumatic experience may need to first incite enough distress to shake the individual's view of the world and his or her place in it. This distressing situation forces individuals to reassess, revise, and rebuild fundamental aspects of their psychological, philosophical, and/or spiritual lives.

Finding Your Own Meaning, Purpose, and Growth

Thinking back to our formative years, many of us were encouraged to envision and strive toward a meaningful adulthood. Our parents and teachers would ask: What do you want to be when you grow up? Of course, life ambitions change as we grow older and more knowledgeable about the options available to us. Ideally, throughout our lives we will have the freedom to choose pursuits that allow us to use our own strengths and interests. If we are fortunate, we will have the leeway to periodically reevaluate how we are using our skills, particularly when we encounter a setback or event that shakes our world view.

In *Man's Search for Meaning* (1963) and *The Will to Meaning* (1969), Viktor Frankl argues that what is meaningful for one person may not be meaningful for another, or for the same person at a different point in life. For Frankl, meaning is not handed to us: We must search for it, in the concrete experiences of our daily lives.

FINDING MEANING AND PURPOSE ALL AROUND US

How can you search for and find meaning and purpose in your own life? Based on the work of Frankl, William Breitbart and his team (Breitbart *et al.* 2010) developed a type of psychotherapy centered on four sources of meaning with the goal of addressing end-of-life distress. But these are just as relevant for someone who is not facing a life-altering illness. Think about how you connect or can connect to them in your own life.

- *Historical*: This is meaning derived from the legacy you have been given as a family member, partner or parent, or member of a particular group; how you live this legacy in the present moment; and how you pass it on to others.

- *Experiential*: This is the meaning found in everyday experiences of love, beauty, humor, and nature. Put simply, it involves being fully in the present moment. It may not involve physically "doing anything" – and even people in their last moments of life can find meaning in these areas.

- *Creative*: This is fostered by using your energy to make things – paintings, poetry, music; work products that live on beyond your years; or a family that brings you pride.

- *Attitudinal*: This type of meaning is to be found in the attitude people take toward their suffering, including when they are face to face with life's limitations. Many of the people we interviewed for the book made a conscious choice to face difficult situations with love, gratitude, active problem solving, and where needed, acceptance.

Conclusion

In his writing, Frankl recommends that we search for meaning not by asking, What is the meaning of my life? but instead by asking, What is life asking of me?; not by asking, What can I expect from life? but rather, What does life expect from me? We did not choose our parents and had no say about the time or place of our birth.

During our lives, of our countless experiences, we chose only some; many we did not, particularly moments of adversity. Nevertheless, here we are, right now, with a unique set of life experiences, skills, and talents. In his view, and ours, meaning is made, not (entirely) given.

What is life asking of us, then? Everything. Everything we have. Or, as Frankl (2019) believed: life is asking us to fill the space in which we happen to have landed. Our station in life, our occupation – they do not matter. What matters is what we do with what we have. We'll revisit these important ideas from Frankl in the book's concluding epilogue.

12

The Practice of Resilience

Resilience is more than an idea – something you simply think about and then it happens. Building it requires practice. But where to begin? We believe that for most people it is best to begin by choosing one or two resilience factors that align with their personal values, feel natural to them, fit well with their lifestyle, and that seem doable. And then we recommend consistent practice and patience because building resilience will take time and sustained effort. At the end of each chapter of this book, we have provided some suggestions about how to work on each of these factors in your own life.

Over time, you can add more resilience factors to your training. As you add factors to your practice, they may interact with one another and enhance your overall resilience. For example, people who become more optimistic often become more likable – which in turn may open up greater access to social support. Increased social support may then provide the safety net and confidence needed to try out new, more active, creative, and effective strategies for coping with a host of challenges.

Building resilience requires the same commitment and persistence necessary to excel at a sport or succeed at following a fitness regime. The qualities and habits cultivated in athletics – persistence, drive, concentration, dogged commitment, and willingness to tolerate some pain – all apply to training to increase your resilience. It also helps to understand that no one can be resilient all the time in all areas of his or her life, as we mentioned in the first chapter. You should also keep in mind that we all have what Chris Peterson and Martin Seligman have called "signature strengths," traits or abilities that come naturally to us and areas in which we excel (Peterson & Seligman 2004). Knowing your strengths (this may require getting feedback from others) can help boost your confidence and fuel further growth.

While we have spent most of the book going into detail about each of our ten resilience factors, we know that they are highly interrelated. You might have noticed that some of the people we interviewed appear in multiple chapters – that's because they've told us about more than one factor that has been important to them over the course of their lives. We know this well from our own life experiences. As we mentioned in Chapter 1, one of us (Dennis) survived an attempted murder in Chappaqua, New York, in August 2016. In his story, we can see many factors that were helpful to him over the course of his recovery.

Dr. Charney told his story in a June 2018 interview for Mount Sinai's Road to Resilience podcast.

I stopped, parked my car in front of Lange's [Deli], and went in and ordered my standard bagel, light on the butter, and iced coffee. And then I went out to go to my car and all of a sudden I heard a loud "boom" and looked at my shoulder and saw that blood was coming out of my shoulder … And I glanced in front of me and saw a person holding a shotgun. But my immediate reaction was the "fight or flight" reaction to get myself to safety.

So I ran back into Lange's and I yelled out, I said, "I was shot." And then the folks in the deli started reacting. One of my friends who works behind the counter, George, immediately called the police. And as he told me later, he was going to make sure that my assailant did not come into that deli one way or the other.

I felt severe pain in my right side, my right shoulder. I really couldn't move my right shoulder and eventually I found out that I had been hit with around 15 pellets from the shotgun. It had penetrated my shoulder. Some of the pellets had penetrated into my lung cavity and through my diaphragm into around my liver. And a couple of my ribs were broken as well. So, it was a pretty significant injury. Ultimately, I lost half of my blood.

There was one moment there [that morning] that still is very emotional to me. One of the police officers, who was actually off duty, followed the ambulance, and sat outside my room to protect me in case there was somebody else who's going to come and try to hurt me. My son is there and he's thanking police officer Davenport for guarding us even though he was off duty. And police officer Davenport said to my son, "I just wish I was there to take the bullets." And that's somebody who didn't even know me. (Earle 2018a)

Dr. Charney soon learned from the police that the person who shot him was a former faculty member who had been terminated in 2009 for academic misconduct. He had been planning the attack for months, stalking Dr. Charney and his family, including his grandchildren. It was horrifying.

Here he was, a well-known researcher in resilience and the dean of a medical school, facing a life-altering event and a painful rehabilitation. Could he practice what he preached?

I had several role models. A couple were people we ended up interviewing and learning from, you know, as part of our research in resilience. They included the POWs from Vietnam who were held for six to eight years in prison and were heavily tortured and many of them, after they were released, achieved great things in their life. We got to know Navy SEALs. I knew those people personally, and so I would think … If they could do it [I can too] – I have one trauma. Many of them had multiple [traumas].

I [also] set goals for myself right away and I learned that from my resilience work. So when I was in the ICU, I said to the doctor who's in charge of my care, I said, "I have to give that White Coat speech." The White Coat speech is a speech to the medical students who are just starting medical school. It's a very moving ceremony where we put white coats literally onto the first-year medical students as they start medical school.

And this sounds silly, but I'm among the millions of Bruce Springsteen fans. And he wrote a song "Tougher Than the Rest." Now the song is not exactly like what happened to me, but that phrase, that I was going to be tougher than the rest, just kept running through my mind when I was in the ICU. That I was going to be tougher than the rest in my recovery from this shooting. (Earle 2018a)

Another part of his recovery was an unexpected opportunity to be a role model for other survivors of violent crimes. Almost a year after his own assault, a former physician opened fire with an AR-15 assault rifle in two floors of Bronx-Lebanon Hospital, killing one person and seriously wounding several others there.

> *A number of people were transferred to Mount Sinai for treatment because their wounds were serious. And one was a young doctor who was like in his first year of training after medical school. And our staff told me that he was having trouble coping in the beginning. And they thought it might be helpful if I were to go meet him … And I walked in and said, "I may be the dean, but I'm your brother." That I've gone through something similar … recovery. And that in the beginning there's going to be a sense of anxiety. And you're going to feel very emotional. But eventually that's going to fade. And this experience, believe it or not, is going to make you a better doctor. Because you treat patients who are suffering, and you're going to be able to recall your suffering and be a better doctor and be more empathetic with your patients. (Earle 2018b)*

Like many other individuals we interviewed in this book, Dr. Charney can attest that recovery – even with all this support – can be rocky. For a time, he felt uneasy at night, in the dark, reliving memories of the trauma. He was startled by loud noises, and together with his family, struggled to make sense of why someone would attack him and if it could happen again. Through all of this, he remained focused on his goals.

After being discharged from the ICU, he did grueling physical rehabilitation daily. He achieved his short-term goal – just two weeks after being shot, he delivered the White Coat speech to rising Mount Sinai medical students (we close the chapter with part of this speech). Soon after that, he set out to do a push-up challenge to support prostate cancer awareness. Each day got a little bit easier.

Resilience in Context

In this book, we have also talked a lot about how individuals embraced certain resilience factors in tough times. However, resilience is also relevant in broader contexts, such as in the family and parenting, or in your career. In the rest of this chapter, we will look at these parts of life in a bit more detail.

The Family

We all need family. Ideally, it is one of our most important sources of resilience, the place where we learn what it is to feel safe, loved, and accepted. The family is also typically the root of values. For some people, though, their early family experience is not so favorable. Some of us may harbor vivid childhood memories of being misunderstood or disappointed by our parents, or on the extreme end, jarring experiences of abuse or neglect. As adults, we may benefit from understanding the struggles that our parents may have faced in raising us. Perhaps they came from difficult or troubled families themselves; they may have been doing the best they could under harsh circumstances. By trying to understand and in some cases "forgive" family members, hopefully we can open the door to rewarding and supportive relationships.

A Son Gains Perspective on His Father's Sacrifices

Tony Chung, a Mount Sinai graduate student, struggled to understand his father when he was a child. Other friends would have parents at ball games, on field trips, or to play with in the backyard; Tony's father, Dennis, a refugee from Vietnam, was always at work. An appreciation for his father's sacrifices, what he had left behind in Vietnam, and what he was building from "scratch" for the family only came as Tony got older.

When I was younger, I felt like I took my dad for granted a little bit to be honest because I always saw him as someone who was always at work. He was never really home or never really there for me ... when I was a kid, I had gone to the park to play Frisbee with their [my friend's] dad and I remember feeling so jealous. And then my dad was only off for one day a week and I forced him to buy a Frisbee and play Frisbee with me in the park.

I think as I got older and especially during COVID, I realized my dad was not working at the restaurant fourteen hours a day for nothing. He was there for the pure love of his family and to support us. I see how much money and effort he spent on putting me through school and bringing me to where I am today. I think I finally have a better appreciation for him.

And what I learned is that nothing could ever be worse than having every single thing in your life taken away by the government. Being forced to take a treacherous journey on a boat to a refugee island and live there for a year eating canned food. Nothing can be worse than that. I just say to myself, if I feel like I'm struggling, not really suck it up, but just hang in there. There will be better times.

Sadly, some families may be so toxic that reconnecting with and forgiving them would only cause us more pain. When this is the case, it may be best to create a new "family" that provides a healthy source of strength. We may do this in marriage or a romantic relationship, with a group of friends, or colleagues at work, or with a religious congregation. Some of us will be privileged to be able to build or participate in teams that communicate well, support one another tangibly and emotionally, and spotlight mutual accomplishments. These well-formed "work families" can be emotionally healing.

Whatever our family history, it is always wise to surround ourselves with allies; people who like and accept us, who treat us with kindness and respect, and who encourage us to be our best selves. In good times, these people provide a framework for sharing goodwill and resources; when troubles arise, we can count on them to "be there" for us – as we are for them.

Family dynamics expert Froma Walsh advocates a "family resilience framework" to handle adversity. It comprises nine key processes that resilient families tend to use when responding to trauma and stress:

- Making meaning of adversity,
- Maintaining a positive outlook,
- Fostering transcendence and spirituality,
- Practicing flexibility,
- Enhancing connectedness/social support,
- Lean on social and economic resources,
- Use clear communication and gain clarity on ambiguous situations,
- Expressing both positive and negative emotions openly, and
- Solving problems collaboratively and learning from setbacks.

From this list, you can tell that there are clear similarities between the ten factors we have discussed in this book and these processes that Froma Walsh sees as key to family resilience (Walsh 2021).

Raising Children

Will our children be prepared for the world they will face as adults? If our goal is to raise a resilient child, we must find the right balance between protecting that child and encouraging him or her to reach their full potential.

There are thousands of books on parenting; and many first-time parents get bogged down in wanting to do the "best" job they can. But they just need to be "good enough." The British pediatrician and psychoanalyst Donald Winnicott coined the term "good enough" to describe a parent who is not overprotective, and fulfills their baby's needs while gradually moving them further away from immediate gratification as they grow up (Winnicott 2005). This style of parenting allows the child to gradually experience and master more challenges, including feelings of frustration, on their own. A good enough parent encourages challenges that the child can master, but not those that are completely overwhelming and dangerous. A "good enough" parent will also make mistakes; they "own" them and move on. The same can be said of "good enough" teachers, coaches, mentors, and bosses.

Dr. Annetine Gelijns, the chair of Population Health at the Icahn School of Medicine, spoke with us about how her parents supported her resilience. Dr. Gelijns was born with spina bifida and severe scoliosis, requiring many surgeries, one of which left her temporarily paralyzed. Her parents never lost faith in her ability to recover and thrive – even when doctors recommended that she should be transitioned to a long-term care home. For long stretches of her childhood, she had to wear orthopedic braces; like with Deborah Gruen, this included a "clamshell" to add spinal stability.

Supporting Independence

Dr. Gelijns described how her parents allowed calculated risks to build her self-confidence.

> And what I really wanted as a 10-year-old was to ride horses. So they gave me a pony when I became 10. And I would ride with my brace, and I would take my pony in the woods. And you know, sometimes when we gallop, you know, I would be caught up with my brace in a tree … but you know, they allowed me to take those risks. And they said, look, you know, you have to do this to really sort of get better. But we will support you and what you want to do. And if you want to take risks, we'll be there and allow you to take them … [T]hat made all the difference, that you know that people were backing you up. And that even where you were different, they said you're not different. If you want to go horse riding and be a competitive horse rider, you can go and ride competitively. So I think that sort of gave an enormous strength to what you do.

Work and Career

Many of us have faced – or will face – difficult situations at work – receiving a negative performance review, being passed over for a promotion, or even losing our job. Business leaders who are now household names, like Michael Bloomberg and Steve Jobs, were fired from firms before they started their own enterprises.

For those who are leaders of any sort, of teams of one other person to thousands, building resilience in this role is crucial to "mission success," particularly in times of crisis. Never was this clearer to us than during the COVID-19 pandemic; and we saw many examples of resilient leadership at Mount Sinai. Our research during the early part of the emergency showed that those frontline healthcare workers who felt supported by their leaders had lower risk of developing mental health symptoms. Being reliable, physically and emotionally present, and communicating information clearly are key aspects of resilient leadership.

Leading in Crisis

Margaret Pastuszko, president of the Mount Sinai Health System, shared some important lessons from the first wave of the pandemic. First, she made clear that it is important to think of employees as people first, with a sense of safety being paramount.

> I think … [an] important thing for our employees was to give them space to make sure that their families were okay. That we could focus on getting the work done, but also, making sure that our families were okay. A number of us moved out of our homes. We had to make sure that we had those accommodations and things like that. That's what I mean by supporting those individuals. Because otherwise, you can't worry that your family's in danger of something you don't understand at the same time you're trying to help all the other people.

She also shared something that is another essential part of resilient leadership – being courageous and decisive. You can always learn from missteps and course-correct when the storm calms down.

Was everything we did for our team perfect back then? I don't know. It was the best we could do at the time with the best information we could gather. And I always say, "It's better to make a decision than let it be made for you." You can wait for the perfect information and the perfect everything, but then the decisions will be made for you.

Even if you are not in a leadership role, most of us can bolster our careers by learning to face fear, cultivate realistic optimism, learn from role models, and give and receive social support. The work environment is sometimes viewed as a dog-eat-dog world, but resilience comes from staying true to one's values and moral compass, even if it means passing up an opportunity for career advancement.

Resilient leaders build resilient teams. In a speech given at Mount Sinai in 2013, retired Rear Admiral Scott Moore shared five attributes of resilient and highly effective teams:

1. They have leaders who clearly communicate a vision and mission for the team.
2. Leaders sincerely care about each member of the team.
3. Coaching and mentoring of future leaders are priorities. Delegation is standard, including tolerance of failure while developing as a leader.
4. Leaders constantly demonstrate trust in team members, which causes a reciprocal trust in leaders to develop.
5. There is a strong desire to always improve, demonstrated by the constant review of team performances while accomplishing tasks, thereby holding teammates accountable, including leaders themselves. (Icahn School of Medicine 2013)

There is nonstop communication by leaders, to include listening, in pursuit of best practices. When the going gets tough, leaders step up and lead through adversity.

Activities That Incorporate Multiple Resilience Factors: A Few Examples

As we have pointed out earlier, resilience factors tend to build upon one another and sometimes operate synergistically. Here are just a few examples.

Become a Volunteer

Volunteering to join with others in the pursuit of a worthy goal has many potential benefits. First and foremost, it can provide aid to an organization, to a cause, or to people in need. But it can also strengthen the volunteer by enhancing one or more resilience factors.

Steve Goes to Camp

After giving a talk on resilience, one of us (Steve) was approached by a board member from the Hole in the Wall Gang Camp, a no-fee outdoor retreat for children with cancer and other serious illnesses that was founded by the actor and philanthropist Paul Newman. The following summer, he volunteered to serve for a week as a camp counselor at The Hole in the Wall Gang Camp in Ashford, Connecticut.

> During the weekly orientation for new volunteers, I was introduced to my two new bosses, college-age counselors, who had both worked at the camp for several years. They made me feel right at home.
>
> Even though all of the kids had a serious medical illness, and in some cases a major physical disability, they knew how to have fun; they invented games, cracked jokes, and made friends in a matter of minutes. They were not entitled, narcissistic, Me-generation types. Instead, they were fun-loving, generous, and kind. Over the course of the week, I don't remember hearing a single complaint from any of the kids about his illness.

When I look back on this week and think about resilience, a number of factors stand out. Serving as a volunteer counselor helped – and at times forced – me to step out of my comfort zone, increase my flexibility, contribute to a worthy goal, receive and give social support, and look more closely at my own purpose and mission in life. However, the most powerful boost to my own resilience came in the form of role models: the devoted, sturdy, and selfless men and women on the staff, and, most important, the boys in my cabin. I continue to be impressed by the degree of resilience, bravery, and grace that I witnessed in these young gentlemen and try my best to imitate them.

Depending on the organization, volunteering may also provide us with opportunities to deepen our religious or spiritual practice by participating in a religious-based mission; to exercise moral courage by joining a group that fights against injustice; to improve physical health by participating in a bike ride to raise funds for cancer research; or to boost brain fitness by becoming a tutor or mentor. And for anyone, the experience may foster cognitive and emotional flexibility.

Athletic Competition

Physical exercise is associated with both physical and emotional resilience. Although we can build resilience by exercising alone, exercising with a friend adds social support, and by joining a competition we actively seek to challenge and test ourselves. Even better, competition involving team sports provides us with camaraderie and opportunities to find new role models. Finally, competing for a cause – for example, a 10-kilometer run for cancer – adds the dimension of altruism. Whether consciously or not, we may put to work at least five resilience factors by participating in such an event.

In the United States today, some teachers and parents believe that competition is destructive to the emotional well-being of children, and they try to create an alternate world where everyone is a winner. However, competition is unavoidable. It permeates modern life: we compete in athletics, for entrance into college, for jobs, even for mates. Sometimes we win and sometimes we lose.

Jeff Gruen's Parenting Perspective

Jeff Gruen, the father of Deborah, the remarkable young woman born with a potentially disabling condition whom we met earlier in the book, learned about the value of competition from both of his daughters. Until his daughters joined the local swim club, Jeff believed that competition was bad, that it undermined confidence, camaraderie, and the sheer joy of learning. Later, he came to understand the value of tolerating and even embracing competition.

> I learned an incredible amount about how to professionally survive [as a pediatric researcher] and about my academic career through their sports. Part of the reason I didn't do sports growing up was that I didn't understand them. If I can't win, I don't want to play, and that was really my attitude for years and years. And with my children, [they weren't big winners] but they loved it. It took me a long, long time to learn that they didn't have to win the race to be happy ... For them, their P.B., their personal best, became really important, and I didn't understand it. If I couldn't get the big paper published, do the big experiment, get the big grant, it made me very angry and very upset, which is a tough way to conduct a professional career, especially if you are constantly comparing yourself with people.

Many of the resilient people we interviewed, including Dr. Jake Levine who we read about in Chapter 8, recognized that competition can bolster feelings of self-efficacy and bring out our best. It can help us learn to recover from "failure," and help us strive toward more challenging personal goals.

Become a Mentor

Mentoring takes the concept of role models and turns it around. As a mentor, you serve as a model for someone who needs skill building and encouragement. In the process, you also develop your own skills, because when we teach, we learn. In addition, mentors typically embrace an optimistic outlook (believing that their mentee's life will get better), practice altruism (giving of their time and talents), and give and receive social support. A large component of mentorship is selflessness. Discussing her mentorship work with junior faculty in her department, Dr. Gelijns told us that she prioritizes "creating an environment in which they can be the best that they can be" ahead of her personal goals.

Perhaps the most widely known mentoring program is Big Brothers Big Sisters of America, which matches children ages 6 through 18 with adult mentors. BBBS also has programs devoted to special populations such as children whose parents are in the military or in prison. The minimum time commitment is one hour per week. Volunteers can meet their little "brother" or "sister" in the community or at school, and the emphasis is on friendship.

Survivor Mission

On January 29, 2006, ABC news correspondent Bob Woodruff was grievously injured in a roadside bomb explosion while embedded with military forces in Iraq. He suffered severe brain trauma and was in a medically induced coma for thirty-six days. After intensive speech therapy and other rehabilitation services, Bob returned to television eighteen months after the injury to host a prime-time special about his traumatic brain injury. With his wife, Lee, Bob co-wrote the book *In an Instant: A Family's Journey of Love and Healing* (Woodruff & Woodruff 2008) chronicling his injury and the process of rehabilitation.

The Woodruffs founded the Bob Woodruff Foundation in 2006 to help military service members and their families recover from the impact of traumatic brain injury. According to its website, the foundation's mission is to "find, fund, shape, and accelerate equitable solutions that help our impacted veterans, service members, their families, and their caregivers thrive." Like Jerry White, who founded the International Landmine Survivor Network, and J. Corey Feist, and Jennifer Breen Feist, who co-founded the Dr. Lorna Breen Heroes Foundation, Bob and Lee Woodruff have chosen to use their traumatic experience as a platform for helping others.

One need not be famous to embrace a survivor mission. On Valentine's Day 2000, after dinner at their favorite restaurant, Carolyn Moor and her husband Chad were driving home when a car carrying four college students in the oncoming lane of traffic drifted into their side of the road. Chad intentionally spun the steering wheel sharply so that his side of the car, rather than Carolyn's, would be hit. They skidded out of the path of the oncoming car but smashed into a lamp post, which collapsed, striking Chad on the head. The other car drove on as if nothing had happened.

Carolyn, a trained nurse, performed CPR on her husband, but twelve hours later Chad died from his injuries in a nearby hospital. Carolyn was left with two children and funeral arrangements; she had no choice but to carry on with the routines of life and did not have the option to take leave from work. Recognizing from her painful experiences how little support there was for widows in the United States, she founded the nonprofit Modern Widows Club in 2011. Their mission is to "empower widows to lean into life, build resilience and make a positive difference in society" (Modern Widows Club 2022). Their mentorship, leadership, educational, advocacy, and support group programs have spread across the US and now have a global reach. They are pioneering widow support, solutions, and research.

In Chapter 11, we highlighted a few other examples of individuals and their survivor missions. From all these stories, you can see that a clear mission and persistence are essential.

Resilience: Parting Words

Resilience is about understanding the difference between fate and freedom, learning to take responsibility for one's own life, and working within your scope of control. Human beings are free, but with freedom comes a responsibility to:

- Find and imitate resilient role models,
- Cultivate positive emotions and optimism,
- Face our fears, and confront rather than avoid problems,
- Learn from failure, and persist when it would be easier to give up,
- Constructively reframe unpleasant, stressful, and traumatic events,
- Seek out social support and build our support network,
- Keep our bodies in shape through exercise, good nutrition, and sleep,
- Use whatever strengths we have and cultivate those strengths,
- Devote time and energy to spirituality and religion,
- Assist others who are in need,
- Find meaning in our day-to-day life,
- Acquire the knowledge and skills necessary to achieve goals through training,
- Accept that achievement rarely comes without enormous work and hardship,
- Build strength of character with a moral and ethical core,
- Find and embrace a survivor mission when appropriate,
- Search for opportunity in adversity, to learn and to grow from the hand that fate deals us,
- Accept what cannot be changed,
- Try our best to bear unavoidable physical and psychological pain with grace and dignity,
- *Or, in summary: Do the best we can with what we have.*

These are the choices that each of us faces, repetitively, throughout life. For some, of course, the burden is much greater than for others.

We hope that we have impressed upon you that there is no one path to adapting, "working through," or recovering from tough times.

Dr. Charney's Speech

We close this chapter with an excerpt from Dr. Charney's speech to the Icahn School of Medicine class of 2020, delivered just two weeks after he was shot. While he was speaking to future physicians, what he says can apply to all of us.

> We are often called upon to show strength during professional and personal tragedy. This is both a burden and a privilege – to show strength, to show courage, to inspire those around us by demonstrating grace under duress. This is a gift unlike any in the world. These next four years of your life will be trying. It will be a challenge to find a balance between achieving success in school and fulfillment in other aspects of life. I know you only get one life, and in anything you do what matters most is that you have integrity and stand for what you believe in. As a doctor this isn't just a choice – it's a commitment we make to our patients. And finally, I know bad stuff does happen. A bad thing happened to me.
>
> You will face tough times, but if you stay the course, nose to the grindstone, eyes to the stars, ultimately you will emerge further down the road tougher than the rest. Or as Ernest Hemingway said, "The world breaks everyone, and afterward many are strong at the broken places." (Earle 2018a)

Resilience Facing Death:
A Tribute to
Dr. Steven M. Southwick

Our colleague and friend Dr. Steven Southwick, passed away on April 20, 2022, at the age of 73, after a five-year battle with metastatic prostate cancer. At the time of his death, Steve was the Glenn H. Greenberg Professor Emeritus of Psychiatry, PTSD, and Resilience at the Yale School of Medicine and Medical Director Emeritus of the Clinical Neuroscience Division of the National Center for PTSD of the US Department of Veterans Affairs.

Steve was born on April 24, 1948 in Boston, Massachusetts. His family showed a clear commitment to service and education. His father, Wayne Southwick, was the founding chair of the Department of Orthopedic Surgery at the Yale School of Medicine. His brother, Frederick, is also a physician, and his sister Marcia, now retired, was a creative writing professor.

During the Vietnam War, Steve served in the United States Army and was stationed in Germany. After his service, he attended medical school and completed his psychiatry residency at Yale University. Steve then remained at Yale throughout his career, where he forged rich collaborations and decades-long friendships.

Steve was beloved by his friends and colleagues, and loved mentoring medical students, psychiatry residents, and faculty at all levels. His wife Bernadette was an incredible source of support.

There is no question as to his impact on the field of psychiatry – with over 400 published papers, books, and chapters focused on understanding post-traumatic stress disorder and resilience, and how to find meaning in suffering. But more than that, he practiced what he preached. Using Steve's own words, and the experiences of those who knew him well, we devote this epilogue to how he *lived* many of the resilience factors that he studied throughout his illness.

Steve Devoted His Full Self to Others

Over five years, Steve pursued aggressive treatments including clinical trials, radiation, and hormones; all of these came with significant complications and the physical pain was intense. Steve's illness refocused his attention – showing his love and giving and getting social support became a priority. In his notes for this book, Steve wrote:

My experience with cancer has forced me to carefully assess the topic of resilience as it applies to me. Occasionally, after giving a lecture on resilience I have been asked by an audience member, "Dr. Southwick, do you personally follow the advice that you and Dr. Charney give in your book?" My routine answer, "All I can say is that you don't have to be a good swimmer to be a good swimming coach." But that answer is no longer sufficient.

I haven't always faced my fears right away. Sometimes I have procrastinated, which has only made the situation more daunting. But not with incurable cancer. There is no time to procrastinate and no time to worry about fear of failure or rejection. There is only time to embrace whatever time you have left and to love as much as you can and to give, give and then give more.

Before [the diagnosis], I was afraid to let people know how much I cared about them and loved them. But not anymore. What's the worst that can happen? My love won't be returned, or someone will disapprove of something I believe in or something I do, or I will be reprimanded, or I will be fired from my job, or I might even die? Well, I am dying. And truly understanding this can be liberating. I have spent my whole life trying to get an "A" in everything, trying to succeed ... And in the end what really matters? What matters is what you love and who you love. That's it – end of discussion. Love is the great motivator. Love is the heart and soul of resilience. At least, that's what I now believe.

[And] I would not be alive today without the unconditional love of my family and friends. For me this is the most important resilience factor. We must have loving support and we must give loving support in order to thrive and live a full life. Social connectedness is the anchor that keeps us from drifting into oblivion.

In mid-2020, as we were hit by the first wave of the pandemic, Steve's expertise in traumatic stress helped shape programs to support the well-being of healthcare workers at both Yale and Mount Sinai. Dr. John Krystal, Steve's long-time friend, and chair of Psychiatry at the Yale School of Medicine, shared:

> His capacity to focus on the needs that others had in our community at that time was just remarkable. And so many times I was thinking as he was talking, how can you do this? How can you talk about the illness and distress and the pain of others when you're in the same kind of situation? And yet, I had the feeling that these kinds of discussions were actually part of the way in which he remained resilient.

In his last month of life, Steve experienced an acute bladder perforation and was admitted to Mount Sinai Hospital for sixteen days. It was not clear he would survive it. Others would show despair. Steve showed love – he told *everyone* in his life that he loved them. He called our colleague Dr. Robert Pietrzak from his ICU bed to check in on him, when he learned that Robb's father had died. One of us (Dennis) witnessed the extent of this outpouring of love: "I got a call from the housekeeping people that I had to go down and tell Steve to stop telling the housekeepers that he loved and appreciated what they were doing."

John Krystal saw this love in the last email he received from Steve, who had partly recovered from the acute issue and been discharged home from Mount Sinai: "He was telling me about what happened at Sinai, and it was just the short, you know, 'Miss you, love, Steve,' because [of] all the things that he had had to sustain. He just really wanted to make sure that I knew how he felt and that's the kind of guy he was."

Steve Used Role Models to Give Him Strength and Was a Role Model to Others

As we shared in the quote from Steve that opened the chapter on role models, he relied heavily on the experiences of people he had met and interviewed over the years:

> Sometimes, to learn from resilient role models, I ask them how they think and how they behave when dealing with adversity, and then I try to imitate them. For example, Deborah Gruen, the young Paralympic swimming champion who we profiled in the chapter on optimism, swam an average of 24 miles per week as part of her high school training. Several years ago, when I was still swimming 1 mile two to three times a week, I can remember thinking midway through my workout that completing half a mile was good enough and that it was time to end my workout. But then Deborah came to mind. Are you kidding? I thought. You wimp, you can swim at least 1 mile. So, I pushed ahead and swam the full mile.

Steve also had strong role models within his own family, pushing him toward a career geared toward helping others:

> I have been exceptionally lucky to be surrounded by resilient role models all my life. First [was] my father, a no-nonsense Korean Veteran and orthopedic surgeon who grew up in a small Nebraska farm town. His advice was always terse, wise, and unambiguous ... [When] I asked him what it takes to live a good life, he replied, "Give 60, take 40." Imagine a world where everyone who has the resources and capability to give 60, actually gave 60.

Steve also served as a role model to many members of his care team. Dr. Ash Tewari, system chair in the Department of Urology at Mount Sinai, met Steve early in his diagnosis. Steve's courage became a comfort when Dr. Tewari himself became the patient – a COVID-19 infection early in the pandemic left him in the intensive care unit for two weeks, and in need of grueling physical rehabilitation.

He Was Optimistic and Used Humor to Reframe His Challenges

Those who had the pleasure of knowing Steve can attest to the optimism he brought to his roles of clinician, researcher, mentor, family member, and friend. This was clear too during his cancer treatments. While he participated in clinical trials and treatments abroad, he remained aware that they might not work and planned accordingly.

Steve savored the life that he had, without clinging too tightly to the chance of a complete cure, particularly as his illness progressed. He wrote:

> I am basically an optimistic person and believe that there is light at the end of the tunnel. However, I am glad that I learned about rose-colored optimism from former POWs because rose-colored optimism can cloud judgment. For someone with an incurable disease this could mean overestimating how much time they have left to live, overestimating potential efficacy of therapies, and inadequately preparing for the future. It might mean believing that there is a cure, a silver bullet just around the corner. It might mean spending your remaining time searching for the next treatment and avoiding being present and attending to important issues like giving thanks and saying goodbye. But, in the end, there is no silver bullet for any of us.

> When I asked one of my doctors if it was time to get my house in order, complete my will, tidy up financial issues, and let my family and friends know how much I love them, he said, "Yes, it's time." That was hard to hear, but I am grateful for his honesty.

Steve's emails with friends and family are also a testament to the way he was actively trying to reframe his challenges in his final year. Dr. Krystal shared examples of Steve's use of humor – cheekily describing the hospital food he was served during his care abroad:

I asked him to keep me in the loop and how it was going and he decided to send me pictures of the food they brought to him at the tables, so, two memorable pictures. One was a ball of something that had been scooped on a tray and he said, "I didn't know what it was before I ate it, and after I ate it, I still don't know what it was."

And then, and I think it must have been a few days later, he sent me another one, which is his dinner, and something brown in the big part of the tray. But for some reason almost the entire rest of the tray was filled with cups of pickled bean salad that just looked horrible, you know? Just horrible. And he said something like, "Lucky to get the pickled beans today. If you want, I'll ask the chef for the recipe."

The notes he left for the book include lists of his favorite jokes. Among them is this well-known line from Woody Allen: "I am not afraid of death; I just don't want to be there when it happens."

He Remained Physically Active – Even in His Last Months

Physical fitness was a large part of his identity; and his high level of physical fitness before and during his treatment may have bought him precious time. Steve shared this love of physical activity with one of us, Dennis Charney, who had the privilege of being his friend and colleague for forty years.

Over the five years of his grueling prostate cancer treatment, Steve and Bernadette would routinely kayak for four to six hours and take 25–30-mile bike rides and 5-mile hikes, when his energy allowed. Dr. William Oh, Steve's medical oncologist, shared that he came to his appointments excited to share photographs of his latest adventures. Reflecting on the role of exercise in his life, Steve wrote:

> I have always loved sports and physical fitness. During Junior High School, on Saturday mornings, I played hockey for a team sponsored by Hamden Auto Body and then immediately afterward for a

team sponsored by Roessler's Hot Dogs; in high school I played football, wrestled, and ran track; in college I played football and wrestled; and in the army I wrestled for a military team in Germany.

Sports and physical fitness have always been a central part of my identity, at times more important than academics or occupation. My wife, Bernadette, and I hike, bike, and kayak. It also plays a central role in Dennis' life ... He and I have shared many challenging adventures such as racing in a 90-mile kayak race in the Adirondacks and kayaking down the Futaleufú river in the mountains of Chile with his wonderful son Alex.

Exercise and sport [have] also helped me to get to know myself, to test my limits, to find out what I am made of, and to be surprised at the strength that lies within. Pushing oneself and reaching down into one's core are part of sport and resilience. And when you are a member of a team there are all of the added benefits of camaraderie and having a common mission ... Honestly, for me one of the most painful consequences of cancer and its treatment has been rapid deterioration of strength, endurance, and of experiencing the many rewards of exercise, competition, and physical challenge.

As his physical condition worsened, long hikes became short walks on the beach with Bernadette. In early April 2022, Steve was captured on video having a moment of pure joy – sitting in his favorite chair, moving his kayak paddles, and imagining being out on the open sea.

No Question About It – Steve Was Resilient

Steve remained intellectually curious and self-reflective. Even in the ICU, he typed up and recorded thoughts for the book, and collected quotes or references he wanted to include. This work gave him a sense of purpose.

What is life asking of me ... Prioritize differently. What things matter and why. Right now, I believe that life is asking Dennis, Jon and me (and all of the people who are helping us) to use all of our past experience to adjust [our] thoughts on resilience and to hopefully help some reader[s]. I try to remember that I still have a certain amount of freedom and with that freedom comes responsibility.

Steve clearly made the most of the present moment, not knowing how many moments he had left. William Oh shared:

> I think he showed how resilience could allow him to get through the toughest times and to basically live a life with dignity, and I think that's the special gift that he gave to his friends, his family, and to me as his colleague and doctor … One of the things I would say Steve taught me was to continue to live your life for the moment.

In his notes, Steve also reflected on the many ways resilience has been defined over the years, seeming to struggle with the question: Am I *resilient* in my cancer battle?

> Resilience has been defined as the ability to bounce back but I can't bounce back. It has been defined as going through a traumatic situation without a drop in functioning, but I have had a drop in function. Does that mean I am not resilient?

We can answer Steve's question for him: *He was resilient.* He inspired, supported, loved, and lived fully. He let go of resentments and connected to sources of meaning. According to Dr. Robert Pietrzak, Steve did "*bounce back* [emotionally] with love, giving to others, service to the field, his colleagues, mentees, all the frontline workers" in his final months. His wife Bernadette added: "he gave – into his last hours – all that he had left to all those around him – words of inspiration, laughs, and love."

We close this book by giving Steve the last words, sharing how he defined resilience. Everyone he knew well agrees that this is how he lived:

> Do the best you can with what you've got. You take it all – success and failure – and use it to do the best you can in the service of others and love.

Abbreviations

ACT	acceptance and commitment therapy
ANS	autonomic nervous system
CBM	cognitive bias modification
CBT	cognitive behavioral therapy
CPT	cognitive processing therapy
DNA	deoxyribonucleic acid (the molecular basis of heredity)
HCW	healthcare worker
HIIT	high-intensity interval training
HPA axis	hypothalamic–pituitary–adrenal axis
LOT-R	Life Orientation Test Revised
MCP	meaning-centered psychotherapy
MRI	magnetic resonance imaging (also fMRI: functional magnetic resonance imaging)
PE	prolonged exposure
PFC	prefrontal cortex
PNS	parasympathetic nervous system
PPE	personal protective equipment
PTG	post-traumatic growth
PTSD	post-traumatic stress disorder
SNS	sympathetic nervous system

References

1 What Is Resilience?

Bhatnagar, S. (2021). Rethinking stress resilience. *Trends in Neurosciences*, 44(12), 936–945.

Choi, U.-S., Sung, Y.-W., Hong, S., Chung, J.-Y., & Ogawa, S. (2015). Structural and functional plasticity specific to musical training with wind instruments. *Frontiers in Human Neuroscience*, 9, 597.

Cunningham, A. M., Walker, D. M., Ramakrishnan, A. *et al.* (2021). Sperm transcriptional state associated with paternal transmission of stress phenotypes. *Journal of Neuroscience: The Official Journal of the Society for Neuroscience*, 41(29), 6202–6216.

DePierro, J., Katz, C. L., Marin, D. et al. (2020). Mount Sinai's Center for Stress, Resilience and Personal Growth as a model for responding to the impact of COVID-19 on health care workers. *Psychiatry Research*, 293, 113426.

DePierro, J., Marin, D. B., Sharma, V. *et al.* (2021). Developments in the first year of a resilience-focused program for health care workers. *Psychiatry Research*, 306, 114280.

Dwyer, J., Lipton, E., Flynn, K., Glanz, J., & Fessenden, F. (2002). Fighting to live as the Towers died. *New York Times*, May 26, retrieved from https://www.nytimes.com/2002/05/26/nyregion/fighting-to-live-as-the-towers-died.html

Earle, J. (2020a). Our finest hour. Mount Sinai podcast, April 10, retrieved from https://www.mountsinai.org/about/newsroom/podcasts/road-resilience/our-finest-hour

Earle, J. (2020b). Workshopping resilience. Mount Sinai podcast, November 6, retrieved from https://www.mountsinai.org/about/newsroom/podcasts/road-resilience/workshopping-resilience

Feingold, J. H., Peccoralo, L., Chan, C. C. *et al.* (2021). Psychological impact of the COVID-19 pandemic on frontline health care workers during the pandemic surge in New York City. *Chronic Stress*, 5, 2470547020977891.

Goldstein, R. B., Smith, S. M., Chou, S. P. *et al.* (2016). The epidemiology of DSM-5 posttraumatic stress disorder in the United States: results from the National Epidemiologic Survey on Alcohol and Related Conditions-III. *Social Psychiatry and Psychiatric Epidemiology*, 51(8), 1137–1148.

Hobfoll, S. E. (2001). The influence of culture, community, and the nested-self in the stress process: advancing conservation of resources theory. *Applied Psychology*, 50(3), 337–421.

Kilpatrick, D. G., Resnick, H. S., Milanak, M. E., Miller, M. W., Keyes, K. M., & Friedman, M. J. (2013). National estimates of exposure to traumatic events and PTSD prevalence using DSM-IV and DSM-5 criteria. *Journal of Traumatic Stress*, 26(5), 537–547.

O'Donnell, K. J., & Meaney, M. J. (2020). Epigenetics, development, and psychopathology. *Annual Review of Clinical Psychology*, 16, 327–350.

Pernet, C. R., Belov, N., Delorme, A., & Zammit, A. (2021). Mindfulness related changes in grey matter: a systematic review and meta-analysis. *Brain Imaging and Behavior*, 15(5), 2720–2730.

Pietrzak, R. H., Feingold, J. H., Feder, A. *et al.* (2020). Psychological resilience in frontline health care workers during the acute phase of the COVID-19 pandemic in New York City. *Journal of Clinical Psychiatry*, 82(1). DOI:10.4088/JCP.20l13749

Southwick, S. M., Bonanno, G. A., Masten, A. S., Panter-Brick, C., & Yehuda, R. (2014). Resilience definitions, theory, and challenges: interdisciplinary perspectives. *European Journal of Psychotraumatology*, 5(1), 25338.

Wolf, E. J., Miller, M. W., Sullivan, D. R. *et al.* (2018). A classical twin study of PTSD symptoms and resilience: evidence for a single spectrum of vulnerability to traumatic stress. *Depression and Anxiety*, 35(2), 132–139.

Yehuda, R. (2022). Trauma in the family tree. *Scientific American*, 327(1), 50–55. DOI:10.1038/scientificamerican0722-50

2 Optimism: Belief in a Brighter Future

Alexander, R., Aragón, O. R., Bookwala, J. *et al.* (2021). The neuroscience of positive emotions and affect: implications for cultivating happiness and wellbeing. *Neuroscience & Biobehavioral Reviews*, 121, 220–249.

Earle, J. (2021). Heart to heart. Mount Sinai podcast, June 25, retrieved from https://www.mountsinai.org/about/newsroom/podcasts/road-resilience/heart-to-heart

Fodor, L. A., Georgescu, R., Cuijpers, P. *et al.* (2020). Efficacy of cognitive bias modification interventions in anxiety and depressive disorders: a systematic review and network meta-analysis. *The Lancet Psychiatry*, 7(6), 506–514.

Forbes, C. N. (2020). New directions in behavioral activation: using findings from basic science and translational neuroscience to inform the exploration of potential mechanisms of change. *Clinical Psychology Review*, 79, 101860.

Fredrickson, B. L. (2013). Positive emotions broaden and build. In P. Devine and A. Plant (eds.), *Advances in Experimental Social Psychology*, vol. 47, pp. 1–53. Amsterdam: Elsevier.

Grosse Rueschkamp, J. M., Brose, A., Villringer, A., & Gaebler, M. (2019). Neural correlates of up-regulating positive emotions in fMRI and their link to affect in daily life. *Social Cognitive and Affective Neuroscience*, 14(10), 1049–1059.

Heiy, J. E., & Cheavens, J. S. (2014). Back to basics: a naturalistic assessment of the experience and regulation of emotion. *Emotion*, 14(5), 878–891.

Keller, H. (1903). *Optimism: An Essay*. New York: Thomas Crowell.

Keller, H., Sullivan, A., Macy, J. A., & Shattuck, R. (2003). *The Story of My Life*. Kindle ed. New York: W. W. Norton.

Krittanawong, C., Maitra, N. S., Virk, H. U. H. *et al.* (2022). Association of optimism with cardiovascular events and all-cause mortality: systematic review and meta-analysis. *American Journal of Medicine*, 135(7), 856–863. DOI:10.1016/j.amjmed.2021.12.023

Oriol, X., Miranda, R., Bazán, C., & Benavente, E. (2020). Distinct routes to understand the relationship between dispositional optimism and life satisfaction: self-control and grit, positive affect, gratitude, and meaning in life. *Frontiers in Psychology*, 11. Retrieved from www.frontiersin.org/article/10.3389/fpsyg.2020.00907

Peccoralo, L. A., Pietrzak, R. H., Feingold, J. H. *et al.* (2022). A prospective cohort study of the psychological consequences of the COVID-19 pandemic on frontline healthcare workers in New York City. *International Archives of Occupational and Environmental Health*, 95, 1279–1291. DOI:10.1007/s00420-022-01832-0

Reivich, K., & Shatté, A. (2003). *The Resilience Factor: 7 Keys to Finding Your Inner Strength and Overcoming Life's Hurdles*. New York: Broadway Books.

Scheier, M. F., Carver, C. S., & Bridges, M. W. (1994). Distinguishing optimism from neuroticism (and trait anxiety, self-mastery, and self-esteem): a reevaluation of the Life Orientation Test. *Journal of Personality and Social Psychology*, 67(6), 1063–1078.

Segovia, F., Moore, J. L., Linnville, S. E., & Hoyt, R. E. (2015). Optimism predicts positive health in repatriated prisoners of war. *Psychological Trauma: Theory, Research, Practice, and Policy*, 7(3), 222–228.

Seligman, M. E. (2006). *Learned Optimism: How to Change Your Mind and Your Life*. London: Vintage.

Sharot, T., Riccardi, A. M., Raio, C. M., & Phelps, E. A. (2007). Neural mechanisms mediating optimism bias. *Nature*, 450(7166), 102–105.

Stockdale, J. B. (1979). Speech to the corps of cadets by Vice Admiral James B. Stockdale. The Citadel Archives and Museum, August 31, retrieved from https://citadeldigitalarchives.omeka.net/items/show/1850

Tabibnia, G. (2020). An affective neuroscience model of boosting resilience in adults. *Neuroscience & Biobehavioral Reviews*, 115, 321–350.

University of Texas at Austin (2014). Admiral McRaven addresses the University of Texas at Austin Class of 2014. Youtube, May 23, retrieved from https://www.youtube.com/watch?v=yaQZFhrW0fU&t=198s

3 Face Your Fears

Coan, J. A., Schaefer, H. S., & Davidson, R. J. (2006). Lending a hand: social regulation of the neural response to threat. *Psychological Science*, 17(12), 1032–1039.

Earle, J. (2020). The givers. Mount Sinai podcast, May 9, retrieved from www.mountsinai.org/about/newsroom/podcasts/road-resilience/the-givers

Everly, G. S., Wu, A. W., Cumpsty-Fowler, C. J., Dang, D., & Potash, J. B. (2022). Leadership principles to decrease psychological casualties in COVID-19 and other disasters of uncertainty. *Disaster Medicine and Public Health Preparedness*, 16(2), 767–769.

Feingold, J. H., Peccoralo, L., Chan, C. C. *et al.* (2021). Psychological impact of the COVID-19 pandemic on frontline health care workers during the pandemic surge in New York City. *Chronic Stress*, 5, 2470547020977891.

Foa, E. B. (2011). Prolonged exposure therapy: past, present, and future. *Depression and Anxiety*, 28(12), 1043–1047.

Gunaratana, B. H. (2002). *Mindfulness in Plain English*. Expanded and updated edition. Somerville, Massachusetts: Wisdom Publications.

Hanh, T. N. (2000). *The Path of Emancipation: Talks from a 21-Day Mindfulness Retreat*. Berkeley, California: Parallax Press.

Hanh, T. N. (2003). *No Death, No Fear: Comforting Wisdom for Life*. London: Penguin.

Kolditz, T. A. (2010). *In Extremis Leadership: Leading as if Your Life Depended on It*. New York: Wiley.

Lane, R. D., Ryan, L., Nadel, L., & Greenberg, L. (2015). Memory reconsolidation, emotional arousal, and the process of change in psychotherapy: new insights from brain science. *Behavioral and Brain Sciences*, 38. DOI: 10.1017/SO140525X14000041

Mandela, N. (2012). *Notes to the Future: Words of Wisdom*. New York: Simon & Schuster.

Moore, S. P. (2021). Denali final update: failure is a key part of success. Blog story, SEALKids, June 30, retrieved from www.sealkids.org/denali/denali-final-update-failure-is-a-key-part-of-success

Resick, P. A., Monson, C. M., & Chard, K. M. (2016). *Cognitive Processing Therapy for PTSD: A Comprehensive Manual*. New York: Guilford Publications.

Speer, M. E., Ibrahim, S., Schiller, D., & Delgado, M. R. (2021). Finding positive meaning in memories of negative events adaptively updates memory. *Nature Communications*, 12(1), 1–11.

4 Moral Compass

Abdollahi, R., Iranpour, S., & Ajri-Khameslou, M. (2021). Relationship between resilience and professional moral courage among nurses. *Journal of Medical Ethics and History of Medicine*, 14, 3. DOI: 10.18502/jmehm.v14i3.5436

Ames, D., Erickson, Z., Geise, C. *et al.* (2021). Treatment of moral injury in U.S. veterans with PTSD using a structured chaplain intervention. *Journal of Religion and Health*, 60(5), 3052–3060.

Aristotle. (1926). *The Nicomachean Ethics*. Trans. H. Rackham. London: William Heinemann.

Beyond Conflict. (2020). America's divided mind: understanding the psychology that drives us apart. Report retrieved from https://beyondconflictint.org/americas-divided-mind

Brethel-Haurwitz, K. M., Cardinale, E. M., Vekaria, K. M. *et al.* (2018). Extraordinary altruists exhibit enhanced self–other overlap in neural responses to distress. *Psychological Science*, 29(10), 1631–1641.

Cutler, J., & Campbell-Meiklejohn, D. (2019). A comparative fMRI meta-analysis of altruistic and strategic decisions to give. *NeuroImage*, 184, 227–241.

Ginges, J. (2019). The moral logic of political violence. *Trends in Cognitive Sciences*, 23(1), 1–3.

Kidder, R. M. (2005). *Moral Courage.* New York: William Morrow.

Lee, S. (2022). Volunteering and loneliness in older adults: a parallel mediation model. *Aging & Mental Health*, 26(6), 1234–1241.

Ma, W., Koenig, H. G., Wen, J., Liu, J., Shi, X., & Wang, Z. (2022). The moral injury, PTSD, and suicidal behaviors in health professionals 1 year after the COVID-19 pandemic peak in China. In-review article retrieved from www.researchsquare.com/article/rs-1327109/v1

Nieuwsma, J. A., O'Brien, E. C., Xu, H. *et al.*. (2022). Patterns of potential moral injury in post-9/11 combat veterans and COVID-19 healthcare workers. *Journal of General Internal Medicine*, 37, 2033–2040. DOI:10.1007/s11606-022-07487-4

Norman, S. B., Feingold, J. H., Kaye-Kauderer, H. *et al.* (2021). Moral distress in frontline healthcare workers in the initial epicenter of the COVID-19 pandemic in the United States: relationship to PTSD symptoms, burnout, and psychosocial functioning. *Depression and Anxiety*, 38(10), 1007–1017.

Sacks, J. (2020). *Morality: Restoring the Common Good in Divided Times.* London and New York: Basic Books.

Stockdale, J. B. (1978). President's notes: firing line. *Naval War College Review*, 31(2), 2.

Stockdale, J. B. (1984). *A Vietnam Experience: Ten Years of Reflection.* Stanford, California: Hoover Institution Press.

Stockdale, J. B. (1995). *Thoughts of a Philosophical Fighter Pilot.* Stanford, California: Hoover Institution Press.

Svoboda, E. (2019). *The Life Heroic.* San Francisco: Zest Books.

5 Religion and Spirituality

Davis, L. W., Schmid, A. A., Daggy, J. K. *et al.* (2020). Symptoms improve after a yoga program designed for PTSD in a randomized controlled trial with veterans and civilians. *Psychological Trauma: Theory, Research, Practice, and Policy*, 12(8), 904–912.

DePierro, J., Marin, D. B., Sharma, V. *et al.* (2021). Developments in the first year of a resilience-focused program for health care workers. *Psychiatry Research*, 306, 114280.

Earle, J. (2020). Workshopping resilience. Mount Sinai podcast, November 6, retrieved from www.mountsinai.org/about/newsroom/podcasts/road-resilience/workshopping-resilience

Killgore, W. D. S., Taylor, E. C., Cloonan, S. A., & Dailey, N. S. (2020). Psychological resilience during the COVID-19 lockdown. *Psychiatry Research*, 291, 113216.

Lipka, M., & Gecewicz, C. (2017). More Americans now say they're spiritual but not religious. Pew Research Centre, research paper retrieved from www.pewresearch.org/fact-tank/2017/09/06/more-americans-now-say-theyre-spiritual-but-not-religious

Long, K. N. G., Worthington, E. L., VanderWeele, T. J., & Chen, Y. (2020). Forgiveness of others and subsequent health and well-being in mid-life: a longitudinal study on female nurses. *BMC Psychology*, 8(1), 104.

Martin, J. (2022). *Learning to Pray: A Guide for Everyone*. London: William Collins.

Mosqueiro, B. P., Caldieraro, M. A., Messinger, M., da Costa, F. B. P., Peteet, J. R., & Fleck, M. P. (2021). Religiosity, spirituality, suicide risk and remission of depressive symptoms: a 6-month prospective study of tertiary care Brazilian patients. *Journal of Affective Disorders*, 279, 434–442.

O'Brien, B., Shrestha, S., Stanley, M. A. *et al.* (2019). Positive and negative religious coping as predictors of distress among minority older adults. *International Journal of Geriatric Psychiatry*, 34(1), 54–59.

Pargament, K. I., & Lomax, J. W. (2013). Understanding and addressing religion among people with mental illness. *World Psychiatry*, 12(1), 26–32.

Pargament, K. I., Smith, B. W., Koenig, H. G., & Perez, L. (1998). Patterns of positive and negative religious coping with major life stressors. *Journal for the Scientific Study of Religion*, 37(4), 710–724.

Paul Victor, C. G., & Treschuk, J. V. (2020). Critical literature review on the definition clarity of the concept of faith, religion, and spirituality. *Journal of Holistic Nursing*, 38(1), 107–113.

Pew (2017). The changing global religious landscape. Pew Research Centre, research paper retrieved from www.pewresearch.org/religion/2017/04/05/the-changing-global-religious-landscape/

Rochester, S. I., & Kiley, F. T. (1998). *Honor Bound: The History of American Prisoners of War in Southeast Asia, 1961–1973*.

Washington, D.C.: Historical Office, Office of the Secretary of Defense.

Schmitt, A. A., Brenner, A. M., Primo de Carvalho Alves, L., Claudino, F. C. de A., Fleck, M. P. de A., & Rocha, N. S. (2021). Potential predictors of depressive symptoms during the initial stage of the COVID-19 outbreak among Brazilian adults. *Journal of Affective Disorders*, 282, 1090–1095.

Sharma, V., Marin, D. B., Koenig, H. K. *et al.* (2017). Religion, spirituality, and mental health of U.S. military veterans: results from the National Health and Resilience in Veterans Study. *Journal of Affective Disorders*, 217, 197–204.

Southwick, S., & Southwick, W. O. (2005). *Southwick Pioneers in Nebraska: A Genealogy of Linus Ely Southwick, William Orin Southwick, Laura Southwick Frantz, and Their Descendants.*

VanderWeele, T. J., Li, S., Tsai, A. C., & Kawachi, I. (2016). Association between religious service attendance and lower suicide rates among US women. *JAMA Psychiatry*, 73(8), 845–851.

Worthington Jr, E. L., & Langberg, D. (2012). Religious considerations and self-forgiveness in treating complex trauma and moral injury in present and former soldiers. *Journal of Psychology and Theology*, 40(4), 274–288.

Zheng, S., Kim, C., Lal, S., Meier, P., Sibbritt, D., & Zaslawski, C. (2018). The effects of twelve weeks of Tai Chi practice on anxiety in stressed but healthy people compared to exercise and wait-list groups–A randomized controlled trial. *Journal of Clinical Psychology*, 74(1), 83–92.

6 Social Support

Amstadter, A. B., Begle, A. M., Cisler, J. M., Hernandez, M. A., Muzzy, W., & Acierno, R. (2010). Prevalence and correlates of poor self-rated health in the United States: the National Elder Mistreatment Study. *American Journal of Geriatric Psychiatry: Official Journal of the American Association for Geriatric Psychiatry*, 18(7), 615–623.

Asurion (2019). Americans check their phones 96 times a day. Research paper retrieved from www.asurion.com/press-releases/americans-check-their-phones-96-times-a-day/#:~:text=Despite%20our%20attempts%20to%20curb,global%20tech%20care%20company%20Asurion%C2%B9

Azmiardi, A., Murti, B., Febrinasari, R. P., & Tamtomo, D. G. (2022). Low social support and risk for depression in people with type 2 diabetes mellitus: a systematic review and meta-analysis. *Journal of Preventive Medicine and Public Health*, 55(1), 37–48.

Brown, S. L., Nesse, R. M., Vinokur, A. D., & Smith, D. M. (2003). Providing social support may be more beneficial than receiving it: results from a prospective study of mortality. *Psychological Science*, 14(4), 320–327.

Cigna (2022). The loneliness epidemic persists: a post-pandemic look at the state of loneliness among U.S. adults. Report retrieved from https://newsroom.cigna.com/ loneliness-epidemic-persists-post-pandemic-look

Darling Rasmussen, P., Storebø, O. J., Løkkeholt, T. *et al.* (2019). Attachment as a core feature of resilience: a systematic review and meta-analysis. *Psychological Reports*, 122(4), 1259–1296.

Fernandez-Jimenez, R., Jaslow, R., Bansilal, S. *et al.* (2019). Child health promotion in underserved communities. *Journal of the American College of Cardiology*, 73(16), 2011–2021.

Fletcher, S., Elklit, A., Shevlin, M., & Armour, C. (2021). Predictors of PTSD treatment response trajectories in a sample of childhood sexual abuse survivors: the roles of social support, coping, and PTSD symptom clusters. *Journal of Interpersonal Violence*, 36(3–4), 1283–1307.

Golaszewski, N. M., LaCroix, A. Z., Godino, J. G. *et al.* (2022). Evaluation of social isolation, loneliness, and cardiovascular disease among older women in the US. *JAMA Network Open*, 5(2), e2146461.

Grey, I., Arora, T., Thomas, J., Saneh, A., Tohme, P., & Abi-Habib, R. (2020). The role of perceived social support on depression and sleep during the COVID-19 pandemic. *Psychiatry Research*, 293, 113452.

Gu, R., Huang, W., Camilleri, J. *et al.* (2019). Love is analogous to money in human brain: coordinate-based and functional connectivity meta-analyses of social and monetary reward anticipation. *Neuroscience & Biobehavioral Reviews*, 100, 108–128.

Kraav, S.-L., Awoyemi, O., Junttila, N. *et al.* (2021). The effects of loneliness and social isolation on all-cause, injury, cancer, and CVD mortality in a cohort of middle-aged Finnish men: a prospective study. *Aging & Mental Health*, 25(12), 2219–2228.

Landa, A., Fallon, B. A., Wang, Z. *et al.* (2020). When it hurts even more: the neural dynamics of pain and interpersonal emotions. *Journal of Psychosomatic Research*, 128, 109881.

Laugesen, K., Baggesen, L. M., Schmidt, S. A. J. *et al.* (2018). Social isolation and all-cause mortality: a population-based cohort study in Denmark. *Scientific Reports*, 8(1), 4731.

Milek, A., Butler, E. A., Tackman, A. M. *et al.* (2018). "Eavesdropping on happiness" revisited: a pooled, multisample replication of the association between life satisfaction and observed daily conversation quantity and quality. *Psychological Science*, 29(9), 1451–1462.

Na, P. J., Tsai, J., Southwick, S. M., & Pietrzak, R. H. (2022). Provision of social support and mental health in US military veterans. *Npj Mental Health Research*, 1(1), 1–8.

Oravecz, Z., Dirsmith, J., Heshmati, S., Vandekerckhove, J., & Brick, T. R. (2020). Psychological well-being and personality traits are associated with experiencing love in everyday life. *Personality and Individual Differences*, 153, 109620.

Pietrzak, R. H., Feingold, J. H., Feder, A. *et al.* (2020). Psychological resilience in frontline health care workers during the acute phase of the COVID-19 pandemic in New York City. *Journal of Clinical Psychiatry*, 82(1). DOI:10.4088/JCP.20l13749

Ratajska, A., Glanz, B. I., Chitnis, T., Weiner, H. L., & Healy, B. C. (2020). Social support in multiple sclerosis: associations with quality of life, depression, and anxiety. *Journal of Psychosomatic Research*, 138, 110252.

Sippel, L. M., Allington, C. E., Pietrzak, R. H., Harpaz-Rotem, I., Mayes, L. C., & Olff, M. (2017). Oxytocin and stress-related disorders: neurobiological mechanisms and treatment opportunities. *Chronic Stress*, 1, 2470547016687996.

Stockdale, J. B. (1984). *A Vietnam Experience: Ten Years of Reflection*. Stanford, California: Hoover Institution Press.

Straus, E., Norman, S. B., Tripp, J. C. *et al.* (2022). Behavioral epidemic of loneliness in older U.S. military veterans: results from the 2019–2020 National Health and Resilience in Veterans Study. *American Journal of Geriatric Psychiatry*, 30(3), 297–310.

Vedanthan, R., Kamano, J. H., Chrysanthopoulou, S. A. *et al.* (2021). Group medical visit and microfinance intervention for patients with diabetes or hypertension in Kenya. *Journal of the American College of Cardiology*, 77(16), 2007–2018.

Wang, J., Zhang, X., Simons, S. R., Sun, J., Shao, D., & Cao, F. (2020). Exploring the bi-directional relationship between sleep and resilience in adolescence. *Sleep Medicine*, 73, 63–69.

White, E. B. (1952). *Charlotte's Web*. New York: Harper & Row.

White, J. (2008). *I Will Not Be Broken: Five Steps to Overcoming a Life Crisis*. New York: St. Martin's Press.

Young Kuchenbecker, S., Pressman, S. D., Celniker, J. *et al.* (2021). Oxytocin, cortisol, and cognitive control during acute and naturalistic stress. *Stress*, 24(4), 370–383.

Zamanian, H., Amini-Tehrani, M., Jalali, Z. *et al.* (2021). Perceived social support, coping strategies, anxiety and depression among women with breast cancer: evaluation of a mediation model. *European Journal of Oncology Nursing*, 50, 101892.

7 Role Models

Bandura, A., & Walters, R. H. (1977). *Social Learning Theory*, vol. 1. Hoboken, New Jersey: Prentice Hall.

Cheung, P. (2020). Teachers as role models for physical activity: are preschool children more active when their teachers are active? *European Physical Education Review*, 26(1), 101–110.

Dietz, C., Zacher, H., Scheel, T., Otto, K., & Rigotti, T. (2020). Leaders as role models: effects of leader presenteeism on employee presenteeism and sick leave. *Work & Stress*, 34(3), 300–322.

Heyes, C., & Catmur, C. (2022). What happened to mirror neurons? *Perspectives on Psychological Science*, 17(1), 153–168.

Iacoboni, M. (2009). *Mirroring People: The New Science of How We Connect with Others*. New York: Farrar, Straus & Giroux.

Larose, S., Boisclair-Châteauvert, G., De Wit, D. J., DuBois, D., Erdem, G., & Lipman, E. L. (2018). How mentor support interacts with mother and teacher support in predicting youth academic adjustment: an investigation among youth exposed to Big Brothers Big Sisters of Canada programs. *Journal of Primary Prevention*, 39(3), 205–228.

Slaughter, V. (2021). Do newborns have the ability to imitate? *Trends in Cognitive Sciences*, 25(5), 377–387.

Werner, E. E. (1993). Risk, resilience, and recovery: perspectives from the Kauai Longitudinal Study. *Development and Psychopathology*, 5(4), 503–515.

Werner, E. E., & Smith, R. S. (1992). *Overcoming the Odds: High Risk Children from Birth to Adulthood*. New York: Cornell University Press.

Xie, H., Karipidis, I. I., Howell, A. *et al.* (2020). Finding the neural correlates of collaboration using a three-person fMRI hyperscanning paradigm. *Proceedings of the National Academy of Sciences*, 117(37), 23066–23072.

8 Mind Your Body

Dawson, D., Sprajcer, M., & Thomas, M. (2021). How much sleep do you need? A comprehensive review of fatigue related impairment and the capacity to work or drive safely. *Accident Analysis & Prevention*, 151, 105955.

Demnitz, N., Stathi, A., Withall, J. *et al.* (2021). Hippocampal maintenance after a 12-month physical activity intervention in older adults: the REACT MRI study. *Neuroimage Clinical*, 35, 102762.

Hall, M. G., Grummon, A. H., Higgins, I. C. A. *et al.* (2022). The impact of pictorial health warnings on purchases of sugary drinks for children: a randomized controlled trial. *PLOS Medicine*, 19(2), e1003885.

Hallgren, M., Kandola, A., Stubbs, B. *et al.* (2020). Associations of exercise frequency and cardiorespiratory fitness with symptoms of depression and anxiety – a cross-sectional study of 36,595 adults. *Mental Health and Physical Activity*, 19, 100351.

Harvey, S. B., Øverland, S., Hatch, S. L., Wessely, S., Mykletun, A., & Hotopf, M. (2018). Exercise and the prevention of depression: results of the HUNT Cohort Study. *American Journal of Psychiatry*, 175(1), 28–36.

Kaye-Kauderer, H. P., Levine, J., Takeguchi, Y. *et al.* (2019). Post-traumatic growth and resilience among medical students after the March 2011 disaster in Fukushima, Japan. *Psychiatric Quarterly*, 90(3), 507–518.

Kaye-Kauderer, H., Rodriguez, A., Levine, J. *et al.* (2020). Narratives of resilience in medical students following the 3/11 triple disaster: using thematic analysis to examine paths to recovery. *Psychiatry Research*, 292, 113348.

Law, C.-K., Lam, F. M., Chung, R. C., & Pang, M. Y. (2020). Physical exercise attenuates cognitive decline and reduces behavioural problems in people with mild cognitive impairment and dementia: a systematic review. *Journal of Physiotherapy*, 66(1), 9–18.

McEwen, B. S. (2017). Neurobiological and systemic effects of chronic stress. *Chronic Stress*, 1, 2470547017692328.

Philpott, T. (2012). *Glory Denied: The Vietnam Saga of Jim Thompson, America's Longest-held Prisoner of War*. New York: W. W. Norton.

Piercy, K. L., Troiano, R. P., Ballard, R. M. *et al.* (2018). The physical activity guidelines for Americans. *JAMA*, 320(19), 2020–2028.

Raynolds, J. (2007). *Leadership the Outward Bound Way: Becoming a Better Leader in the Workplace, in the Wilderness, and in Your Community*. Seattle, Washington: Mountaineers Books.

Scott, A. J., Webb, T. L., Martyn-St James, M., Rowse, G., & Weich, S. (2021). Improving sleep quality leads to better mental health: a meta-analysis of randomised controlled trials. *Sleep Medicine Reviews*, 60, 101556.

Stamatakis, E., Lee, I.-M., Bennie, J. *et al.* (2018). Does strength-promoting exercise confer unique health benefits? A pooled analysis of data on 11 population cohorts with all-cause, cancer, and cardiovascular mortality endpoints. *American Journal of Epidemiology*, 187(5), 1102–1112.

Svensson, M., Brundin, L., Erhardt, S., Hållmarker, U., James, S., & Deierborg, T. (2021). Physical activity is associated with lower long-term incidence of anxiety in a population-based, large-scale study. *Frontiers in Psychiatry*, 12, 714014.

Takehara, K., Togoobaatar, G., Kikuchi, A. *et al.* (2021). Exercise intervention for academic achievement among children: a randomized controlled trial. *Pediatrics*, 148(5). DOI:10.1542/peds.2021-052808

Wang, Y., Chung, M. C., Wang, N., Yu, X., & Kenardy, J. (2021). Social support and posttraumatic stress disorder: a meta-analysis of longitudinal studies. *Clinical Psychology Review*, 85, 101998.

Zlatar, Z. Z., Campbell, L. M., Tang, B. *et al.* (2022). Daily level association of physical activity and performance on ecological momentary cognitive tests in free-living environments: a mobile health observational study. *JMIR MHealth and UHealth*, 10(1), e33747.

9 Challenge Your Mind

Bonnechère, B., Langley, C., & Sahakian, B. J. (2020). The use of commercial computerised cognitive games in older adults: a meta-analysis. *Scientific Reports*, 10(1), 15276.

Goldberg, S. B., Lam, S. U., Simonsson, O., Torous, J., & Sun, S. (2022). Mobile phone-based interventions for mental health: a systematic meta-review of 14 meta-analyses of randomized controlled trials. *PLOS Digital Health*, 1(1), e0000002.

Iacoviello, B. M., Murrough, J. W., Hoch, M. M. *et al.* (2018). A randomized, controlled pilot trial of the Emotional Faces Memory Task: a digital therapeutic for depression. *Npj Digital Medicine*, 1(1), 1–7.

Iacoviello, B. M., Wu, G., Alvarez, E. *et al.* (2014). Cognitive-emotional training as an intervention for major depressive disorder. *Depression and Anxiety*, 31(8), 699–706.

Jackson, S. B., Stevenson, K. T., Larson, L. R., Peterson, M. N., & Seekamp, E. (2021). Outdoor activity participation improves adolescents' mental health and well-being during the COVID-19 pandemic. *International Journal of Environmental Research and Public Health*, 18(5), 2506.

Kabat-Zinn, J. (2009). *Wherever You Go, There You Are: Mindfulness Meditation in Everyday Life*. New York: Hachette.

Maes, M. J. A., Pirani, M., Booth, E. R. *et al.* (2021). Benefit of woodland and other natural environments for adolescents' cognition and mental health. *Nature Sustainability*, 4(10), 851–858.

Nicholson, A. A., Rabellino, D., Densmore, M. *et al.* (2022). Differential mechanisms of posterior cingulate cortex downregulation and symptom decreases in posttraumatic stress disorder and healthy individuals using real-time fMRI neurofeedback. *Brain and Behavior*, 12(1), e2441.

Pi, Y.-L., Wu, X.-H., Wang, F.-J. *et al.* (2019). Motor skill learning induces brain network plasticity: a diffusion-tensor imaging study. *PLOS One*, 14(2), e0210015.

Stojanoski, B., Wild, C. J., Battista, M. E., Nichols, E. S., & Owen, A. M. (2021). Brain training habits are not associated with generalized benefits to cognition: an online study of over 1000 "brain trainers." *Journal of Experimental Psychology: General*, 150(4), 729–738.

Sudimac, S., Sale, V., & Kühn, S. (2022). How nature nurtures: amygdala activity decreases as the result of a one-hour walk in nature. *Molecular Psychiatry*. DOI:10.1038/s41380-022-01720-6

Sullenberger, C., Zaslow, J., & McConnohie, M. (2009). *Highest Duty: My Search for What Really Matters*. New York: HarperAudio.

Verhaeghen, P. (2021). Mindfulness as attention training: meta-analyses on the links between attention performance and mindfulness interventions, long-term Meditation Practice, and Trait Mindfulness. *Mindfulness*, 12(3), 564–581.

Voth, M., Chisholm, S., Sollid, H., Jones, C., Smith-MacDonald, L., & Brémault-Phillips, S. (2022). Efficacy, effectiveness, and quality of resilience-building mobile health apps for military, veteran, and public safety personnel populations: scoping literature review and app evaluation. *JMIR MHealth and UHealth*, 10(1), e26453.

Zhang, K., Liu, Y., Liu, J., Liu, R., & Cao, C. (2021). Detecting structural and functional neuroplasticity in elite ice-skating athletes. *Human Movement Science*, 78, 102795.

Zhu, J. L., Schülke, R., Vatansever, D. *et al.* (2021). Mindfulness practice for protecting mental health during the COVID-19 pandemic. *Translational Psychiatry*, 11(1), 1–11.

10 Cognitive and Emotional Flexibility

Ben-Zion, Z., Fine, N. B., Keynan, N. J. *et al.* (2018). Cognitive flexibility predicts PTSD symptoms: observational and interventional studies. *Frontiers in Psychiatry*, 9, 477. DOI: 10.3389/fpsyt.2018.00477

Chan, Y.-C., Hsu, W.-C., Liao, Y.-J., Chen, H.-C., Tu, C.-H., & Wu, C.-L. (2018). Appreciation of different styles of humor: an fMRI study. *Scientific Reports*, 8(1), 1–12.

Emmons, R. A. (2016). *The Little Book of Gratitude: Create a Life of Happiness and Wellbeing by Giving Thanks*. London: Gaia.

Frankl, V. E. (1963). *Man's Search for Meaning: Revised and Updated*. WW Publisher.

Gloster, A. T., Walder, N., Levin, M. E., Twohig, M. P., & Karekla, M. (2020). The empirical status of acceptance and commitment therapy: a review of meta-analyses. *Journal of Contextual Behavioral Science*, 18, 181–192.

Hayes, S. C. (2022). Acceptance and defusion. *Cognitive and Behavioral Practice*. DOI:10.1016/j.cbpra.2022.01.005

Kalia, V., & Knauft, K. (2020). Emotion regulation strategies modulate the effect of adverse childhood experiences on perceived chronic stress with implications for cognitive flexibility. *PLOS One*, 15(6), e0235412.

McGuire, A. P., Fogle, B. M., Tsai, J., Southwick, S. M., & Pietrzak, R. H. (2021). Dispositional gratitude and mental health in the U.S. veteran population: results from the National Health and Resilience Veterans Study. *Journal of Psychiatric Research*, 135, 279–288.

McRae, K., Jacobs, S. E., Ray, R. D., John, O. P., & Gross, J. J. (2012). Individual differences in reappraisal ability: links to reappraisal frequency, well-being, and cognitive control. *Journal of Research in Personality*, 46(1), 2–7.

Millstein, R. A., Celano, C. M., Beale, E. E. *et al.* (2016). The effects of optimism and gratitude on adherence, functioning and mental health following an acute coronary syndrome. *General Hospital Psychiatry*, 43, 17–22.

Reeck, C., Ames, D. R., & Ochsner, K. N. (2016). The social regulation of emotion: an integrative, cross-disciplinary model. *Trends in Cognitive Sciences*, 20(1), 47–63.

Secinti, E., Tometich, D. B., Johns, S. A., & Mosher, C. E. (2019). The relationship between acceptance of cancer and distress: a meta-analytic review. *Clinical Psychology Review*, 71, 27–38.

Southwick, S. M., Sippel, L., Krystal, J., Charney, D., Mayes, L., & Pietrzak, R. (2016). Why are some individuals more resilient than others: the role of social support. *World Psychiatry*, 15(1), 77–79.

Steward, T., Davey, C. G., Jamieson, A. J. *et al.* (2021). Dynamic neural interactions supporting the cognitive reappraisal of emotion. *Cerebral Cortex*, 31(2), 961–973.

Stockdale, J. B. (2013). *A Vietnam Experience: Ten Years of Reflection*. Stanford, California: Hoover Institution Press.

Tabibnia, G. (2020). An affective neuroscience model of boosting resilience in adults. *Neuroscience & Biobehavioral Reviews*, 115, 321–350.

White, J. (2008). *I Will Not Be Broken: Five Steps to Overcoming a Life Crisis*. New York: St. Martin's Press.

Wu, X., Guo, T., Zhang, C. *et al.* (2021). From "Aha!" to "Haha!": using humor to cope with negative stimuli. *Cerebral Cortex*, 31(4), 2238–2250.

11 Meaning, Purpose, and Growth

Breitbart, W., Rosenfeld, B., Gibson, C. et al. (2010). Meaning-centered group psychotherapy for patients with advanced cancer: a pilot randomized controlled trial. *Psycho-Oncology*, 19(1), 21–28.

Feingold, J. H., Hurtado, A., Feder, A. *et al.* (2022). Posttraumatic growth among health care workers on the frontlines of the COVID-19 pandemic. *Journal of Affective Disorders*, 296, 35–40.

Frankl, V. E. (1963). *Man's Search for Meaning: Revised and Updated*. WW Publisher.

Frankl, V. E. (1969). *The Will to Meaning: Foundations and Applications of Logotherapy*. New York: New American Library.

Frankl, V. E. (2019). *The Doctor and the Soul: From Psychotherapy to Logotherapy*. New York: Vintage.

Graber, A. V. (2009). *The Journey Home: Preparing for Life's Ultimate Adventure*. Purpose Research.

Greenberg, J., Tsai, J., Southwick, S. M., & Pietrzak, R. H. (2021). Can military trauma promote psychological growth in combat veterans? Results from the national health and resilience in veterans study. *Journal of Affective Disorders*, 282, 732–739.

Keegan, W. (2007). *Closure: The Untold Story of the Ground Zero Recovery Mission*. Greenwich, Connecticut: Touchstone.

Masterson-Duva, M., Haugen, P., Werth, A. *et al.* (2020). Adapting meaning-centered psychotherapy for World Trade Center responders–CORRIGENDUM. *Palliative & Supportive Care*, 18(6), 764–764.

Southwick, S. M., Gilmartin, R., McDonough, P., & Morrissey, P. (2006). Logotherapy as an adjunctive treatment for chronic combat-related PTSD: a meaning-based intervention. *American Journal of Psychotherapy*, 60(2), 161–174.

Tedeschi, R. G., & Calhoun, L. G. (1996). The Posttraumatic Growth Inventory: measuring the positive legacy of trauma. *Journal of Traumatic Stress*, 9(3), 455–471.

Tedeschi, R. G., Cann, A., Taku, K., Senol-Durak, E., & Calhoun, L. G. (2017). The Posttraumatic Growth Inventory: a revision integrating existential and spiritual change. *Journal of Traumatic Stress*, 30(1), 11–18.

12 The Practice of Resilience

Earle, J. (2018a). An unexpected trauma. Mount Sinai podcast, June 27, retrieved from www.mountsinai.org/about/newsroom/podcasts/road-resilience/unexpected-trauma

Earle, J. (2018b). The prescription to my recovery. Mount Sinai podcast, July 25, retrieved from www.mountsinai.org/about/newsroom/podcasts/road-resilience/prescription-recovery

Modern Widows Club. (2022). About, website page, https://modernwidowsclub.org/about/

Peterson, C., & Seligman, M. E. (2004). *Character Strengths and Virtues: A Handbook and Classification*, vol. 1. Oxford University Press.

Icahn School of Medicine (2013). Teamwork – a life and death necessity, speaker Rear Admiral Scott P. Moore. YouTube, 22 November, retrieved from www.youtube.com/watch?v=JXGz00IMzTY

Walsh, F. (2021). Family resilience: a dynamic systemic framework. In *Multisystemic Resilience*, pp. 255–270. Oxford University Press. DOI:10.1093/oso/9780190095888.003.0015

Winnicott, D. W. (2005). *Playing and Reality*, 2nd ed. London and New York: Routledge.

Woodruff, L., & Woodruff, B. (2008). *In an Instant: A Family's Journey of Love and Healing*. New York: Random House.

Index